TWIN FLAMES

TWIN FLAMES

THE STORY BEGINS . . .

BOOK ONE

THE LOVERS OF THE ARCHANGELS

J.L. BERKOWITZ

First edition.

Paperback ISBN: 979-8-9916591-0-9

Hardback ISBN: 979-8-9916591-1-6

EBook ISBN: 979-8-9916591-2-3

https://JLBerkowitz.com

ACKNOWLEDGMENTS

This book is a product of my imagination assisted by vivid dreams with sexy male angels and beautiful females. Even though I am a writer of fantasy romance novels, I enjoy allowing love to test the boundaries of the unknown in this series, The Lovers of the Archangels. It is sure to deliver beyond expectations.

I would like to express my deepest gratitude to my family and friends who have supported and encouraged me in life. Pushing me to achieve my dreams and to share my skills for storytelling through writing books.

This gratitude is extended to the fans and bloggers. Thank you for your support with your honest reviews. The response to create the New Edition of *Twin Flames* touched my heart dearly.

A tremendous shout out to my editor Nadene Seiters. Your personal touch and professionalism was exactly what this New Edition of *Twin Flames* was missing. It is always so enjoyable to be able to work with you. I could not of done this without you.

FAWS! Dr. Laura Garrison, Christine Alston, Naydaliz Soto, Cindy Wilson, and Jade Castrinos. I have never in my life had a group of women mean so much to me. The constant support and rally for me to keep writing and share my stories is priceless.

I am grateful to myself for sensing and responding to the constant pull of energy that guided me to my mentor, Dr. Laura Garrison, of La Alza Health and Wellness in Sarasota, Florida. Thank you for teaching me how to have inner peace with myself so I can enjoy life and thrive as a published author and storyteller and an entrepreneur.

At last to my wonderful and supportive husband, Michael, of almost thirty years. I am so blessed and grateful to have you as my husband and soulmate. Our romantic love story is cherished daily as we go through life with our family we have built together. I love you for loving me every day of our amazing journey in this wonderful, incredible life.

—J.L. BERKOWITZ

CONTENTS

Nature Realm
Of
Faermorreya
Falls
Trolls
Wise Old Oak
N
W
E
S

ONE

A ree hung over the edge of an old fishing dock, studying the curves of her reflection along with the brightness of her teal-colored eyes glistening in the still waters. After a moment she sighed, looking for something interesting to catch her eye. Finding nothing more than a pebble, she tossed it into the water, watching the ripples spread. Bored, she scrunched up the skirt of her white linen dress so it wouldn't get wet. Sitting between two wooden rails, she began tucking the hem of her dress under her left butt cheek.

Lost in thought, she kicked her legs back and forth so just the tips of her toes touched the surface of the chilly water, each brief splash making her smile's reflection framed in deep red locks wiggle on the water. She looked at the old fishing dock weathered by time; the railing held a familiar engraving—an M and A inside a heart, found by her fingers. She smiled at the memory as her feminine, slender fingers traced the etching. Her dear Michael would meet her here soon, once the set of suns tucked beneath the horizon. She took a deep breath and released a decompressing exhale.

She got up, releasing her ankle-length, flowing dress, brushing off the dirt. Twirling like a delicate ballerina, her skirt billowed and fluttered around her. Intent on escaping boredom, she spun and spun until dizziness consumed her.

Stepping off the dock, she walked up to a very special spot. Atop a hill in a rolling meadow stood the most unique tree in the realm, her favorite, the tree of different colors. The tree had bark as dark as chocolate and roots resembling octopus legs curling through the earth. Creepy Jenny vines crawled up the roots to encompass the enormous trunk. The tree branches reached out, touching the sky, strong and wide enough she could walk on them. Vibrant colors, as if with a paintbrush, the tree grew leaves of purple, red, yellow, and blue, bursting in colors.

Aree picked pieces of wet grass off her feet before she sat down on the blanket she had spread out under her tree. Enjoying the smell of blooming wisteria clumping around the old fishing dock nearby, the delicate fragrance eased her mind. While she watched, the fireflies blinked from the canopy top, frolicking with happiness through the branches.

Feeling peaceful, she filtered through her memories of this place. Some of her favorites are shared romantic nights here. Michael would play his violin in a soft, romantic tune. They would dance in the twilight; she would fall in love with him once more.

The tree is special for both Aree and Michael. Long ago, they had made a bond with each other and planted a seed. As their love grew, so did the tree. They enjoyed climbing up the massive, dark branches deep into the tree canopy, playing chase or lounging on branches with their heads touching and their fingers entwined, oblivious to the world around them. Energy danced around them like layered halos moving up the tree, thriving from their love for one another.

Smiling, she loved this place. Her fingers stroked through the wild lavender covered in dew, leaving liquid diamonds all over her hand. She inhaled the smell of lavender with delight and sighed. Leaning back on her arms, she wiggled her toes in the furry blanket as she looked up, admiring the brightly colored leaves.

With a smile from ear to ear, Aree sensed an incredible, warm energy approaching, Michael. Patiently, she waited for the perfect moment. Then, she leaned her head back into the warm and comforting hands of her protector, companion, soulmate.

Michael smiled down at her as he cradled her head. Gently, he outlined the curves of her face as he turned her chin upward. She tilted her head back in full submission as he placed his warm and soft lips on hers. He held her close, burying his face in her hair, taking in the orangey rose scent causing his eyes to glow brilliant shades of blue, swirling full of passion and pleasure. He watched the red shimmers of her hair as it moved through the warm breeze. Speechless in happiness, he joined her on the blanket.

Soon, they rested side by side, relishing the early evening sounds. He leaned over her body, kissing her softly. First, he kissed her forehead, then slowly rubbed the tip of his nose with hers, then continued to kiss each rosy cheek. He kissed the very tip of her chin when she wrapped her arms around his powerfully muscular neck and shoulders, crawling her fingers across his upper back and dragging her nails softly down his muscular arms.

Life was perfect in the little piece of heaven they had created. Being in his presence and feeling his heavenly glow gave her security. There was no pain, no fear or anger, just the most intense feeling of a beautiful, never-ending love. It continued to grow without limitations.

Together, they loved taking long walks along the shoreline of the sea, where the water reflected liquid silver waves rolling onto the beach, holding hands and kicking the diamond sand as they chased each other around in the receding waters.

She loved spending time in nature, communicating with flowers and trees and even animals. Aree owned a unique ability. When she meditated, she connected with nature, controlling everything with her breathing.

Michael, on the other hand, enjoyed being in the stables, where he could ride Nokomis, his winged stallion of Heaven. He loved riding bareback over the beautiful hills.

They never once worried about their future or time, blessed with the immortality of Heaven. Soulmates, Aree and Michael shared the first bond of a human soul and celestial light being together forever.

Lying on the furry blanket, they laughed and told each other stories, when in the distance they heard a faint sound of flutes and harps coming from the city. The crystal singing bowls continued to grow in vibrations on the F note—a call to Michael.

"The Elders are requesting me?" he spoke in a soft, concerned, deep voice. His energy halo swirls had stopped and dissipated from the tree.

Old thoughts started running through his mind. It had been a long time since he had heard the call from the Elders. Last time he heard the crystal singing bowls vibrating so rapidly, they had requested Michael prepare for war, a war no one saw coming. Deep in the back of his mind, he always knew the time would come and the battle would begin again. He just hoped it wasn't now.

Putting space between them, he stood, grabbed the blanket, and turned to her. "We must go," he said.

Before she could speak, he wrapped his arms around her waist, laid a firm, reassuring kiss on her plump, soft, pink lips, and then, with a swooping sound, his wings appeared, spread out, ready for flight. He held her tightly against his body as he shot straight into the air above the treetops.

Michael looked toward the Grand Cathedral. In the distance, he saw the majestic city, Celestrian: the Holy City of Angels, a city of a thousand angels and Archangels. It sat deep among the clouds of color. Different crystals formed a brilliantly bright city, located in the middle level of the heavenly realm. The trails of Celestrian were created from the finest crushed Jade. In the middle of Celestrian, a Grand Cathedral was the source of Michael's summons.

Michael turned and flew to the Castle of Archangels, their home nestled against a grassy knoll on a small cliff overlooking the sea. The medieval castle builders had carved it from black granite, and ivy and moss covered the towering walls. Landing softly on the dewy grass in the middle of the courtyard, he released Aree and kissed her forehead.

"I will be back soon, my love." He gave her a wink and a smile and then took to the sky to answer his call.

Aree turned and ascended the castle's front steps, tucking the blanket under her arm, when she noticed the smell of jasmine around the castle was stronger than usual. She enjoyed the fragrant air. She pushed open their chamber's doors, accessible through a left archway.

"Aree, wait!" a familiar voice called out. She turned around to see Michael's brother Archangel Gabriel coming up behind her, exposing his welcoming smile with his priceless dimples.. "I didn't mean to startle you; I just heard the crystal singing bowls. Do you know anything about what the Elders want?" he asked. As he approached the doors, she invited him in.

Placing the blanket on a table, she looked up at him with a blank face. "I don't know anything," she said. "We were sitting under our tree when we heard the crystal bowls. Michael dropped me off here and headed to the Cathedral at once. Do you think I should worry, Gabriel?"

He looked at her. "No! No! I'm sure it's nothing to worry about. Don't worry." There was a strange silence. Then he said in a convincing voice, "I will let you get back to what you are doing. Kindly relay to Michael my search for him."

She gave him a reassuring smile. "Is there something I can do?"

Gabriel grinned, showing his charming dimples, shaking his head no. "I was just curious."

Aree smiled as Gabriel left, and she pulled the doors shut. She tried not to let her mind go crazy with nonsense thoughts, so she thought a hot bath would help her relax before dinner while enjoying a big, chilled glass of a new fruit elixir Michael's brother Raphael had created. This would ease her mind for sure.

As she enjoyed her drink, she could not keep her mind from wandering, knowing Elders spoke only with the Archangels to relay important orders from the Creator.

She recalled hearing Michael speak about the Elders, also known as the Wise Ones or the Empyreans. Hundreds of Elders maintained records for all the realms, including every human on earth. Others were astrologers for all the realms. Some worked as monks, studying the secrets of the ancient history of all the realms.

The Elders were the oldest beings, closest in age to the Creator. They had been with him before the beginning, before the Creator had manifested the universe and its realms with different dimensions. Since the beginning, they had always been there.

The Elders were tall, smoke-like beings reaching ten feet in height, usually dressed in a veil of the thinnest satin and silk robes of pale blue. Their eyes were bright violet, with hair of white and glistening silver strands reaching to their feet, and long facial hair to match. They radiated blue mist and smoke rising all around them. They could appear in a form with boney appendages showing under their robes and disappear at will, using their mystical powers. Most contact with the Empyreans happened in the Grand Cathedral.

The Grand Cathedral sat above the middle of Celestrian, elegantly embraced by its magnificent cloud bank. It shone bright like a sun, created from the gold and silver mountains.

Massive stained-glass windows lined the main narthex in the center of the Cathedral. Statues of mighty angels stood sentinel along the many levels of the Cathedral, some dressed in war attire, some with trumpets turned up to the sky.

Statues of gargoyles stood on each corner, hiding in the mist from the colossal fountains shooting holy water hundreds of feet in the air. The fountains themselves resembled Celestial Beings of all kinds throughout the universe gathered in unity. Carved from iron, the fountains showed their age through the turquoise patina enhancing their appearance.

Outlining the ascending steps to the Cathedral were golden, lower-level angel statues in armor holding swords pointing toward the doors. White linen draped in a frame around the doors adorned by a dove.

In the center of the Grand Cathedral, two towering spires of crystal stretched toward the sky, carved with angelic hieroglyphs sparkling like glitter. Each day, the sounds of flutes, harps, and violins filled the air as Celestial Beings hummed on cue.

***

Michael arrived just as the singing bowls slowly faded. White owls flew down from their perch, signaling Michael's arrival. As the bowl's vibrations stopped, this alerted the Elders of Michael's presence on the grounds. Landing softly, he made his wings disappear as he walked up the stairway.

There was a commotion near the altar sitting in the middle of the Cathedral. A group of lower-level angels stood in deep discussion and quieted their voices as they saw Michael approaching. Michael, with deep respect, stopped at the altar and bent his knee. He scanned the area for hints about the purpose of his call. Finding none, he turned around and headed into the west corridor where the Elders gathered. Walking down the familiar marble and rose quartz hallway, he admired every stained window lining the massive walls.

Glancing up, he saw the earth through the crystal dome, magnifying the ancient blue and green orb. It took his breath away every time he looked at its beauty, and it reminded him of how important it was to keep the orb and all its unique creatures living there safe.

Earth was a planet of matter where all creatures had feelings of love and loss, compassion, and pain. Humans were special, for they had fascinating minds of curiosity. Seeking love, they had the ability to learn from mistakes and keep peace with other creatures. Angels were light beings created to protect, to follow orders, and to help guide humans peacefully to protect their planet. He stood there admiring the orb and took pride in protecting it. He wondered if the earth was the reason for his summoning....

He turned toward the doors of the west chamber, the entrance to the Hall of Records. The massive doors were made of antiqued sycamore covered in gold and ornamented with carvings of angelic script, glistening across the keystone connecting the double doors, morphing into beautiful vines with inset diamonds covering the door frame. As he looked, he never noticed all carving and script before. Personally, it was a little much for his taste.

Inside the Hall of Records, Michael's anxiety rose as he looked across the room. He hadn't met in this room for a while. Beautifully carved columns stood every twenty feet across the hall, reaching up to meet in a point in the middle of the ceiling where a single stained-glass window hung, creating a soft kaleidoscope effect across the walls. Hundreds of scrolls stacked on old shelves lined the edges of the room.

The Elders sat on their engraved thrones around a large ruby table in the center of the room, awaiting his arrival. He walked in, bowing his head in respect as he approached his throne, created from the finest lapis. Other Elders came and went freely around the room. None had names or held leadership titles, all equal beings of identical form and function and mind.

The room settled into silence as a bright light streamed through the stained-glass window on the high ceiling. It forced Michael to cover his eyes as the light grew brighter. The second moon shone directly on the Cathedral. He lowered his arms, adjusting his eyes to the intense colors reflected in the room.

An Elder stood and spoke, looking directly at Michael. "There is trouble in Faermorreya that could cause devastation in the earthly realm. We need your full cooperation and complete understanding of this mission.

"There has been a breach of the seal of Faermorreya, nature's invisible dimension of the earth. This seal must remain shut for the earth and its dimensions to survive. Demons discovered a weakness in the seal. Watchers have informed us the demons are planning on destroying the creatures and magical beings of nature in Faermorreya, destroying the dimension and killing the earth's oxygen supply.

"As you know, we do not interfere with politics or issues as nature dimension keeps the peace between all magical beings. But since this threat includes the wellbeing of the outer realm of the earth, we must act."

A different Elder rose and spoke. "If demons succeed in their mission, they will have what they need to start the big war. But first, they will cause mass killings and destruction. We must act fast yet draw no attention. All evil entities are expecting our angels to be watching. We must stay calm and do the unexpected."

This intrigued Michael. Sitting straight up with his back against his throne, resting a fist under his chin, he felt the sharpness of his unshaven face. "Inform me of your requirements; I'll guarantee their fulfillment," he spoke with authority.

The court of Elders nodded in agreement, their murmurs acknowledging each other. Michael looked around at the Elders, seeing them stroke their long silky beards with their boney appendages, deep in thought but showing some anxiety....

An Elder turned to study Michael's expression and manner. They rose and declared, "We have a plan, but it excludes you."

Michael raised an arched eyebrow, confused, asking, "Why am I here?"? If I am not going on a mission, I do not understand how this concerns me?"

An Elder sitting across from Michael leaned over the top of the table toward Michael, his mist and smoke swirling around him. His violet eyes grew brighter, then he, too, started stroking his beard. In a loud voice, he said, "It's Aree, your soulmate! She is the chosen one for this mission!"

In complete shock, Michael pushed his throne far away from the table, shouting out, "No! She knows nothing of warfare with demons on earth! She has no knowledge of Faermorreya's existence. There must be another you can send!" Breathing heavily in defiance, he stood his ground, defending his mate and trying everything not to lose her to the earthly realm.

He pleaded and pleaded for another possibility. When he finally realized this was an order, he sat down in defeat. His love for Aree was important, but he would always obey any command given to him; he had never disobeyed an order from the Elders. Michael quietly slumped down on his throne with his hands clenched into fists, turning his knuckles white. His knee bounced anxiously. His arms glistened from sweat, his forehead slicked with anger. He gazed into a room corner, aware of this mission acceptance.

In a calm, peaceful voice, one Elder said, "Michael, we request you bring Aree to us so we can proceed with the mission." Speechless, Michael nodded his head.

The bright light dimmed, and all the Elders considered the proceedings satisfactory. They vanished one by one, returning to their daily duties. The doors closed, leaving Michael alone in the room. He pushed his throne slowly away from the table, stunned. Dropping to his knees, he knew he couldn't do this. Tears burned his angry eyes and his cheeks flushed as he settled into a silent melancholy. He did not want, nor was he ready, to let go of his love. How would he break the news to her that she had to go back to earth, beginning afresh without any recollection of him or their love? He must tell her that night! How did he tell her they had given an order?

TWO

Back at the castle, Aree hummed a tune she often heard the birds sing and swayed back and forth, enjoying the breeze as it blew across their balcony. The balcony spread across a wide-open marble floor the color of moss. Braids of silver railing intertwined with ivy and moon flowers enclosing the perimeter. Aree stood, glancing off in the distance seeing the majestic snow-topped ruby and garnet mountains.

Combing her hair, she wove a fishtail braid she laid over her right shoulder, giving her the illusion of a smaller neck and exposing her defined collarbone for Michael to kiss upon his arrival. Chills coursed throughout her body at the thought of his mouth on her neck. She placed small white and violet flower clusters throughout her braid. She had put on a cream, thinly translucent silk gown; she loved to tease Michael. The gown exposed her tiny, toned frame with her natural curves, arched back, and full hips around her tiny waist. Her breasts were barely covered, especially tonight, as she stood in the gentle breeze. She knew he loved it when she wore this dress.

Leaning over the balcony, looking for Michael, she tried to wait patiently. She desperately desired to understand his sudden departure. Awaiting his arrival, she went into the kitchen and made two tall glasses of fruity elixir. As she sipped hers, letting the elixir cover her lips, she allowed it to tingle just before she swallowed.

His footsteps appeared to get heavier as he entered their living quarters after locking the doors. Aree scurried over and handed him a huge mug while dousing him with kisses, clinging onto him like she looked at him after a lengthy estrangement.

"WELL?" She drew away with beaming eyes. "Well, TELL ME!"

Guzzling a vast sum of elixir, turning, searching for the vessel which it appeared from, he began pouring another. "Aree, do you need some extra?"

She nodded yes. "Why don't we relax on the terrace so we can savor our drinks and the tranquil air while you inform me of everything?"

Refilling the two mugs to the perimeters, he lifted his head in time to observe her turning and walking toward the rail so she could enjoy the cool air. Tracing her frame with his finger in midair, he thought to himself, She is so gorgeous. The precise wife for him. She was consistently cheerful with such a pleasant personality. He also thought it adorable she interacted with creatures and trees. Her natural vitality pulled all individuals near to her. She was peculiar that way, and she stood by his side.

He approached the table as Aree sat down. Pulling out a chair across from her, peering at the miniature flecks of shadowy blue in her teal-colored eyes, he sought to speak. His tongue felt giant in his mouth.

"Aree, I strolled into the Hall of Records to meet the Elders there, awaiting assembled around a table. I accompanied them on my throne at the table." Choosing to offer her the brief report, seeing her eyes fastened strongly on him, adhering to the later news, Aree was all ears.

"I sat there as an Elder informed me about trouble with an invisible dimension of earth, named Faermorreya, the magical world of nature." There was a pause. He had another sip and hesitantly glanced aside as tears sought to obscure his vision.

Reaching across the table, Aree lifted his hand in hers and with baffled eyes said, "Michael, I didn't realize the nature world was real. I understood it was all a delusion that mothers instructed youngsters with as stories!" giggling with another meager snicker.

"What's so amusing, Aree?"

Smirking in between giggles, she proceeded, "That doesn't sound like anything you couldn't handle."

Michael, lifting an eyebrow, studied her as she babbled on about leprechauns and elves when he sought to hinder her. "Honey, you are a warrior. I don't think leprechauns are going to give you an issue. It's going to be OK love; I can handle a few days while you carry out orders. I can take care of myself! So who is traveling with you? Gabriel, Raphael?" she babbled on repeatedly.

Michael got up and went around to her and clutched her arms. "Aree!" She stared at him, stunned by his action. "I need you to listen to me, please! I am not traveling anywhere, babe." A bewildered smile darted across her face just as he spoke. "It's you." Her smile instantly vanished.

Aree rose, glaring at him. "What do you mean me? What can I do? I'm a lover, not a warrior! Michael, there must be a mistake! You must have misinterpreted. This isn't conceivable." Taking a step back, leaning on the rail, guzzling the remains of her elixir so swiftly a bit splashed all over her collar and stained her gown. She reached for the big jug, wiping her mouth with her hand. Michael remained there, powerless, observing her, not realizing what to do.

The third moon soared. The silence between them broke from a soothing murmur. "OK, I'll do it. I will adhere to orders issued to me, honey. It can't be that dangerous, or they wouldn't send me, right? Do you know when I leave?"

Michael avoided eye contact as he peered into the distance, saying, "There's more.". My love, while you are gone from the heavenly realm, you will not have any remembrance of me or our love."

In an instant, a freezing sensation raced across her body. She released the jug to the floor sending elixir in the air. "WHAT!" fell from her lips, but he didn't see through her stone demeanor.

"You will remember everything when you come back. I have served on many missions. It has always been conducted this way for thousands of years." Michael stepped up behind her, encasing her in a violet, long, fleece shawl around her shoulders. Pushing himself taut against her body, pushing her hair off her shoulder, he murmured into her ear, "I am uncertain when they require you to go, my love."

He forced his lips against her collarbone, cherishing the touch of her delicate, pale skin on his lips. Massaging her arms, turning her around but keeping her tight in his arms, he pressed her against his chest. Never could he ever choose to let her leave. She shuddered slightly on the inside. He recognized it as her fear of leaving behind all she appreciated and treasured. Realizing she needed a diversion to ignore the emotions in this dilemma, scanning toward their master suite without her knowing, he took her up in his arms.

"Right now, you are with me, my love. This is our time." He had her attention with a passionate kiss as he strolled to their bed.

In the room's rear, a large four-post bed made of onyx stood, with rhinestones placed every two inches around the poles shimmering like twinkling stars in the night sky. Misty, violet, velvet blankets and silver pelt throws were strung across the bed with feathery pillows of varied sizes. He steadily released her next to the side of their bed.

Tossing the violet shawl on a chaise near a wall-sized fireplace, he glanced over again, confirming it landed on the chaise, not in the fire. Aree watched every motion Michael made as he loosened his cloth pants and let them settle to the floor. Remaining still, he let her appreciate him nude. His shadow attracted her attention to the superficial contour formed from the moonlight and the glow of the fire reflecting his masculine physique.

Michael removed the gold tassels keeping her gown on her shoulders, following it with his eyes as it slipped off.. The gold tassel dangled on the tip of her hard nipple before it settled on the floor, instantly giving Michael a surge of blood to his groin with every pulse of his heartbeat. He induced his eyes to churn a blazing, neon blue with desire, never dropping eye contact with her. Placing his fingers on her neck, he moved her hair off her shoulder, uncovering her slender neckline, tipping her head into position so he could enthusiastically savor her sweet lips and kiss behind her ear.

Tracing the contour of her sensual torso, he felt and kissed every part of her. He glided his hands up her outer thigh, then suddenly clutched her plump rear. He picked up her up in his brawny arms, lying her on the silvery white pelts and kissed her intensely, compassionately maintaining the contact between them.

Aree caved into his seductive touch and the warmth emitting against her body as he arranged himself on top of her, pushing his solid erection against her outer thigh as he adamantly kissed her breasts, delighting her nipples with his tongue, giving her a tantalizing sensation seizing her soul, provoking her to moan and close her eyes in sheer gratification, forgetting all about the mission.

Michael forced his mouth against hers, planting his hand between her upper thighs as she opened them for him. He slid his arm downward so he could slip his fingers to where he could receive the warmth as he began penetrating her tenderly.

Enjoying her satisfaction, he took over the penetration with his tongue. This shot her into complete euphoria as he taunted her, making her crave more. She lifted her hips in passion, presenting herself to him. He tenderly slid her legs open as he positioned himself on his knees. Gripping her hips to pull her to closer to him, he thrusts himself into her moderately at first, concluding with his animalistic penetration deep inside her, forcing out moans of orgasmic bliss. With their bodies quenched, a glistening glow emitted as they move simultaneously in perfect synchronicity together throughout the night.

Lying there cuddled in his arms, she knew his mind teemed with intentions of keeping her right there permanently so he could protect her. Aree could feel his anxiety and knew images of losing her had seized his mind. Lying her head on his chest, she put a hand around his abdomen. Their heart beats and breathing slowed enough they picked up on the same breathing patterns. This allowed them to ease into a deep sleep, secure in each other's arms with weeping eyes.

THREE

Dawn appeared too promptly. Michael hurt from thinking apathetic thoughts and not choosing to let her leave. Peering back at her sleeping so quietly, he shrouded her with furs as she slept. Remaining on the edge of the bed, he shoved his sandy blonde hair off his forehead, noting the red streaks heightening his royal blue eyes as he gawked at himself in the full-length mirrors.. Standing there studying himself, sporting nothing but thin cloth pants, he looked. Pondering his person without his armor, he saw nothing but an angelic light being in human form. He stayed there, stretching before flexing his arms and legs, posing.

Thinking to himself, I am an archangel with arms of steel and an impressive, powerful frame.". If desired, he could display and extend his wings ten feet from his body. The magnificent archangel could not alter the approaching event, but in a split second, could divide an attacker in half with a spiral of his wings. Turning elsewhere, he reached for an appropriate linen shirt matching his pants, exposing just enough of his muscular pecks.. Standing and looking at himself, he looks chilled but mentally is not holding up so well. He is so afraid she will see him weak. He thought, She cannot look at me like this. I must make every minute perfect. He lowered his head as he dropped his arms. He sulked.

Softly kissing her on her forehead and pushing a few wild strands of red hair off her face, he swept the back of his hand across her cheek, and with a smooth motion, he turned, stepping out, closing the doors softly. He headed to the stables to brush and bath Nokomis. His mind reeled with worries of what ifs. Spending quality time in the stables would help ease the painful feelings he experienced.

Michael wandered along the gravel trail to the stable of Celestrian. It was a beautiful morning. He glanced up and noticed two of the highly majestic and magical creatures of Celestrian. He saw an adult griffin and winged stallion nibbling on fresh, cool grass growing in the feeding pastures. He paused, leaning on the fence observing, astonished at such creations of exquisite abilities with enormous power and intelligence.

An incredible creature, with the head of an eagle, the body of a male lion, the tail of a dragon, and silver scales tapering to an arrow-like point, the stallions' massive size put them around ten feet at heart height. They had the strength of a mighty freight train with wings twice the length of their body. Instructed in warfare, these stallions were the utmost weapon for the archangels. They could move at the speed of light, exploding through the clouds, creating thunder rumble with every step from their heavy hooves, generating lightning to explode across the sky. The creatures could fly through all dimensions.

Nokomis scampered out of a stall and through the stable's passageway, making his way across the field. Sensing Michael's off energy, he sank his head and inserted it under Michael's arm, demanding rubs from him. Eyes of blended gold, Nokomis was the hue of a thunderstorm, with the spirit as well. He had been with Michael since he was a filly, gaining respect and learning the rules from his master.

Nokomis grunted and eagerly strutted around, searching for sweets. Michael smirked. "Come over here, you big lug," he said, handing Nokomis a carrot and sugar cubes. "Let's go to the stables, boy."

He relished brushing the grand breast, feeling much better. He settled his head against Nokomis, hinting "I desire to fly." Neighing, it delighted Nokomis the need was mutual. Snatching a handful of luxurious black mane on Nokomis, he mounted him, leaning tight against his muscular frame. They were off, leaving stardust as their trail.

***

Aree woke in her routine way, in wonderful spirits. Reaching out her arms, she spread her fingers across the silver pelt blankets shrouding her perfectly. Observing the beautiful songs of the morning birds and feeling grateful for another day with Michael, she took on a cheery attitude and added a smile. Thinking about upcoming events, Michael's missions were never too long, so hers should be the same. . . . Stretching then slipping into her favorite sheer wraps, she put her long, silky red hair in a messy bun on top of her head with wisps sticking out around her face. She stepped outside onto the balcony and took a deep breath in and out, nice and slow.

Enjoying the peace she felt, Aree decided she was not going to worry about the unknown of her new mission, and she was going to enjoy the day. She noshed on some fresh fruit, wondering where Michael was. Maybe she should walk down to the stables and check on him. Quickly she shoved the last of the fresh berries into her mouth and went to get dressed.

Later that morning, Aree left the castle grounds, walking by the olive and orange trees where her little garden of flowers and herbs grow. This was her special place. She meditated and fed birds and other creatures. She watched squirrels race around the oak trees in a game of chase, knowing she had nuts and dried fruit for them.

Realizing how much she enjoyed being with the animals, she practiced feeling and communicating with nature. Sitting on the ground motionless, she closed her eyes, lifting her arms up above her head in a bowl formation, swaying her arms in a circular motion. Sitting still and quiet, she opened her eyes to watch flowers swaying in the same motions of her arms and her breathing. She communicated with nature. She orchestrated the movements of the flowers and trees to the dancing yellow Spanish moss resembling gold, basking in sunlight.

Eventually, she rose and scattered a mix of seeds, nuts, and dried corn for the gathered critters. Enjoying the bright violet sky and the sun, Aree replayed last night's conversation between Michael and her. She wondered about Michael, concerned by his activities yesterday as they were odd, relatively distant. Why is he so worried about this mission they have chosen me to do? What is he not telling me . . . ?

***

They walked along the shore, talking and sucking up every moment. Aree stopped. Turning toward him, she gently swept the light dusting of diamond sand on his cheekbone off. Smiling, she kissed every inch of his face.

Holding his face in her hands, she whispered, "I love you, Michael, forever and ever. Our love is strong and unbreakable. What we have lasts lifetimes." Looking into his eyes, she continued saying, "We are soulmates. I could never forget you or our love. I promise to never forget our love."

His eyes of royal blue were glossy and watery, reflecting the diamond sand in his hair. He kissed her hard and pulled her into his bare chest, holding her tight. He could feel her breasts against his skin and the heat rising off her body as he ran his hand to the small of her back before lifting her higher into him. Throwing her arms around his neck, she returned the same force of affection to him as well.

At the castle on his balcony Gabriel stood, gazing across to the east wing. Gripping his fingers tightly around the silver filigree decorating the railing around his balcony, he looked on. With a stature smaller than Michael's but just as muscular and tone, he looked on with chiseled features. His emerald-green eyes would hypnotize anyone with their beauty. His wavy, dark-brown hair lay perfectly over his shoulders.

Currently, he fretted over his brother and the meeting's purpose. Just then, Raphael knocked at his door as he pushed his way in. "Gabriel, they have informed me of the meeting yesterday between Michael and the Elders. Sit, my brother. This is going to shock you!"

Now Gabriel knew the mission. "Aree must go on alone! Michael is going to miss her. Not able to protect her from danger from the hands of evil entities! He knows they will know who she is!" Gabriel cried out. "Being the soulmate of Michael the Archangel isn't something of a secret. She is someone they want to get their grubby crawls upon."

Raphael said, "Sartael wants to torture Michael with her soul. His hatred for Michael is vicious. Any harm to her endangers the realm's safety. It could destroy everything, even Heaven." This concerned Raphael and Gabriel. They finished their discussion right before Raphael had to meet Uriel, the older and wiser brother.

***

The two brothers, Uriel and Raphael, walked on, holding onto braided satin ropes attached to young Griffins. Raphael had concerns regarding Michael and his emotions.

"Michael has been tense," Raphael said, as he looked up and noticed Aree and Michael giggling and laughing in their favorite tree.

Watching on from a distance, Uriel spoke, "She is the one. She can do this; her ability to connect with nature is very strong. She is the only one. Until she returns, emotions aside, Michael will wait whether he likes it or not...."

As they continued their walk, Raphael started noticing the trail led to an open field. "Is this meant to be a special experience?" Raphael chuckled. "Your aren't expecting help with these youngsters!"

Uriel didn't joke around, so his silence wasn't something new. Taking the braided satin rope from Raphael, he suggested he go sit over by a crystal pergola dripping with huge yellow and peach Angel Tree flowers sitting atop a grassy knoll. "And see, you will be out of harm's way there."

Raphael's chiseled jawline cracked into a smirk as he took a seat, pushing aside his reddish-brown locks sticking out of his braided hair intertwined with gold and royal blue satin rope, intensifying the golden color of his eyes. He replied sarcastically, "Carry on!" to Uriel.

Uriel was a strange loner. One hundred percent devoted to order. If he was not patrolling the different realms, he trained Griffins when they reached a defiant age in their youth. Uriel had a way to make them obey and stay obedient, to not so aggressively snap their huge, powerful beaks when they wanted something.

At first, he led the young griffins to an open part of the field. Whistling the griffin's language, he had their full attention as he continued training them. He used raw meat in chunks as treats. Young Griffins were dangerous. They acted like baby goats, playing and jumping around as their dragon scales came in and their front claws started growing talons. Uriel showed them self-control around others and while eating.

It wasn't long before he finished training. Uriel said, "The Elders wanted you and Gabriel to be with Michael. Soon Aree will be leaving. They ask the both of you to distract him as I escort her myself to the earthly realm, making sure she arrives safely."

Facing, his brother, Raphael agreed and said, "We will do it, Uriel, my brother; I will not disappoint you."

FOUR

A couple of days passed. Anxieties ran high. Aree, looking straight ahead, took a deep breath as they neared the entrance to the Grand Cathedral. Squeezing Michael's hand, she anxiously stayed near his side. Passing the altar and looking at the massive stained-glass window's effect, the array of colors took her breath away.

She whispered to Michael, "My palms are sweaty."

He looked and smiled at her with a loving gleam in his eyes. Turning the corridor, she looked at the marble and rose quartz flooring leading them to majestic doors with such ornate, angelic scripture. On the other side of these massive doors were the Elders awaiting to deliver her quest.

Michael kissed her forehead, then pushed the doors open to colored mist and heavy chattering among the Elders. "Welcome, Aree," an Elder stated, "please take a seat next to Michael's." Eyes were on them as they started walking around the huge ruby table surrounded with big thrones. She was both amazed and nervous in the presence of the Elders.

Throughout history, only Archangels had been in the Elders' presence. Aree felt tiny compared to the ten-foot-tall beings with mystic movements fading in and out. She tried not to stare, but she had never seen Elders. They scared her when in full figure showing their white, boney appendages.

Seeing the brothers present and in their armor, with wings outlying flat against their backs, this made her sweat even more. As she and Michael took their seats, the brothers made a sudden movement closer, taking one step, standing behind them. Not speaking, Michael lifted an eyebrow at Raphael with a quizzical look. They never put the brothers at attention behind him at a meeting. His fears for Aree quickly intensified. What was she being called to do? How dangerous was this quest? His anxiety was at a breaking point.

"Welcome to this urgent meeting," an Elder spoke. "The Watchers brought to our attention a rip in the seal of a dimension belonging to the earthly realm. Demons have entered the nature dimension, known as Faermorreya. What we know is that they plan on causing massive destruction to Faermorreya, killing its creatures and landscape. If this was to happen, it will destroy the oxygen given to the outer realms of the earth needed for all survival.".

"As we know, Aree has been called upon to help protect Faermorreya in this mission."

Aree felt confused. What could she do to save the earthly realm? This was a mission for an experienced warrior, not a selfless, nature-loving soul! Before she could speak, Michael stood in defiance, shouting "NO! I WILL GO! THIS MISSION IS NOT FOR HER!" Standing and pushing his throne back, Michael faced resistance from his brothers, who pushed him back onto his throne.

"ORDER! ORDER!" an Elder stood and shouted. It quieted when a different one stood, turning to Michael and Aree.

"Please, Michael, know your place. If we didn't believe Aree was the right choice, we wouldn't have made this decision. Aree feels things and energies we don't understand. She knows how to communicate with nature and understands the needs of trees and plants. There is no one with her abilities left. She is very special. She has powers to protect Faermorreya, which cannot protect itself in this matter....

"This mission requires free will and a special love and connection for nature and the earthly realm. Angels lack understanding of free will. Aree is our only hope."

Placing his head in his hands, Michael understood she experienced nature differently. She was special, not like any human soul.

The room was silent when Aree stood nervously and said, "OK, I'll do it!" Turning to Michael, who was in complete shock, she reached out to cradle his chin in her hands. "My love, my destiny calls. I know nothing of my existence before I found you. If I can save the nature realm of the earth, then I know of no other decision. I must go." Looking for approval in his eyes, she hid her fears from her warrior mate.

"Aree, we will make arrangements and explain to you your return to the earthly realm," an Elder spoke. "The next day is your departure from the heavenly realm. Return to your chambers and mediate for clarity from any distracting thoughts, trust in your love you both have created, and never lose faith in that. This will keep you together. Uriel will call on you tomorrow. We will pray for a quick and safe return." An Elder slammed a gavel on the ruby table, which echoed throughout the room. They adjourned the meeting.

FIVE

Happy Birthday Sassy Hudson!" the banner used to read stretched out across the porch railing. It was that time again, her birthday, but she didn't celebrate it anymore. It was the last happy memory she had of her parents before they left the planet.

She reminisced, thinking of the stories her father used to tell her of their family. Her name was short for Sasalia, her father's mother's name. As a child, her parents used to call her Sassy. A little-miss-know-it-all with her head in a book or outside somewhere exploring nature, her dad called her "Miss Sassy Pants" because she loved to debate everything with everyone. These sudden thoughts had her missing her parents; she lovingly smiled, remembering.

It was a gorgeous day. She lay on the hood of her metallic-blue pickup truck parked high on a hill in the country overlooking her little town. Born and raised in the country, she loved being in nature. The fresh air, birds chirping, the smell of fresh cedar trees spread across the landscape, even the smell of wet gravel.

Tiny white butterflies fluttered around the mounds of clover leaves. Spring was here. It was one of her favorite times of the year. Everything felt fresh after months of a melancholy, long, wet winter and being stuck inside from the weather.

The winters caused the landscape to go through major transformations. It turned darker and mysterious as everything went dormant. Sassy referred to it as the sunless weather season. Dark-gray skies filled with heavy snow and sleet pellets banged against the windowsills, making a binging sound. To her, when the deciduous trees dropped their leaves, they resembled creepy old witch fingers sticking up out of the ground. The Junipers trees were the only things green left with their needles.

Now everything burst with life and colors along with cool breezes. It was so refreshing for the soul. Sassy felt rejuvenated, seeing bright-blue skies and green pastures with new hay or grasses swaying in the breezes. It resembled waves moving over the ocean. She got that same hypnotic feeling when she was on the beach as she did as she looked over the grass fields growing in pastures.

Today was a special treat for her. Sassy chilled, tapping her finger nails on the beer bottle she held while sipping on the ice-cold beer, looking deep into the clouds. She looked deeply into the clouds searching for her angels. She noticed them lounging and being playful deep within the clouds dressed in flowing, long gowns blending into the color of the pale-yellow clouds, along with a peachy glow and golden, glistening ropes as belts around their waist reflecting in the sunlight. From time to time, they blessed her with their presence. They appeared to her in human form in the clouds.

They visited her time and time again throughout her life. The angels watched over her. She didn't know why or what made her so special. She just knew they were there. On a day the sun was bright, and she needed a pair of sunglasses to look up into the clouds moving across the sky in different origami shapes the angels created.

She recalled this one time she experienced seeing tons of angels in thunderstorm clouds. It was a late afternoon. The sky turned a creepy gray-green color with strange energy. She remembered the low clouds swiftly rolling across the sky as the winds intensified. As the thunderstorm grew, she felt the electric energy in sky.

The angels were on enormous horses, wearing armor with swords held high in the air, riding into battle. They became visible only during lightning flashes as thunder roared in the skies. She recalled sitting on the front porch watching the storm as it crept over the hills and trees.

She never knew where the angels were going. It was a sight burned into her memory.

Her attention quickly shifted when she noticed a red hawk flying over. Sassy, being a quirky nerd to some, demonstrated communication with the hawk, thanking it for the greetings from above. She wasn't the average person who only saw nature; she associated and communicated with nature with her energy and feelings.

Flowers bloomed if she requested this of them. An angel showed her this power when she was the age of five. It was a secret she had never told or shown anyone, even her parents. Keeping her secrets caused her to live a lonely life, never having close friends to share this power with. Even at present, she found it difficult to be around people and engage in dating. No one understood her abilities. Although the angels had always been around, doing their best to love and protect her, knowing Sassy truly wanted security and love.

Watching the angels, she envied how they played in the clouds. Smiling down to her, one angel telepathically whispered, "In time. Your life on earth is very important. Be patient, enjoy life."

Sassy smiled, finishing her beer in two big gulps. She looked up to see the angels begin to fade deep into the clouds. A different one smiled, placing its hands in prayer formation before it disappeared.

Rolling off the hood of the truck, throwing the beer bottle in the back, she opened the door and climbed in. Looking in the rearview mirror at herself, she saw blood shot eyes matching her red hair in a messy bun. Her teal-colored eyes looked tired. She mumbled out loud, "Boy, Sassy, you are showing your age today, that's for sure." With a crooked smile, she glanced into the mirror. She still looked good. She would make a great partner for a man, any man. If only there were any available men near her.

That was her twenty-fifth birthday wish this year. She was tired of being lonely and desperately wanted to fall in love. Never feeling or experiencing being in love physically, she was sick of waiting for her knight in shining armor. Her life lacked both family and a spouse. She got glimpses of her dream soulmate she saw only in visions and in her dreams now and then. He first appeared to her on her thirteenth birthday. She referred to him as "her protector."

Starting the engine and rolling down the window, she began driving through the winding hills, admiring the bright-green leaves and the sunbeams shining through the trees. Taking a deep breath, this was one of her favorite dead-end roads. It was secluded and tucked back off the side of a rocky hill near train tracks. When she wanted to withdrawal from society and the chaos of daily living and just needed to be alone, she found comfort being in nature, far from humans here. For a brief moment she imagined life in the bustling city. Driving on her favorite gravel road made her realize living in the country just felt so right. She would always be a country girl.

Approaching home, she turned onto the long, narrow road leading up to the ranch she inherited when her parents passed from old age. She was much younger. That was the downfall of having a child in your older years. They grew into adults alone. Not having any siblings or family left on the planet, they left Sassy with everything, giving her a good, comfortable life.

Sassy admired the once-working ranch with the main house in a barn-style home with a gray-green color with moss covered wooden shingles. She thought about all the times as a child she would lounge on the huge, white, wraparound porch extending to the back of the home with rocking chairs and hanging flower pots placed in sunny spots. Turning the engine off and pulling the keys from the ignition, she stepped out of her truck under the shade of the gigantic oaks and maple trees surrounding the property, working as a wind block for the home.

A huge red barn was the center of attention here. Everything happened around the barn. It used to be a working ranch with cattle, chickens, and horses, always bustling with cattle trailers and cowboys on horses, very busy when her parents were there. Nowadays Sassy lived alone with her two dogs, Wookie, a Great Pyrenees, and Scotty, a labradoodle, who pranced and barked in happiness as she exited the truck…. Normally they spent their days lounging on the front porch watching the world go by.

Barney, a golden palomino horse, poked his head out of the barn to investigate the commotion. Being the son of Sassy's father's prized winning race horse who had passed on the farm, he was special to Sassy, and he knew it. He saw her and strutted over to the fence line with his golden pale-yellow mane and tail swaying in the breeze. His huge, dark, golden eyes greeted and fluttered in her direction. He sought treats and a neck scratch.

"Good evening, Barney." She pulled an apple from a tree and fed it to him as she took a seat on a hay bale, cracking another beer. She hung out with Barney and watched the dogs play, admiring the gorgeous sunset. The sky was a treat with pink- and peach-colored clouds against the setting sun stretching across the western skyline for miles.

Barney reached over and nudged her back. They shared a powerful connection with each other. He understood her thoughts and talked to her. Turning to look at him as he eyeballed another apple, Sassy giggled. "I'm so lucky to have you in my life, Barney. You fill that empty spot in my heart with your craziness."

Opening up another beer and quickly slugging it down, she spit out the beer as it foamed over flowing out of the bottle. Barney neighed out loud laughing! She stood up and called out, "Ha-ha! Goodnight, my friend, see you in the morning!" and headed for the house. It was getting late, and she was tired. Tomorrow would be another day at earthly Creation, a quaint candle shop selling crystals and incense she had inherited from her mother.

* * *

Sassy awoke, covering her eyes with a pillow from the sunlight beaming through the bedroom windows, making her realize she was late for work! Jumping out of bed, she splashed her face with cold water and hurried to put on a pair of jeans and a white t-shirt. She created a mess as she quickly made a cup of coffee to go while feeding the dogs hurriedly and rushing out the door. She had hair blowing in her face as she ran to her truck.

She exhaled a gigantic yawn as she started the truck. The air had a slight chill this morning. It helped Sassy wake up as she frantically rubbed the small goose bumps on her arms, waiting for the heater to warm the truck up so she could head into town.

Other shops, including the grocery store, emitted the scent of fresh-baked bread in the morning. There was a charming flower shop with delightful holiday window displays and a deli owned by a robust man named Tony from Philadelphia, Pennsylvania. He always said cheesy pickup lines to the females. Sassy acted shy and played nice, just a smile and wave hello. Tony must have known of her lack of interest in him.

He had a bold and loud personality. Convinced the people of Texas are picky eaters and they needed to broaden their taste palates and try more Italian cheeses and meats, he struggled to understand the need for BBQ and fried chicken.

Sassy enjoyed having Toni and his deli in town, with his loud-talking Philly slang. He always wore an apron covering his enormous beer belly and a long, black mustache to make up for the baldness on his head. He had no shame! Creating attention from all wherever he went.

The local hair salon had all the gossip on everyone's personal business and kept the gossip lie open when it came to Toni. Sometimes Sassy wondered what they said behind her back. She, besides Toni, was probably the only person in town that had never gone to the salon since she didn't cut her hair.

Downtown Valley Mills was not busy, with about five thousand residents. It had enough to release stress and make for comfy living. Mature Crepe Myrtle trees lined the streets with benches and flowerbeds under every black antique streetlamp, kinda like a Thomas Kinkaid picture with a Texas touch and one stoplight.

Morning time, children waved hello while crossing for school. The town hall and post office were always busy in the morning. Additionally, a lovely central park had annual fireworks in July and a Santa at

Christmas time who inquired about children's behavior. It was a quaint little town, just no single men there, unfortunately.

Pushing the door open and turning on the lights, she took a deep breath, closing her eyes. Ahh, "Invigorating . . . I love the smell of this shop. It evokes memories of woods, beaches, and winter holidays simultaneously." At the rear of her shop, she designed distinctive candles in different sizes and shapes. The smells of wax and different fragrances filled the air in there. The room had a worktable for projects, an oven, stove, and a couch for occasional naps. She had covered the walls with different plants and ivy sitting on shelves in between candle molds and slimy bottles of oils stacked in alphabetical order. The scents gave this shop a mystic vibe, along with the sound of the wind chimes.

Sassy called out, "Good morning, Archie!"

Archie enjoyed the pleasant spring crisp breeze as he stayed lying near the door. He lazily rolled over on his back with his four paws in the air. He looked at Sassy upside down as he released an enormous yawn. After doing his stretching exercises, Archie approached her for his morning treats. Sassy gave him a good rubdown and then gave him chunks of cheese for his treat. Occasionally he got roast beef, his favorite, but after smelling the cheeses, he decided it was good enough for him today.

Archie was Sassy's partner in crime. With the body of a large gray panther and gold-streaked pea-green eyes, he could be a bit of a Cheshire cat and lived and worked in the shop, always watching and keeping evil and negative energies at bay. Sassy had spoiled him since she found him in the wild as a cub. As he grew, she allowed him to create a puss-in-boots protective role with her.

Rubbing his enormous belly, she spoke with a grin, telling him, "People in town are still nervous about you walking around alone in town. Stupid town gossip," she said in a baby's voice while playing with his tail, irritating him. "Maybe later, I will take you on a walk to show these people how cool you are."

The bells rang out from the ceiling above the shop door, announcing a customer had entered. A breeze played the wind chimes, making it loud for a moment. Sassy looked up from the backroom when she heard the ringing. Wiping her hands off, she stepped out from the back room.

"Good morning!" she called out. There was no response. Looking around for someone, she called out, "Hello, is anyone here?" Still no answer. Walking to the front door to check the bells, she heard Archie cry out!

Sassy turned in his direction, noticing a dark, old, wooden box sitting on the floor in the middle of an aisle of mystic books of potions and ceremony candles. As she approached, she noticed it had no return label on it. Looking at it, she preceded cautiously, picking it up and placing it on the front counter near the register.

Checking it over, it impressed her with the smoothness of the wood. It was obviously handmade with old architectural techniques and carvings. The stain and texture on the box seemed to be produced from a dark-brown plant dye, and with age, it had now turned into an ashy, black tone. The lid was sealed shut with maybe a solvent or wax, she thought. It was not modern candle wax. It reminded her of the medieval times when waxes were used to seal letters closed. That was the texture, though much stronger. The lid was attached in an unknown way. Looking over the sides, she noticed carved, ancient scripture around the entire box about an inch below the lid.

Making a mental note of the box décor, Sassy was anxious to look it up on the web later. Out of the corner of her eye, she saw Archie pacing back and forth, swinging his tale. He could see its strange faint yellow aura giving off a strange vibe. Only he could see the faint aura appear, then disappear for good. Sassy picked up the box with Archie hot on her heels. They both headed to the backroom.

Looking for space on her working table, she placed the box on the couch. She quickly cleared space on the table to place the box. It stirred up weird feelings felt by both of them. For a moment, it stopped Sassy in her tracks.

Checking the logbook for deliveries, she didn't anticipate anything until a week out, and her packages would arrive through UPS. Her normal UPS delivery driver was chatty and wouldn't just drop off a box, especially without a return address label, or leave it on the floor in a isle of books on spells. Sassy was confused as she tried to put all the weird pieces together. The UPS driver loved seeing and interacting with Archie when he made a delivery. This delivery was unusual. The box having an aged appearance was strange enough by it itself.

After thinking about it, she decided it was best to wait to open it. "Maybe it's been delivered to the wrong address," Sassy mumbled, bothered now from wasting so much time on it. Pushing the black box aside, frustrated, she decided to be patience and wait to hear if someone expected this black box. Right outside earthly Creations was a park bench where two elderly gentlemen sat and people-watched. But they didn't recall seeing anyone carrying a black box into her shop.

A couple of days passed and no one claimed the black box. Archie's attention shifted; he remained focused on the box since it had arrived and refused to let her open it. At the top of a tall shelf, he lay there, glaring at it. His behavior was far from normal. He neglected to watch the door or socialize. Sassy wanted his focus removed from it. His actions bothered her.

The day ended, and Sassy was tired. Locking up the shop, she remembered she was going to take the box home with her. Walking in the backroom, she saw the box. Just as Sassy reached for it, a crashing of candle molds fell off a shelf, scaring her!

"Shit, Archie!" she yelled out.

After taking a minute to calm herself, she picked up the box. Turning toward Archie, who now was on the table, the hair stood up on his neck as he released a growling hiss at the box! Sassy had never seen this side of him. An energy existed only he could sense. She knew big cats had superior vision, different from humans' ability to see. Arching his back, he hissed again, then slapped it with his enormous claws out, trying to slice it. His sharp nails did not penetrate the wood.

"It's petrified!" A rush of dopamine hit Sassy! Standing, frozen for a minute . . . multiple thoughts raced through her mind. Whatever was in this box must be extremely ancient and important. She never saw a scripture carved into wood. It was lovely; maybe it was Latin? Pushing her hair off her face, she tied it in a bun on top of her head. She looked at Archie excited.

"What is this? Archie, I am going to remove the black box from the shop. I didn't order it, and it clearly bothers you, so I am taking it home with me tonight." Looking at the box closely, she was intrigued by it. Archie bumped his head against her hand; a slight purr of thanks could be heard. Looking up at her, pleased, blinking his eyes at her. She could tell he felt more comfortable knowing she would remove it from the shop. Sassy mumbled out loud, "I will put it in the barn. I hope you can relax; sleep well my fuzzy friend. I will see you in the morning." Sassy kissed her fingertips, then rubbed his head, turning off the lights and locking the door. She loaded the box into the truck and headed home.

****

For the next few months, everything was normal at the shop. Just as it was prior to box's arrival. Archie was back at work guarding the shop. He seemed OK. The energy in the shop was positive and loving. It returned to normal days of making candles and selling protective stones. Days blended and seasons changed, repeating the same routine endlessly.

Sassy yearned so badly for love. Her work day ended, and she went in the back room and fell on the couch. "I am so unhappy. Today's sales were good, yet I am so lonely. . . ." She began thinking that maybe love was not for her. Maybe she was supposed to be alone. Recalling that day's sales, there was a high demand for crystals and love candles. Sassy thought to herself, I wonder if I was to create a love candle for myself, could I find love?

As she drove, looking at the changing landscape with the days getting hotter, she lowered the driver's window and held her arm out against the wind. The warm sun on her arm made her feel so peaceful, boosting her mood. But as she drove up the driveway, it was a different story. Her dogs didn't greet her when she drove up.. Barney didn't greet her either; she noticed he was at the farthest part of the land with the neighbor's horses.

She parked her truck, confused. She quizzically watched them through the windshield, wondering what they were doing. Exiting the truck, she closed the door and entered the house. Walking into the kitchen, she opened the fridge and grabbed a Dr. Pepper as she turned and headed outside to find out what was going on with her animals....

She shook her head, confused, as she went to check it out. Placing her Dr. Pepper on a table, she opened the squealing barn doors, creating the eerie sound of an old, rusted car door being wrenched opened. Walking her fingers along the wall feeling around for the light switch in between 2x4s, she turned on the lights, and on cue *POP! POP! POP!* The overhead barn light bulbs blew out one after the other, fast. Startled with fear, she squatted down to the floor, covering her head with her hands. Summoning the courage to enter, Sassy expected to find something like a burglar or gigantic snakes or even a rabid skunk. But she saw nothing. Everything appeared OK except the broken glass from the blown bulbs on the floor.

Her tension eased. She felt calmer. Pushing the doors open wider to get more natural lighting inside, she saw the broom and grabbed it to clean up the glass. Carefully sweeping, she ensured no small glass fragments remained on the barn floor. While inspecting for glass in the hay, something caught her attention. The black box had a shadow around it vanishing before she could investigate further. Placing the broken glass in the trash, she put away the broom and dustpan. Sassy walked over to where she had placed the box on the floor and held it in her hands. She walked out of the barn and placed the box next to her Dr. Pepper. Turning, she pulled one door shut in the barn and latched it. Picking up the box and her Dr. Pepper, she headed to the house.

Later when she glanced out the window, Barney was in the barn and the dogs ran and played in the yard as happy as ever, as if nothing had ever happened. Watching them confused her. Scratching her head, now all her animals had been affected by the box. Pleased the problem was solved, Sassy knew the box was the cause. Facing the room with the box, she spoke, "What is in that box?"

Sassy placed the mysterious box next to the fireplace in the living room. It fit in there. Her mother was fond of old antique farm tools, so she displayed different ones above the fireplace, adding a Texas rustic farm appearance to the room. An old antique box always added allure to any living room. With hands on hips, she surveyed the box, her head shifting side to side. After admiring the new piece, she made her mind up to keep it. Pleased with her decision, blowing hair away, she turned and headed to the kitchen. Opening the fridge, she reached for a plate of leftover meatloaf and sweet potatoes and reheated it in the microwave, then grabbed another Dr. Pepper from the fridge door. Turning off the lights, she headed into her bedroom to watch the local news.

SIX

Michael spun around, noticing the nice, deep trail he had created from pacing back and forth on the diamond sand right where they used to walk and talk about plans together. He had stopped keeping track of her being gone. It'd been forever since he last held her in his arms. He experienced for the first time the feeling of losing a loved one. It caused him to struggle to stay focused and positive.

"Is Aree ever coming back to me?" Kicking the diamond sand, he tried to hold back tears from falling.. Unsure of what to do with himself anymore, he took off running in a full sprint on the sand, trying to outrun his feelings.

Standing on Gabriel's balcony, they watched over Michael from afar. "We are struggling to keep Michael focused on anything but the return of Aree. His impatience is rising, Gabriel." Raphael's voice took on a melancholy tone. "He is giving into a secluded lifestyle, avoiding normal dining times, not attending commanders' meetings. This mission of Aree's consumed his thoughts. No return date has been announced. It's been over twenty earthly years. I worry about him, Gab."

"Maybe we should alert the Elders of Michael's behavior." Looking on over the balcony, they both watched as he faded from their site, nothing but a trail of glistening diamonds running parallel to the beach.

The next morning Gabriel and Raphael went to the Cathedral seeking advice from the Elders. Multiple groups moved about. A handful of them all worked with scrolls and recorded secrets. Hundreds of Elders faded in and out. An intimate group of Elders stood in a circle of colored smoke in a far corner near shelves storing thousands of scrolls of angelic scriptures' deepest secrets. It seemed like miles and miles of scrolls.

The only sound Gabriel heard was "Shh, shh, try to speak softly; here they come." At once, the room filled with glistening violet eyes directly focused on Raphael and Gabriel. Boney appendages appeared out of a mist, waving them both in. The brothers prepared to act, giving their best performance, willing to give the Elders what they wanted to know.

"Please, please, take a seat. Since Aree left, we have been paying more attention to Michael. We find him distracted by memories they created. Michael is displaying mortal emotions, and we are concerned about it. We understand he is not checking in with his commanders for reports across the realms. Questions are forming about his loss of appearance. What changes have you both noticed in Michael?"

Gabriel stood first, rubbing his hands together quickly. The feelings of betrayal weighed heavily on his tongue. Raphael could see he was anxious. After a quick glance at the Elders and his brother, he paused before speaking. "I have been trying to spend time with Michael in a way that doesn't seem like I'm watching him, but Michael doesn't go out, and he has missed many meals."

In that instant, Raphael stood and assumed command of the conversation. "I too have been watching Michael. I have seen him sitting on the dock where they used to dance together. Or I'll see him taking long runs on the beach." Raphael and Gabriel nodded in a synchrony, agreeing.

An Elder felt the need to explain. Sensing the passion Raphael and Gabriel expressed for their brother's well-being, he continued, "Michael is a light being, not designed for what he is experiencing. With Michael, we are observing something never recorded before. It's unfamiliar territory when angels experience loss or loneliness from loving a human soul. This concerns us. This is a delicate situation. Michael has attached himself to her soul, developing emotions created for mortal souls. His bond with Aree is very interesting, yet confusing. His celestial light is fading from the aching he feels for Aree's soul. We must be very careful with him."

A peculiar energy lingered in the air. An Elder leaned into Gabriel and Raphael, looking deep into their eyes. "We all know that Aree will return someday. Now she is a young woman unsure of her future. She does not know we have picked her to save a realm. She finally accepted her situation. The departure of her parents from the earthly realm was hard on her. I will tell you she possesses the gateway.

"As for Michael, we have discussed all options to control his absence from his commander's curiosity. We ordered him to the Ruby Mountaintops. The business he will conduct there will occupy his time and not offer the opportunity to sulk over her absence. This is his new order."

***

Both brothers, being aware of Michael's new orders, were uncomfortable telling him. They shared mugs of passion fruit and elderberry elixir. Raphael was doing push-ups, unsure of how they were going to tell Michael he was being sent to the Ruby Mountaintops.

Gabriel said, with an excited tone in his voice, "Not to mention the extreme weather that is changing constantly in the Ruby Mountains! The perfect place for the Imperial Eagles to raise young eaglets high on the snowcapped peaks. The stallions roaming free on the mountains along with the Griffins until we assign them their warriors, but NOT PERFECT for Michael!" Gabriel recalled younger years when they trained them to manage flight in the extreme weather up and down the mountains with a warrior in armor swinging an enormous sword on their backs.

The Monastery stood massive, like a small city, deep in the mountains, protected from weather and hidden from sight. "Hey, Raphael, remember when they were building it? You can see only bits and pieces of the protective walls blending into red granite rocks." Crafted from mountain crystals, it seamlessly camouflaged and deceived the gaze. "You know they used wizardry, creating and cracking open the side of a mountain and carved its crystals into the Monastery."

Raphael responded. "Really? I didn't know that."

Gab responded, "I can remember being a mastery cadet, learning distinct elements of war, meditation, and control as well. We trained for what felt like an eternity. We share many memories there, long, long ago." Raphael turned to Gabriel. "Maybe I should let you tell him alone."

Before he could finish the sentence Gabriel interrupted, stating both of them needed to explain the decision made about him while they were all betraying him.

Heavy banging on huge oak doors vibrated the walls. "Gab!" Michael called from behind the door. He banged again harder on the doors.

Gabriel rushed over and swung the doors opened. "What are you trying to do? Knock my door down?" Gabriel yelled at Michael while he walked by Gabriel with his head down, not answering or even acknowledge him.

He threw himself down on the lounger with his hands, rubbing his eyes. Covering them like a child, in a monotone, he spoke, "Gabriel, you will never understand what I am going through. I won't be making it to dinner later, so just explain to everyone that I had other things to tend to."

"Hello, Michael." Immediately the energy was altered when Raphael spoke.

Unaware of Raphael's presence, Michael kept his hands over his face, unable to turn his head. Startled, he rapidly sat up, returning a hello to his brother. Raphael, on high alert, walked over to him, taking a seat in a chair next to the lounger. "Michael, it's good to see you."

"You too, Raphael," Michael mumbled kindly. Taking a long drink and an even longer pause, Raphael studied, taking a long look at Michael. He noticed he was a little smaller, much thinner and unshaved. He deeply sighed. . . . "We need to tell you something, Michael."

With a sudden rush of adrenaline, he asked, "Is she returning? Say something, Raphael."

Gabriel handed a glass of elixir to Michael and said, "No, she is OK; it's not about her. It's about you."

"ME!" Michael snapped back, appalled by the attention put on him. Raphael jumped in front of Michael and calmed him down, informing him of the meeting they both had with the Elders.

"They're concerned about your behavior, Michael. It is reaching ears on the edge of our realm. The Elders continued to tell us of the conversations they had among themselves. Upon agreement and feeling that this is the best action to pursue with you."

Michael glared at Raphael like a hungry cave dweller, cracking his knuckles, anticipating his next words. "You must report to the Monastery in the Ruby Mountaintops."

Michael stood in silence.

"Pack for the long journey. Nokomis will take you there." Uncomfortable silence controlled the room. They could feel the tension rising from Michael's energy he radiated.

Looking in his glass, he drank the rest of the elixir, leaving some running down the corner of his mouth and dribbling onto his unshaven whiskers, dripping onto his chest, staining his shirt a hot pink color. He didn't his mouth, leaving droplets of elixir hanging on to the ends of his untamed mustache. With care, he set the glass on the table before making his way to the balcony. In the distance, he could see the Ruby Mountaintops. He glared at them.

It felt like forever to Gabriel. Slowly, he walked over, extending his arm to reach for Michael's arm. Michael tensely pulled away, not looking at either of his brothers, still staring at the mountains, then in a loud firm voice, he asked, "When do I report?"

Gabriel, in a low tone, responded, "The day after next."

Michael dropped his head, allowing his untamed hair hang down to blow in the wind, knowing they could not see his eyes as he squinted at them in rage. Clenching his teeth, his fists wrapped around the balcony railing. Realizing everyone worried about what he did, instead of how he felt, angered Michael. Gabriel's hearing picked up on the metal twisting sound Michael created before he walked out, slamming the huge oak doors behind him so hard it again shook everything on the near walls.

SEVEN

The seasons changed, and with this Sassy liked to clean her crystals to refresh the energy in her home. She sat outside, her quartz crystal catching the sunlight perfectly. A rainbow of colors danced on its surface. Sassy admired the colors when it reminded her of a certain stone she recently looked for. Placing the crystal down, she quickly rose and entered the house, slamming the screen door shut.

Looking over at her books, she noticed how unorganized her shelves were. As she scanned the book titles, she saw theology, candle making, oils, and crystals books all mixed. She was getting frustrated with her organization. Finally, she saw the one book she wanted.

As she stretched for it, she realized it was out of reach. Stepping on the fireplace and trying to bury her fingernail tips into the binder of the book, reaching and reaching, the book moved, and she lost her balance, falling backward and hitting the black box with her heel, sending it rolling across the floor. Getting up from the ground and seeing the box tossed across the room, she was upset thinking she damaged the box, which had become a fixture in her home décor. She had forgotten the box for a while until now. Hastily she picked it up to inspect it; she noticed a corner had lifted from her accidently stepping on and kicking the box.

Sassy placed the box on the table and gently tried to peer into it but could see nothing. She wedged her finger under the top and could pop it off. Shocked, she stood there holding the lid and saw black, old, silk material wrapped around an item that had formed an indentation into the wood from its weight.. Laying the lid on the table, she reached in and picked up a heavy object. Slowly, she unwrapped the item, seeing a spire from a crystal sticking out.

After unwrapping, Sassy was in awe! It was the most gorgeous, unique cluster of crystals. Dark green with gold veins running through it like tiny tentacles seeking food. The closer she looked, the more it amazed her. It almost looked like fluid inside. She had seen nothing like this before. Sassy looked at it and wondering why it was in a wooden box. Her curiosity overwhelmed her, and she had to find out. She went in search of something long enough to reach all her books. Finding her broom, she walked back into the living room, held it up near her bookshelf, and swept the shelf clean of books, sending them all over the floor. After returning her broom, she sat among her books, diligently searching for any available information.

After spending hours searching through books for the crystal, she got up and stretched her legs. She walked, picked up the crystal, and left through the front porch screen door. Sassy placed the cluster of crystals on a table to cleanse itself with the full moon rising. She left it there overnight. She cleaned up her mess from earlier when she noticed Wookie laying on his back with his four paws in the air so the early evening breeze blew across his belly. He watched the leaves falling off the trees and chewed on one just to hear the crunchy sound. It pleased her to see her fuzzy friends so content.

Sassy tidied up her book mess before searching the web for crystal information. Searching and searching and typing in anything to find the crystal, she finally typed in *ancient crystal myths* and *BAM!* A picture of the same cluster appeared on a website about mythical tribes. What connection does this crystal have with the Kona Tribe of Alaska?

Sassy read on and on until she noticed late night had turned into early morning before she shut the laptop and lay down on her arms and fell asleep. She woke in a puddle of drool running down her arm. Wiping her face and arm, she got up and went to bed, not noticing the amazing magic going on outside on the front porch.

The green crystal cluster had gold swirls coming from it. Spirals resembling multiple glitter ribbons reached out across the land into the treetops. The full moon had activated the crystal cluster.

Sassy woke refreshed and excited about the crystal. She instantly went outside, picking up the cluster that had returned to its non-active state and went back inside to continue researching this beautiful gem. As she got back on the webpage, she read about how the Kona Tribe was a tribe worshipping nature and was magical. Then one day, the entire tribe disappeared. But not before they destroyed the Forest Crystals.

"Forest Crystal! That's it!" She compared the picture with the cluster in her hand. She was quiet for a moment, then on another website, she purchased a plane ticket. Feeling good about her adventure, she began dancing and singing a little tune she made up, feeling happy.

Sassy came home from the shop with Archie. She closed it until she returned. She had reached out to Mr. Whitey, a good old cowboy that was also a dear friend of her late father. He always watched the ranch when needed. Mr. Whitey would take care of the animals. He was a gentle, grouchy man, always wearing a cowboy hat and a big belt buckle. It was his conversation piece of his younger bull riding days.

Back in her bedroom, Sassy dug out her suitcase to prepare for a trip to Alaska. Knowing she was going to have to hire a guide when she got there, she dreamed of him being her true love. She looked over at Archie, who chewed on her suitcase. "Archie, what if he became my dream man?" Archie responded with a loud purr.

Sassy lay down on her bed daydreaming. . . . Suddenly, her thoughts changed, and she focused on "her protector." If she allowed it, he would flood her thoughts. He made it hard for her to date men. He was so perfect, but it was the feeling she got when she saw him she craved the most.

"Archie, will I ever find love?" She felt melancholy. She curled up with her pillow for a nap.

Sassy lay on the couch holding the cluster in her hands, turning it and looking at its colors. She held it up in a stream of sunlight shooting across the room. A beam caught the crystal, and a gold reflection appeared.. It was so dense, Sassy noticed, and when she placed her fingers in the gold reflection, they disappeared.

Stunned by what she just witnessed, Sassy dropped the crystal on the floor. She grabbed it quickly off the floor, afraid she had ruined it. She held it up again, and it reappeared. The gold reflection was almost hypnotic. Sassy was so impressed and filled with anxiety over this magical forest crystal. Studying the reflection closely and carefully, it vanished. It wasn't until Sassy saw the sun's shift that she grasped what had occurred. The sun hit the crystal by coming through the windows. Sassy immediately ran into her bedroom and placed the forest crystal on her windowsill so the morning sun would reflect off it again.

Preparing for bed, Sassy rechecked everything. Ticket to Alaska waited, Mr. Whitey called, shop closed. Everything was prepared. Lying in bed next to Archie, Sassy felt like things benefited her.

"Maybe the crystal will lead me to my Him. Maybe the crystal wanted to be found by me?" Reaching over and rubbing the top of Archie's head, she kissed her fingers and rubbed them on his head as he closed his eyes, smiling at her.

Sassy rose earlier than usual. Last night, she saw him again surrounded by clouds. He touched her cheek with his warm hand, saying, "Don't forget me or our love," then he faded away reaching for her. She made a cup of coffee and thought hard about him.

"I know he is real." Slowly she sipped her coffee, glancing out the window and noticing it was still dark out. She went into her bedroom and turned on the news, looking to see a weather update in Alaska. After she finished her coffee, she started her day with a shower.

Sassy perched on her bed, observing the sun rise over the hills. Archie sat on the bed waiting too. He wanted to see this gold reflection. Patiently waiting, the time had come.

The forest crystal sat on her bedroom windowsill when a beam of sunlight hit it, shooting a gold reflection across the room. Sassy, all excited, jumped up and down.

"Archie, watch this!" Sassy placed her entire hand in the stream of gold, and it disappeared. She giggled while moving her feet and hands in the stream when a wicked little thought popped into her pretty little head.

"What if I stand in the stream?" Nervously, she put her whole being into the gold fluid reflection. Looking at Archie, she counted down from five and stepped into the gold reflection.

Sassy heard electric popping as she moved around, feeling no different, then in a flash, everything went black.

EIGHT

High pitch noises with a disabling, piercing pain cursed over her as she lay on the ground curled up covering her ears. Nausea brought on by the dizziness she felt on top of the tingling sensation lingered from the fall. Sassy tried to adjust and focus her eyes. Everything was blurry.

"Am I OK?" She pushed herself up from the ground but was no match for the gravity. Blinking her eyes over and over, not able to focus, she rubbed her eyes again, noticing the smell. . . . "AHHH, IT STINKS!" The dirt odor was so intense! This was not a smell she knew. Nervous and scared, "Where am I?" she mumbled quietly.

Scared to stand up while her vision hastily returned, she saw the ground coming into focus and realized she lay in black, rich dirt. "I'm outside?" Looking around, rubbing her eyes as her vision cleared, the overwhelming size of the rocks and blades of grass intimidated her.

"WHAT THE FUCK!!" Looking and touching her arms and legs, feeling all over her body, exhaling relief, everything felt normal with no broken bones. She was pretty sure she had dropped from the sky.

"The sky!" Glancing upward, the sky looked the same but different. Slowly standing on her feet, she was astonished!!!! "Where am I?" Everything was enormous, just not her.

Her mind was flooded with questions: Am I crazy???? How could this be? I think I shrunk! How could I be so small???? What the fuck is going on? Where am I?

Feeling nausea, she couldn't hold it anymore. After she finished throwing up from the nerves jumping in her stomach, she sat back down in the dirt, pulling her knees to her chest, then wrapped her arms around her legs.

Taking a couple of deep breaths, dropping her head closer to her chest, she started looking around. Up high in the sky, she saw what looked like umbrellas opening and blowing away in the wind. As she looked harder, she almost screamed when she began realizing there were a lot of them, and they were fluffy. They reminded her of dandelion seeds she would blow in the air, making a wish. She watched them go by. One floated closer to her, noticing her.

"Oh my! They are bigger than me!" She froze for a brief second before she hid behind a blade of grass! Hearing high-pitch giggles in the breeze, Sassy peeked around the edge to see who made the giggling and laughing sounds. She caught sight of their beautiful tiny faces with bodies and legs!

"They are alive!" Astounded and scared, she scooted back up into the green blades of grass the size of an adult tree. Overwhelmed, she felt tiny and vulnerable. Quietly, she watched the dandelion creatures float by, chatting and giggling. She saw them waving their hands at her in what Sassy thought maybe was a friendly motion.

Peeking out through this massive swaying wall of greenery, she reflected on what she just witnessed, then figured it out. She was not on earth anymore. "Where am I?"

Replaying in her mind what she could remember, she recalled standing in her bedroom when she stepped into the flowing, gold reflection from the forest crystal. "The crystal!" She felt instant panic.

A sudden noise caught her attention, and she froze in fear, afraid to turn and face the cause of the noise. She sensed movement all around her. There, out of the grass blades across from her, huge hairy beasts the size of trucks came bursting through the blades, sending Sassy stumbling backward and landing on her butt on the ground.

They crept up on her so well, stealthy in their movements, blending into the surrounding lands with pointed horns resembling broken old tree branches. Big, black, shiny eyes with yellow mandibles and long antennas wiggled in Sassy's direction. Their stench was powerful. Politely placing her hand over her mouth and nose, it was that bad.

Sassy's eyes focused on the riders on their backs, noticing they were bipedal creatures resembling wood chips with squinting, glowing, pea-green eyes. If he stood next to a tree, she would have never noticed him. Holding still, one dismounted from a beast by sliding down the long, stringy hair, landing on the ground. Sassy watched the thick figure with big ears of leaves with moss hanging from them. It had sharp, tiny teeth in a mouth too large for its face. Her eyes spotted weapons too. The creature stood there looking at Sassy, communicating with the other creatures sitting upon the beasts. They gave Sassy the feeling she was about to become a prisoner. Keeping their distance from her, she could sense they wondered what or who she was.

A larger one, maybe a male, approached her, keeping one arm across his chest, holding on to what looked like a weapon. Sassy panicked, looking around for an escape. As she fought her fear; she struggled to be calm. She considered running for the massive trees. He stopped about ten feet away from her, giving her the opportunity to see him better and possibly calm down. Under the bark, she saw muscular arms and legs with a green-tinted skin. He even had holographic wings. The skin on his face blended with the wood surrounding his neon-green eyes hiding behind the moss hanging from him.

Something gave Sassy a sensation that calmed her. Easing her fear and replacing it with the feeling of being safe with the situation, she approached as he waved her forward. As she walked by the colossal beasts, she held her breath. "Wow!" She gasped for fresh air. The wood creatures communicated in tones where she couldn't tell if it was good or bad. They clicked and whistled. Commotion started as the beasts started moving again. She kept her distance but followed them, walking down a beaten path leading toward a magnificent tree.

Sassy was in awe at the beauty of the tree. It was enormous. She looked at the oversized flowers covering the tree when she witnessed it moving. The tree bark was in the motion. Moving in, then out. She watched, thinking the tree breathed. She had to stop walking to focus on an unbelievable sight. Holding still, she studied her surroundings. They were everywhere. The closer they walked to the tree, Sassy saw thousands of fairies showing themselves and looking right at her.

Millions of them took part in a fake 4D visual of the landscape they showed her. They played tricks on her, pretending to be the bark of the tree itself, wore flower petals on their heads, resembling flowers, and others wore tree leaves.

"Absolutely amazing!" Sassy was astonished. Laughing, she said aloud, "No wonder people can't see them as tiny as they are. I can't believe fairies are real. Oh my gosh!" She realized she was the same size as them! More came out, showing themselves. She saw fairies looking like what she read from books and movies, pale skin with black eyes and the bodies of tiny elves. But they had iridescent wings of different colors. Some fairies in the trees wore acorns as hats.

Their voices were high pitched as more joined around. They whispered among each other; it made Sassy feel a little uncomfortable with all the chatting. Without notice, the beasts stopped walking when within ear shot of the tree line. The beasts in line stood still as a feminine, older-looking fairy approached, studying Sassy.

She emitted beauty in all white. With huge blue eyes and dressed very elegant with a regal walk, her longer wings touched the ground. Her headdress reminded Sassy of a white orchid, and she moved with such fluency. She gave off a soft glow all around her. To Sassy, it felt like a comfortable vibe coming in small waves.

A small voice spoke, "Sassy, please do not fear us. My name is Gladys. I am nature's matriarch, born of a seed. I've waited for you a long time. Please, don't feel scared. No one will harm you here. There is much to discuss, but first we must get to safety. Your arrival, I'm sure, went unnoticed by others, so if you will, please follow us to safety. I will gather my guardians to protect us. We must hurry." As she turned around, she waved her hand in the air. Just like magic, all the fairies disappeared quicker than they appeared.

Sassy had the feeling she needed to follow her and began walking through the tall grass and uneven terrain, which got harder for Sassy, who felt very tiny. But she watched as the different creatures did it with ease and silence. A massive shadow covered the sky as a lizard-like creature with feathers flew over them. Sassy grabbed her ears at the screeching, feeling like she stood next to a speaker playing loud music. It appeared she was the only one affected by the screeching. Noticing the pace slowed down, the guardians on the beasts started gathering closer to them, forming a circle of protection as they entered a long, dirt tunnel at the base of a rosebush.

Sassy looked around at the oversized plants thriving and noticed thorns the length of Viking ships as sharp as double-bladed swords. The thorns on the vines were next to the massively huge white roses of York covering the entrance to the tunnel. Facing Sassy, Gladys communicated with her. "The York rose is very fragrant and used to mask odors." Sassy looked up hesitantly. Its pollen had attracted bumble bees the size of German Shepherds buzzing above, collecting all the pollen from the roses.

Sassy trembled with fear at being that close. She was not used to seeing the bottom side of a honeybee covered with pollen. Gladys looked at her, smiling and waving her in. She explained to Sassy, "They provide perfect protection for the tree and its occupants, and we provide them with pollen. It is a splendid arrangement." They continued walking right under a host of honeybees collecting pollen from roses. Sassy took one more look up, amazed. Her whole body vibrated from the fast movement of their wings.

Inside the rose bush deep underground, they walked through tunnels in the roots. It reminded her of walking through beautifully carved caverns in central Texas. An opening with a crack appeared in a very old tree. Sassy again stopped in amazement.

Inside the tree was a secret city. Her neck was getting strained looking straight up, trying to see all the different branches with crystal arched walls and walkways to different areas of the tree. Everything was made so elegantly. The ability and construction of this crystal castle built right into the tree was breathtaking.

A huge variety of different plants and vines thrived together in harmony. Water pipes with a little trickle of water wept down a Willow tree, forming a perfect pond with a smoky, white mist dancing off the banks of the water, making small clouds rising high into the tree leaves. Over by the bank was a group of green and red fly trap plants swaying in ferns as the breeze blew by, causing them to open their mouths, remiding Sassy of a nest of baby birds too small to fly and wanting to eat. Everywhere she looked, there was something new. It was a fairytale land, but real! Jasmine vines assisted for food and shelter for small creatures. It was like each distinct branch was a jungle full of insects and creatures.

As she touched and felt, taking everything in she saw, it surprised her when she noticed a face on this magical tree. A wise man, old, long beard, hiding his grin. It shocked Sassy when it winked at her! This was a real world here! It was her dream world. She had always had a unique bond with nature. Being a witness to the uniqueness of life here was incredible.

Gladys, who watched Sassy's amazement, turned toward her and said, "Welcome to The Wise Old Oak of Faermorreya."

As she moved a huge oak leaf aside, Sassy was exposed to an enchantment wonderland on the inside. Speechless for the first time, she looked around, able to see for miles inside the tree. There were thousands of different species along with the fairies, creatures with eyeballs and long appendages, others looking like hairy ears with wings, so many magical creatures. Most had the figure of humans. They all lived there together in peace. She looked up and noticed different levels, lit up by a luminescent glow from lightning bugs. The tree functioned like a well-oiled machine on the inside.

This is the most impressive place! she thought, with beaming, bright eyes.

Sassy touched the smoothness of the wood creating a stairway to an open foyer. They built this palace from the inside out with ancient magic. Carvings of scenery in the walls played mind tricks with her eyes. Sassy literally touched it to make sure it was not a separate room or levels. The tree carvings were like this everywhere.

"It's made to confuse invaders so they lose their way and make it easier to capture them," Gladys spoke as she took a seat upon a wooden throne made for a queen. She offered the one next to her for Sassy to sit. They had intertwined the thrones in a beautiful braid of Morning Glory vines, copper strands, and jewels with the huge blue-and-white Morning Glory flowers hanging overhead for privacy. Gladys asked her to relax and take it all in.

"There will be a celebration for your arrival later, but for now, just adjust, and I will answer all your questions soon. Welcome to FAERMORREYA, my human friend." Sassy thought she heard every other word Gladys said as she sat and watched all the bustling going on. Faermorreya, what a cool name, and it was REAL!

She saw different beautiful creatures working, collecting food. Others played. Females wrung out flower petals to collect the flower oils. Inch worms measured the steps and levels with tools. Slugs moved and left a trail of slime for a different creature shoving moist moss into cracks. Everyone had a job, a reason for being there. There were even soft tones of music being played.

A handsome male approached them and took a bow in front of them. Gladys waved her hand for him to rise. They spoke in a foreign language, but Sassy could sense it was about her. He reached for her hand. She was unsure on what to do, then he spoke English to her.

"Please, follow me. If you are OK, I will take you to your quarters so you can freshen up, if you would like?" Looking at Gladys, waiting to be introduce, looking at him caused Sassy to have sweaty palms. His presence made her nervous. She accepted and followed Alex.

She started chewing on her lower lip, thinking, "Oh my gosh! He is so sexy and good looking! He has a body of a man!" She got so tongue-tied around good-looking men. She replayed anything she said over and over in her head, making sure she didn't sound dumb. . . . Walking, she stumbled over her own feet. Alex grabbed her waist with brawny hands, lifting her up to steady her steps. She thought he smiled at her when he told her to watch her step.

"Walking through the tree can be difficult for some not familiar with their surroundings." Sassy knew she changed three shades of red from blushing; she was so embarrassed! She managed a thank you.

He was so human-like, except his eyes were black with neon-orange streaks, his hair a dark rust color and sleek, laying on his firm, flawless skin around his well-defined jawline. His wings were that of a wasp, turning orange and gray. Alex was so sexy. Standing next to him made her stomach feel warm. She knew she perspired. He reached out to hold her hand, and she hesitated, brushing her palm on her pants fast without him noticing. She hated touching clammy hands; no one enjoyed that!

She took his hand and followed him deep into the tree to what looked like living quarters. He turned, smiling, telling her that her hand felt warm; it was nice. It'd been a long time since he had held the hands of a human.

Smiling back, she noticed everyone watched them as they passed by, smiling with excitement and whispering like giddy children sneaking around. They came to the corner of a half circle room. Alex pushed aside a huge oak leaf. There, a chamber appeared. Cut into the walls of the tree were unique carvings of fairies and plants, but more suitable for a king and queen's chamber. A beautiful framebedframe made from a walnut shell with sheets and pillows made from velvety rose petals. There was a three-tiered changing wall in front of a bathroom made from a dried lily pad, with a sugar cane shoot for dispensing water.

Sassy just couldn't help herself; she touched everything. It was just unbelievable woodwork!

The silence broke when Alex said, "Please, there is no need to be nervous here. I can only imagine how you are feeling about being in a different world. You are safe here."

Excited, she turned to face him to say thank you, but he had hastily disappeared.

He was right. I am a little nervous and feel a little strange, she thought. Why did the crystal send me here??? Now what happens; how do I get home?

The excitement faded, she became overwhelmed with thoughts. To relax, she decided some meditation would do her good. That's what she needed. Maybe she would receive visions with an answer to all this.

NINE

Later, Sassy heard the same commotion outside her door, giggles with excitement in their voices. Pushing aside the oak leaf, she followed the voices and ended up back at the center hall. A celebration had started, dancing in circles and music played by guardians with string lap guitars and wood flutes. Tons of food and drinks lined the tables. Everyone indulged in the moment. Beautiful spider webbing draped over small branches like silk ribbons, which lit up when hit by the iridescent lighting from above. Feeling completely underdressed in dirty jeans and a t-shirt, Sassy took a seat next to Gladys, now in her formal wear, along with all females.

This intimidated her. Sassy was never popular with girls, and she could sense the same feeling here. The females were gorgeous, flawless features and all in their elegant flowing gowns matching the color of their wings, with flower petals on their heads. Their beauty was nothing for her to compete against.

She admired the males' dark outfits with red maple leaves as capes. The guardians even dressed in lily leaf capes. The whole place looked like a fairytale ball, creatures in costumes dancing in sync with each other. Sassy thought it was such an elegant and an orderly way of life. The evening festivities continued into the night. Sassy hadn't moved at all but enjoyed the fruity, sour drinks, smiling and watching as they danced in their unique and beautiful way.

Out of nowhere, Gladys stood. In her hands, she held a forest crystal. Instantly, the room quieted. She could have heard a pin drop. They were overcome with the energy of anticipation as Gladys held it for all to see. The crowd clapped, pleased! Bringing it down to chest level, she turned, looking back at Sassy, speaking out loud.

"Only someone special could activate the crystal that has a special bond and connection with nature, with love and peace in their heart. The forest crystal has found the young woman named Sassy from the outer earth. It transported Sassy to our dimension." Looking at Sassy, Gladys continued saying, "The forest crystals have been the lifeline between our dimension and the outer earth. We need it to live, and the earth needs us to survive. For centuries, we have lived in fear of demons. Our time for peace is here! Sassy will find the last crystal, reuniting it with the only two left in the universe!"

As she held the crystal up high, the crowd clapped and cheered, "Sassy, Sassy, Sassy!"

Standing, and reaching for Sassy's hand, she began leading her down through the center of the ballroom. Cheers happened as they passed. They walked through a long, poorly lit corridor to get to a small den. Meantime, Sassy thought, Find a crystal? I want to find my soulmate!"!

In a small room with massive, floor-to-ceiling columns on each wall, the columns, bonded together by the vines, grew over cubby holes sporadically placed in the walls. Gladys explained the vines. "Covered with magical poison ivy that can sense negative energy. If it feels negative energy, it will strike with deadly force, wrapping its vines around its prey, injecting its poison through curly thorns, waiting until the prey has swollen from its organs turning into liquid before it absorbs it." Leaning closer, Sassy could see scarlet in the veins.

"This is where the forest crystals belong, deep in the walls of the tree." Gladys handed the crystal to Sassy and motioned for her to walk toward the wall. Placing the crystal in the palm of her left hand, she raised her hand up.

Fear took over Sassy when the poison ivy vines moved, exposing the cubby for the crystal. She closed her eyes and slid the forest crystal into it, watching it glow. The glowing energy emitted from the two forest crystals intensified throughout the room. It gave Sassy the experience of dizziness, with an awesome, euphoric high. With her eyes closing and smiling her lazy smile from ear to ear, she laid her head back and fell into a trance, having no control of her movements.

Swirling green light surrounded her whole being. Sassy's body transformed into something different; the soft green color appeared to consume her and change her appearance and clothing. Her arms stretched out in front and her eyes closed; a thin, iridescent netting appeared, forming into new skin tightly to her body. A gown of the purest white softly reflecting different colors formed itself to her body. She awakened, coming out of this trance as her mind became clearer and clearer. A necklace formed from forest crystals appeared around her neck. Slowly regaining her movement, Gladys rolled a full-sized mirror of gold in front of her, showing her new reflection. Sassy looked and touching her skin on her arms, making sure this was real.

"I am so beautiful!" Her eyes had turned black and narrower, resembling an almond. Her hair was now white, waist-length, and woven into different braids lying over her wings matching the net texture on her skin.

Quickly, turning to face Gladys, she asked, "Is this real?"

Standing there holding her hands in front of her waist, Gladys answered, "Welcome home, Sassy. You are now known as, The White Queen." Sassy could not stop looking at herself. She was now the most beautiful fairy of them all here in Faermorreya. Immediately she stood straighter, prouder in her new confidence.

An electric vibe emitted around her, causing her to get a little nauseous. Looking herself over, she reached back and touched her wings, realizing the vibration came from her wings. She could not believe how delicate they looked, like tissue paper and felt like satin. Two sets of wings reached the ground, light gray with purple to green shades running throughout them, intensifying with her heartbeat. Her wings started flapping at just the thought of flying, which caused her to stumble forward. She was amazed by her transformation but still learning to control her wings.

Gladys waved her hands, and the room changed. "I want to show you something."

They were now in a hidden secret room in the tree. Stunned, Sassy looked at gold room with one long, beautifully carved gathering table with many benches and bookshelves for miles. The bookshelves held all their secrets wrapped in scrolls with green ribbons on them. It reminded her of a wizard's library.

"This is a room full of all your secrets!" Gladys displayed a smile. "Sharing the history of the invisible dimension known as Faermorreya feels right. Please, my dear, sit down and listen to me.".

"Long, long ago, forest crystals only grew in outer earth subterranean in extreme conditions that included fire and ice, deep in the mountains with lofty peaks. There was only one place on outer earth these conditions existed.". The outer earth had an open connection to our invisible world, where we, the guardians of nature, live.

"A magical land ruled by a queen from the Kona Tribe. This queen would come to the invisible dimension, opening the veil from the magic of the crystals. She gave open travel for all. She was loving and allowed us to reseed the planet, creating nature on the outer earth. The two dimensions thrived in peace and happiness, realizing the strength building as the two became one."

Squeezing Sassy's hands, making sure she listened closely, Gladys continued. "Three fully aged crystals are required to maintain control of the veil and protect us and the outer earth from demons. We only had possession of two." The queen knew that.

"The day came when demons found out about the two dimensions and the peace treaty between worlds. They grew jealous of the way fairies and humans had built trust in one another. So they started transforming themselves to resemble magical beings and causing havoc and pain to humans. The humans outside of the Kona Tribe started viewing the mystical creatures as tricksters and liars. They would seek us and kill many, leaving the queen no choice but to seal the veil, forever protecting us from her world.

"For protection, the Kona Tribe destroyed any crystal growing and ordered ruins of the land so no crystals would grow. Their queen called upon their shaman to save one crystal and place a spell on it so one day, when needed, it will choose a pure soul to find the hidden forest crystal in Faermorreya.".

"A shaman wrapped the last crystal in a special cloth with magic that hid its energy, placing it in a sealed box with a spell placed on it, buried deep in a mountain, keeping it safe from demons. Now it has returned; it found you! Trusting in you to find the other one and bring it to us! One on outer earth found you. You opened the veil."

Gladys took a breath, looking at Sassy, who was speechless, glued to the story, twiddling her fingers around the necklace. "Please, Gladys, continue."

Gladys, happy with Sassy's enthusiasm, continued. "Evil entities had joined forces and started a war, seeking the forest crystals on earth. A war like no other." She stopped there.

Sassy sat there thinking about Alaska and the Kona Tribe. She had been on the right track about Alaska! Gladys got up, looking for a certain scroll. She released a sigh in deep thought. Sassy scanned over everything in the room; everything was draped in what resembled gold, but Gladys said it was fairy dust. The same fluid dust she had stepped into back in her earthly bedroom. She sat there with her palms open, trying to collect some in her hand, stopping when Gladys giggled from watching her.

"The gold dust is a protection barrier; it helps keep wandering eyes at bay. It also neutralizes energy around you so nothing negative will engulf you. The fairy dust from the forest crystal has its own magic, powerful; if it gets in the hands of some wrong beings, it can give them access to destroy us and our realm."

Walking around Sassy, Gladys had a scroll in her frail, tiny hand as she took her seat. Studying Sassy's eyes, she said, "My dear, you may research our history anytime. I want you to feel at home here inside the wise old tree, as the rest of us do. OH! But remember, never take the necklace off! It chose you, so it will also protect you."

Concerned, Sassy said, "I'm confused Gladys; is someone or something searching for this crystal right now? The one around my neck? Did I hear you say someone wants to hurt me?"

Gladys could see the fear in Sassy's eyes. Gladys grabbed her hands firmly and seriously. "My dear, not just someone, the evilest of evil and his minions."

"What? Demons are looking for me?"

"Yes, my dear, I will explain everything, but first we must assign a protector for you so you may relax and enjoy this evening."

Sassy stood there blank faced, then told Gladys, "I was hoping the crystal was going to lead me to my soulmate. I was SO wrong. . . ."

Gladys reached out and took Sassy's hands in hers, began patting them, and smiled at Sassy, giving her a quick wink. "You never know, my darling; you are in the dimension of magic!" This changed Sassy's thinking process quickly; she wondered who her protector was.

They both reentered the celebration hall, the music and dancing still going on. No one even noticed they had been gone. Standing across the room under a chandelier of scarlet gems with a beautiful hue of red shining down on him, making his physique glow, was Alex. She was so drawn to his beauty. It was oblivious to anyone around her. Watching him, her gaze glued onto him through the crowds.

Sassy's stare was so strong, he felt it and turned to look in her direction from across the room. She tried not to notice him walk through the crowds, making her mouth go dry from anxiety. He had the slight strut of a confident male, just radiating sex appeal. His eyes glowed a brilliant orange, causing her to experience a warm tingling sensation. He got closer, and she blushed with sweaty palms again.

Talking to herself, "Hold it together, girl; my god you are a queen now!" Their eyes locked just before he knelt in front of her.

Oh my gosh! As she took a deep inhale, He smells so good, she told herself.

Slowly rising, he hesitated, then leaned closer to say, "Hello, my queen." He reached, taking her hand and giving a soft and seductive kiss on her skin above her ring finger. She could feel his presence causing her wings to pulse light with every heartbeat. She managed only to smile and prayed her hands were not sweaty or her wings didn't cause her to stumble again.

"My queen, you are stunning. No other could compare in all the realms. Your beauty is hypnotic." He nonchalantly moved around her, looking at her with such intensity. She just stood there letting him. . . .

Gladys approached them and was pleased to see Alex. She informed Sassy they had decided Alex would be her protector. "I hope you approve."

Nodding with a smile, Sassy agreed, trying not to look excited, turning to him. "Well Alex, so you are the lucky one."

In a deeper than normal voice, he whispered close to her cheek, "No, my queen. I am the honored one." Just then, the sexual tension between them showed a sinful side.

They took their seats at the thrones. Gladys looked around at the dancing, then demanded attention from both in a calm voice; she didn't want any attention drawn to their conversation.

"I must warn you; we worry. Our fears are that the evil ones noticed your arrival. With their greedy need to destroy our world, Faermorreya, and their will to kill all of us guardians of nature. They will destroy all the living plants and trees, causing a death of the earth from losing its oxygen field that came from our dimension. If they felt her arrival, they already know that the white queen has activated a crystal. They will seek her out."

Sassy looked at both. "What happened to the other queen before me?" Gladys paused, her manner changing. She did not want to answer Sassy's question.

With a lingering loss for words, Gladys responded, "Demons killed her."

Sassy took a quick glance at Alex, hoping he could ease her fear, at least make her feel better about having protection, especially from him!

She mentally wasn't ready to hear all of this. She excused herself, needing privacy. This was heavy news. Her mind spun, replaying over and over, "Why me? How do decisions get made by crystals?" Pushing herself through the crowd, she found an opening leading outside where she could get some fresh air. Also, so no one witnessed how scared she was. After taking some deep breaths to calm herself, she felt Alex standing behind her.

"I am going to be around. Do you think you could get used to that?" he said, smiling.

She started dumping her fears on him. "If you think it will help me not have any fear fighting, then yes. But I am not a leader, let alone a queen! This is impossible!"

Alex placed his hands up on her shoulder, turning her so her back faced the crowd and they were face to face. The heat from his hands soothed her skin as he looked into her eyes.

"I am going to prepare you for attacks, to protect yourself with the crystal, and to control energy using the environment for protection." He reassured her of her strength. "You will be fine, not to fear." Sassy felt that same calming sensation giving her some trust in him.

Back in her room, she struggled to understand. Her thoughts went to her true love. Thinking of him always calmed her. "If you are here in Faermorreya, please find me. I don't want to find a crystal. I just wanted to find you," she whispered out loud as she curled up into the fetal position on her little bed, begging him to come and visit her that night.

The next day, early in the morning hours, Sassy spent it with some female fairies showing up in her room with thin armor and new clothing so she could move around more efficiently. It amazed her how they made their clothing from plant material. Her favorite were the boots lacing up with thin strands of palms. After getting dressed, she felt like a badass wearing her new tight bodysuit made of some dark-green, shiny, sleek plant. She noticed her exposed skinchanged colors to camouflage her to her outfit.

Walking with a spear in hand, she was full of anxiety about the day's lessons. She followed close behind, entering a distinct part of the tree that was wide open and had sand on the floor. Sassy looked around, seeing many fairies in sparring pairs dressed like her, but in a different color. It was hard to hear talking over loud clashes as their spears collided in battle moves. Their bodies moved so fast she struggled to keep track of them.

She noticed two females fluttering over to her. One took her hand, guiding her to a far corner. Here they show her how to hide her wings tight to her back and how to hold and swing a spear. After she pleased them with control, it was time to show her how to use her wings as a weapon. They showed her how to vibrate her wings faster and faster until they created an electrical arch around her wings, then release it.

Feeling empowered after a while, Sassy's confidence was at a ten. She even impressed them with how quickly she learned. The fairies displayed jealousy, and all had short tempers, showing in Sassy's knuckles, swollen from being hit with spears if she messed up while they taught her a lesson. Some hits felt more personal, obvious they had strong attachments to Alex.

The time was right. Alex helped Sassy learn how to concentrate on the crystal to control energy with her hands. She couldn't believe it was possible, but it was! Closing her eyes and bringing her hands up to chest level and feeling the energy between her palms facing each other, she could visualize the energy by swirling her hands in a circle, moving her hands closer together, then far apart again in the motion of playing an accordion. She engaged with the energy as she pulled and pushed it between her palms. The feeling was pleasurable, electrifying. She spent days on training with the crystal, learning to fight with a spear, running fast, and moving objects out of her way with the wave of her hands.

She learned to do the same techniques in flight. Flying turned out to be a favorite for her. She liked to flutter around like a butterfly. Life was so different not being a human, being small in a vast world of nature. Sassy found herself not missing the person she used to be. She now had fresh worries and responsibilities affecting an entire realm. All of this happened because this amazing crystal picked her to wear it around her neck.

"I am the Queen of Faermorreya. This is who I am now. Sassy Hudson is no more."

Time passed, and she became a warrior queen able to listen to nature clearly, hurrying to hide very well. She adjusted well in her role as the White Queen, developing more leadership qualities, earning respect across the realm. Alex and she grew closer than a teacher with a student. They spent hours patrolling together.

Taking a casual walk, Sassy's attention drew to admiring the colors of the leaves changing into reds and golds. Faermorreya changed seasons like on earth, except this place had eight seasons in a year and the weather changed now. Alex stopped so they could watch the leaves transforming. Pulling down a branch, she could see the color run through the leaves changing in live time, a miraculous site. It was a domino effect across the land as they watched.

Hearing a deep humming from above them drew their eyes up; they saw it came from a mega dragonfly buzzing high in the tree. It dove right at them. Sassy thought it was going to crash into them. Instead, it hovered over their heads. The humming turned into a vibration running through their bodies from the dragonfly shaking its legs and covering them with some nasty, black, slimy mud. Splashing it all over them, the dragonfly flew upward and away!

Wiping her face and hair, Sassy exclaimed, "What the heck! What is this??? What kind of slimy stuff is this?" At once, the smell of the mud replaced their oxygen! It smelled of rotten egg and sour meat! Covering her mouth and nose, she looked at Alex as he knelt on one knee, rubbing the mud between his fingers in deep thought.

"Alex, what is this?" she snapped, trying to get the smelly mud out of her hair.

Intensely his eyes glowed orange and flickered as his jawline tighten. His body swelled from his muscles tightening; she could see anger across his face. Kneeling in the mud, he turned looking up at her, saying, "DEMONS!"

He got to his feet and demanded she follow him back to her chambers so she could wash the smelly mud off her and her clothing. They arrived. Alex talked in a stern voice, "My queen, when you finish, I will gather warriors. Please, wait here for me to come retrieve you." She stood there nervously but agreed by nodding her head fast. She knew he was in a hurry.

He quickly left her, heading to the gathering room. Behind closed doors, he made his plans to find and attack the demons. He didn't want to alarm everyone. He couldn't handle a full panic breaking out in the tree.

TEN

The Elders had a long discussion on the matter of the relationship forming between Aree and a protector named Alex. They had not planned for the human feelings of lust in Faermorreya. The only chance of this happening would have been before her transformation into the White Queen. Major concerns about this relationship were on everyone's mind. One Elder spoke of her actions not being recorded.

"Is this a sin? Has she sinned? Will her actions affect her reentering the Heavens? We must consider all sides." Aree from the Heavens was Sassy in the earthly realm, and the White Queen in Faermorreya all shared the same soul.

"So how do we account for the actions of one? We sent her on this mission. The responsibility lies with us!"

"There will be no blame, and we will record all actions happening. The only wise decision is to pray for her. We will never discuss this with Michael."

Arriving at the Ruby Mountains was a welcoming sight for both Michael and Nokomis. The trip had been long. Both were reminded of how rugged the mountains were on foot. It was a decision Michael had made to extend his arrival date, dreading being forced to report there. The weather was freezing, and he disliked the bitter cold causing icicles to form on their faces.

Nokomis wasn't pleasant himself. He was unhappy with Michael because they had walked the whole trip basically in silence. Michael wallowed in self-pity, and Nokomis needed a break from the emotions Michael experienced. The trip was almost over.

The bridge to the Ruby Mountains was in front of them. They crossed over the bridge and pushed through the enormous iron gates on the passageway to the monastery. The front entrance was in view. Nokomis picked up the pace, ignoring Michael. He knew exactly where to go, wanting Michael to off load. He stomped his hooves, wanting faster movement from Michael, who removed his last bag. Setting it down, he turned to Nokomis, who did not wait for a goodbye rub. Nokomis trotted off over to the stables for some warm climate and food. Michael watched on, knowing his attitude put everyone on eggshells. Even his stallion couldn't wait to get away from him.

The monastery always amazed Michael. It was the one place in Heaven hidden with secrets deep in its walls. It created its own mystic powers. Here, young soldiers learned about evil and its intentions. There were places here resembling evil dwellings. Only here would young soldiers see and feel some evil, learning how to combat it.

"Michael, is that you?" Turning around, Michael saw Captain Ishmael approaching him. "Ahh, it is you. Welcome to the monastery, my prince," Ishmael spoke in an echoing, deep voice coming from the jaws of a lion.

Michael nodded with an approving smile, rolling his eyes. He was not in the mood to be social or even talk. "You look good, captain," Michael whispered under his breath before Captain Ishmael could hear.

Having six pairs of wings, beige and brown feathers, with a body of a giant man dressed in purple and gold armor, he could morph his head into a lion or an eagle, depending on the mood he was present in and stood around twelve feet tall. Michael felt smaller in stature standing next to him. In the angelic rank, they were right under the Archangels, and they lived a military lifestyle.

Michael looked around the grounds, seeing many Seraphim here at the monastery involved in the teaching and learning of all new cadets. "Captain Ishmael, you look well, my friend," Michael spoke.

With a lion's heads three times the size of Michael's head, he pointed, directing Michael to his quarters with his massive hands. Grabbing Michael's gear for him, Captain Ishmael led the way through long hallways and stairways deep into the chambers of the monastery. The captain shared small talk as they walked down a thin, dark hallway lit up with candles all the way to Michael's door. He placed Michael's gear down and turned to explain the dining times and location. Backing up and bowing to Michael, he turned and walked away, barely fitting through the hallway.

Shutting the door behind him, Michael settled into a familiar room from centuries past. He lay down on the bed, staring at the ceiling with a mural of the constellations showing the different realms. Gabriel had painted this when they trained here. He remembered some good times at the castle, putting him in a nice nap before dinner.

Later that evening, Michael saw Captain Ishmael in the dining room. It was a huge, open floor plan with tables and benches in long lines with blue sapphires placed into the floor between tables. Michael looked up at the tall, onyx beams racing across the roof like a monkey bar. Hanging from each beam were at least a dozen or more diamond chandeliers reflecting beautiful lights across the room. Everything looked the same as years ago.

They covered each table with tons of fruit and vegetables, breads, and meats of all kinds. Fresh water and elixirs were in silver canisters spread out every six feet on the tables. Its looked like a feast for a king. This was daily dining here. Everyone ate together here; no one ate alone. This was very important for the bonding and trust building as a unit.

Joining the table of mixed-rank angels, Michael looked around at all the smiling, boyish faces reluctantly making him feel old. He sat down and started filling a plate with food when a young cadet seated across the table asked Michael to tell them some of his best war moments. Michael hesitated, looking at the young cadet, seeing the excitement in his eyes as the table erupted with chants saying, "MICHAEL, MICHAEL!" He then wiped his mouth and began a story from long ago. He moved his arms up and down, quieting the table. Glancing at all the peering eyes on him, he started.

"This was a war from long, long ago. Our mission sent us to the earthly realm. As we entered, it was a blinding rain and sharp hail, with tons of lightning and thunder colliding.

"Demons in those days had raised and controlled dragons. We hunted down and killed every living dragon in all realms, but demons had gotten ahold of some dragon eggs and raised them on earth, teaching them to seek us and kill.

"We were in an aerial fight, becoming outnumbered from the dragons and their fire. They forced us to form smaller groups so we could hide and fight in small numbers. It was dark, and the hail was problematic, feeling like razor blades in the wind as we flew fast, looking for others in our group. It was a long, hard battle, and I found Nokomis and myself alone, separated from our group.

"Which we know that fighting alone is never smart." Michael looked at all the youthful faces listening to him. "We trained you all not to lose focus on your brothers." Michael continued with his story.

"We were alone in the air, getting pelted from hail in a blinding thunderstorm. There were three dragons that noticed that they had separated us. One was to the North; one to the West, and one to the East. All at once, they stopped in midflight, screeching as they were coming up with a strategy so they can attack us. I couldn't think how we were going to get out of this mess.

"My stallion, Nokomis, took control. He stopped in flightmidflight, levitating, waiting for the dragons to make a move. He stopped flapping his wings; instead, he spread his wings straight out. I knew then what his plan was. I also spread my wings to the same position."

Captain Ishmael, with much excitement, saw and heard Michael telling the cadets, so he pushed his drunken body onto a bench where they ate and forced himself to take over the storytelling while spilling elixir everywhere. He exclaimed in a loud, belligerent voice!

"Nokomis took a dive in between the dragons, and we went into a spin faster and faster. Michael, with all his strength, held his sword straight up as they spun down in the middle of chaos!" Ishmael slammed his hands down on the table, causing the vast table to shake! "It was over! All three dragons were nothing but six pieces falling from the sky. This event stopped the war, and we won! We praised Michael and his stallion Nokomis for their bravery!"

The table stirred with excitement and chattering. At that moment, Michael saw an opportunity to excuse himself and head off to his quarters. Captain Ishmael watched as Michael walked away. He waited until Michael was out of earshot. He interrupted the chattering so he could finish the story. . . .

"LISTEN ALL, NOW LISTEN! Now that the war was over, Michael and Nokomis were in terrible condition. During the fight in the sky, as they sliced the dragons in half, this event caused the dragon's blood to fall all over Michael and Nokomis, causing Nokomis to scream in pain and Michael too. Nokomis could barely land them both safely. The pain of his burning flesh was excruciating.

"Dragon's blood is like acid. You can't wipe it off or stop it from burning, as you will learn in training." Reaching for the canister of elixir, Captain Ishmael started, slurring his words.

"We tried to wipe the dragon's blood off them, but the damage was already done. It had covered Michael and Nokomis. They both had long recoveries. But once they healed, they carried no scars. They are actual warriors!" Slamming the last canister of elixir and wearing half of it, Captain Ishmael, with his drunkenness, looked at each cadet, demanding them to remember this story. Letting out an enormous belch, he grabbed a big buttery dinner roll and stumbled off to his room.

Time passed slowly. Day after day went by, then week after week. Michael remained busy, and he returned to his warrior mentality. Maintaining a routine. Spending time here helped him remember his purpose and what was required of him. Feeling stronger and normal, he grew tired of scheduled meetings on a teaching syllabus and doing appearances in a classroom to tell some war story. He longed for home. He wasn't told how long he needed to stay at the monastery.

One morning he left his quarters earlier than usual; he wanted to take Nokomis for a ride before he had to appear in the sword-training classroom. Today he would pass out swords, and the cadets' training would begin. Michael had his sword on his side. He had spent hours polishing it to show it off, but right then, he wanted some personal time with Nokomis. Turning to walk down a huge spiral staircase with a runner of gold covering each step, he slowed down, counting the steps he took and to respect the Elders descending in front of him.

One Elder spoke, not noticing Michael was only a few steps behind them. He continued his discussion about Aree in a low tone.

"The word coming from the Holy City is that we are going to be recording Aree's journey, even though she is the White Queen in Faermorreya. Not only that, but she also has a personal protector, Alex, who has become close to her."

"OH MY GOSH!" the other Elder spoke. "I hear demons have found a way to Faermorreya. We have much worry that she is being distracted by Alex. She must continue with her mission."

Michael felt like someone had just punched him in the stomach, grabbing the railing so he didn't fall. "WHAT DID YOU SAY?" His voice startled the Elders. Michael descended quickly on to them. "WHAT DID YOU SAY? IS AREE IN DANGER? WHO IS ALEX? WHAT—WHAT IS GOING ON?"

Michael was three steps away when the Elders vanished in a quick panic into the thin mist. He stood there in shock! Breathing heavily, his mind spun as he stood there in a cloud of blue smoke. He turned and rushed back to his quarters. Looking around for his belongings, he packed his things and prepared to leave, replaying what he had just heard over and over in his head. His anxiety ran high. His thoughts were of her being in danger and no one around to help.

"DEMONS, oh how they will pay if they touch even a hair on her head.... And Alex! Who the hell is this?" Not even shutting the door behind him, he ran down the stairway with his bags.. He passed others, not even seeing or hearing them, focused on one thing only: Aree.

Entering the stables, he spotted Nokomis and whistled him over. Nokomis read Michael's energy. He knew they were leaving before Michael had the chance to say anything. Lowering his head, he patiently waited as Michael loaded his gear before mounting. Turning Nokomis to the north in the direction of the Celestrian, Nokomis expressing excited for the trip home; he spread his wings and gives a little prance.

Rubbing Nokomis's neck, Michael spoke, "We are flying on this trip, so take to the skies, my friend!" Nokomis reared up and neighed, spreading his massive wings horizontally. Like a flash of light, they were gone.

Flying through the snow and breaking free of the crazy changing weather, Nokomis flew higher and higher. He felt free when Michael allowed him to take control. Gliding through the celestial skies, he began climbing higher and higher, then turned into a dive. They sped up faster into a nice flight pattern. Michael was being a little pushy on speed, but Nokomis knew how to handle Michael when he was anxious.

ELEVEN

The decision was made for Alex to get together with a squad of warriors. They would find where the demons stayed, along with the plan of a sneak attack to kill them all. Alex explained to his men the importance of not allowing the demons to come to them when he looked up and locked eyes with Sassy. She couldn't stay in her quarters anymore. Patience was one thing she didn't have, so she had imposed herself quietly, hoping he wouldn't notice her, but he had.

She could sense his fear but couldn't tell if he was upset with her for not listening to him. She knew there was something important he was not telling her. Alex could be very secretive about issues and showing feelings. This was different. She knew he hid something.

She watched as the meeting ended. The guardian of the woods and a mixture of pixies and male fairies gathered in groups, talking among themselves. One group prepared to leave as soon as possible, gathering their weapons and shields. This group was Alex's men. They started their journey tomorrow night. Others prepared for battle and started protection duties around the tree. They sent two fairies to guard the room with the forest crystals. Gladys sent word out across the land to all creatures to take shelter and remain hidden. Sassy stood there holding the beautiful gold filigree crystal necklace around her neck as she overlooked all the hustling and chattering going on around.

Twirling it around her fingers, she didn't know how to feel. All this time she had in training for moments like this but never wanted to experience it. A warm hand slid into hers, giving her a gentle squeeze, reassuring. Closing her eyes and giving a brief grin, she knew it was Alex. He spun her around with his hands on her hips. Staring at him, she got lost in his eyes, then he whispered close to her ear, which sent goose bumps all over her body. "Come with me. . . ."

He took her hand and led her to her chambers, which for a long time had been next to his quarters too. She chose Alex as her advisor too; they had announced it to everyone in the tree, and they received it well. It helped eases gossip among the females looking to cause problems. They expected to have the advisor's chambers near their queen. Everyone respected and trusted Alex. He was a natural king. . . .

He pulled the leaf down in the doorway, turned, took her hand, and walked over near her bed. Not saying anything, he sat down, looking at her intensely. "My queen, I sense you're bothered and scared, and I am telling you nothing will harm you, but I know there is something deeper racing through you mind. I am here to listen," he said, caressing her cheek and looking into her eyes.

Feeling safe, she shared her fears. "I thought the forest crystal brought me here to connect with my soulmate. I was coming here to find him, to pursue a life with him. Since I have been here in Faermorreya, my gut feeling is off, as if he is hurting or I did something wrong. I know you must think I am foolish for believing in visions." She turned away from Alex, embarrassed.

He grabbed her hand before she walked away and assured her visions were no laughing matter but a gift only given to special beings. "Alex, I fear demons!" Sassy blurted out.

"My queen, I must ask, do your visions have anything to do with demons?"

She sat still for a moment, thinking, then replied, "No, why?"

A guardian stood in the doorway, banging on the wall. "Lord? We need to speak to you alone."

Standing, he turned facing her. "You're nervous, my queen. Please try to get some sleep. You need your rest. I will check in on you later."

With half a grin, she watched him as he turned and looked at her one more time before he walked away with his soldier.

Sitting on her bed, she heard his footsteps get faint. Sassy took his advice. She had no clue what was going to happen now that demons had announced their presence. Hugging her cotton pillow, she felt scared and struggled to get demons out of her head. She found the strength to do some meditation to soothe her. It wasn't long before Sassy slept and dreamed....

***

Seduced, he pulled her into his body, radiating so much neat. Not wasting any time to tell him how she felt, she showed him by pressing her lips on his neck as she placed her hands around his waist, using her fingers to feel his muscles in his lower back around the base of his wings. She kissed his neck. Bringing her hands back around to the front of his waist, moving upward, feeling his biceps, then his rock-hard abs creating his beautiful chest. He gently squeezed her breasts, sending a tingling sensation down to her hips as they kissed with such passion.

Hearing him groan in pleasure created her to feel aggressive, wanting more, so she slid her hand down to his groin area. He untied her straps crisscrossing under her breasts and holding her top on. After her straps and top landed on the floor, he stepped back, admiring her beautiful, perky breasts. He wanted to violate her.

Rubbing her breast and kissing her neck, he picked her up and placed her on the edge of a bed. She smothered him, kissing every part of his torso, pulling the string keeping his pants on. Looking down, she noticed his huge, hard, bulging muscle begging for her touch. She couldn't resist; she wanted to please him. He knew what she was going to do and moaned pleasurably.

Sinking his finger into the bed pillows, he watched her going down on him with such a perfect amount of suction as she stroked his cock in a steady motion. His legs started to tighten up and tingle with the approaching orgasm. He grabbed her head, moving her hair out of the way so he may watch her movements. She saw him watching, pleased with the pleasure he received from her.

Breathing heavier, he felt ready to explode deep in her mouth as she stroked him harder and harder. Shaking in ecstasy, his animal instinct kicked in, and he aggressively pulled her up and placed her on his lap. He wanted her to reach orgasmic pleasure with him.

He started on her breast, nibbling on her nipple, causing her to yearn for more. Turning to lay her naked body on her back so he may have his way with her, he looked at her beautiful body, then took position over her. He kissed her soft, warm lips, ready to thrust himself into her when she watched him open his eyes. Piercing white eyes!

White eyes that shook her to her core, she screamed herself awake, overtaken by the trembling fear from those glowing white eyes!

"Those were not Alex's eyes!" Sassy noticed her bed was damp from sweat. She sat there, confused by her erotic, fearful dream. That was not a vision but a nightmare. She got up and changed into warmer clothing and replaced the blankets on her bed. After pacing the floor in fear of what was to come, she tried again to get some needed sleep.

The next morning, she was still confused. She had waited for Alex to return last night, but he hadn't. Smoothing her hair over her right shoulder, she hoped to stop Alex before he started his busy day.

Later that morning, he arrived back at her quarters. Sassy kept the white eyes nightmare a secret from him. Alex wasn't responding in the way she had expected. He knew Sassy had something to do with demons. "What is her connection? Why are demons here? Is it Sassy they want?"

Confused, she went to approach him. He looked at her. "Please pack lightly and put on your armor. We will leave soon." He reached for her hand, looking at her calmly.

The time had come. The scouting expedition left the tree walking through tall grass until nighttime arrived. Sassy realized walking through the forest at night when you were one inch tall was very intimidating. She noticed she wasn't the only one feeling this way.

So they took to the trees offering more protection. Walking along branches in straight lines, they wore leafy headdresses so, from an aerial view, they looked like worker ants carrying tree leaves above their heads, on their way back to their home. They walked quietly and for a very long time.

Below on the ground were creatures assisting in the expedition, the ungars, weird beings that didn't speak and had unpleasant attitudes. Alex caught up to Sassy, walking next to her. Seeing her curiosity about the large beings, he began whispering in her ear. "They live in grassy knolls on the forest floor replanting seedlings everywhere and are incredibly strong beings that can carry a lot at one time. They live in clans with unique, characteristic features from the next."

Sassy looked down and focused her attention on their appearance. They had tiny noses with big fat lips, maybe three fingers instead of four, and wore the same clothing and hats. Some had coarse, long, curly whiskers, fat hairy feet, and huge lashes surrounding gigantic brown eyes. Sassy learned they communicated with each other with their eyes.

It had been hours of moving from tree to tree under the cover of darkness. With no sign of demons being around, Alex called in the aerial scouts to fly out head of them, checking for any signs ahead. One returned hastily to inform Alex an ungar had spotted trolls some distance ahead of them. Alex told Sassy the news.

"Trolls have set up residence in the swamps that lead into caves in the back of the waterfalls. The shaggy ink cap mushrooms grow in abundance around the falls and trolls love living in the tall mushrooms with wide ridges all over the tops that provide shade and shelter. Most of them have a nasty smell, so living in fungi that has its own powerful odor gives them the ability to mask their personal stench, a musky, fishy stench."

Sassy looked at Alex. "What do they look like?"

Alex quieted his voice to a whisper as he leaned closer to her. "Very nasty beings with a huge, bulbous head with only a few whiskers, but mostly bald. They have greasy-looking skin and fat rolls, oozing warts all over their bodies. They have long ears with massive metal hopes hanging from them. Tiny hands with stubby fingers resembling tiny wood stumps. As they age, they get uglier. Oh, and they like to eat fairies and mosquitos."

Alex warned Sassy to keep a distance from them. "The time has come. This is where the dark mud came from. It looks like the evil demons are hiding behind the falls and working with the trolls." Alex kissed her hand and turned to gather some guardians from the woods and fairies to discuss the next step.

Screeching howls high above the trees echoed down to the forest floor. Banshees flew and created the terrifying howls. Sassy stood in a panic. Alex ran back to her, squeezing her hand tightly as they hid from danger in a small hole in the side of a branch on the tree. She started seeing light explosions in puffs of smoke. He explained the lights were the spirits of fallen fairies and pixies. It was like one after another exploding in air. She felt his fear; they were under attack from different directions.

Sassy's heart started racing when Alex asked her to stay hidden as he went to fight. There were many demons and evil creatures! The sky looked like a dark shadow covering the treetops from the swarms of banshees flying. Down on the ground, trolls had many guardians surrounded. Sassy witnessed a troll ripping the wings and the head off a fairy before he dropped its body into his mouth. She could even hear the bones cracking as it chewed with its mouth open. She covered her ears from the screams and closed her eyes, wanting nothing more than to be anywhere else but here.

Slowly opening her eyes, she could see an evil creature resembling shadow dogs chasing the Ungars like balls. There was terror and evil everywhere. Black banshees flew while others transformed with distinct features with different attack techniques. She tried to stay hidden in a tree, but a gremlin landing on the branch in front of her spotted her. Sassy could not believe what she saw!

Yellow glowing eyes of fire-charred skin, body of a dogman, all bloody with dripping saliva from its razor-sharp fangs. It landed on all four legs but stood in front of her on two legs. Looking closer, it saw her, showing its strength and power. It tried to tell her something, but it was in tongues with a deep, crackling voice.

Before it received a reply, Sassy had raised her hand to her chest and pushed outward, causing a force of invisible energy to move in the dogman's direction. She hit it right in the chest with such force, causing the creature to yelp and shake uncontrollably before it exploded, sending small pieces of flesh to the ground.

Sassy was SOOOO empowered! . . . Having a blast of confidence felt great! She began killing flying banshees and gremlins in the trees and hitting the trolls with tremendous energy. Alex stood behind her, keeping her close to him. They were back-to-back fighting for their lives. He reached back and grabbed her hand, squeezing it tight. She turned, looking at him, praying they made it out of this battle. She somehow knew he thought the same thing. Her mind kept playing over and over, "Please, Lord, help us!" There were just so many. . . . Fighting went on all around them for hours. The sky looked like a fireworks show with the loss of fairies and pixies.

Alex was hit and fell to a branch below them, wrestling with a dogman. Sassy wanted to help him but had too many evil beings attacking her at once. She closed her eyes and pushed hard outward against the energy, causing them all to explode around her. It took a brief while for the air to clear. She couldn't see Alex anymore!!! She feared, not knowing if he was alive. At some point, she panicked, causing her to tire quickly. Every time she pushed energy, it took a toll on her.

"Where is Alex? I need my protector! Please, Lord, help me! There are too many!" She started vibrating her wings, building power to shoot out rays of electricity just when she stumbled to her knees from being hit.

A burning sensation intensified; the same sensation turned into horribly excruciating pain in the side of her neck. She placed her hand to touch her neck and felt and saw a spewing, warm, green liquid shooting between her fingers, instantly covering her hand.

"What the!" Her eyes were blurry, and sounds faded in and out. She struggled to stay alert, seeing the green liquid running down all over her body. She went numb, fighting to hold her head steady. She saw a red, creepy, burnt finger reached out from a black shadow. Laughing, *"HAHAHA!"* then ripped the necklace right from her weak, limp neck with no fight from her.

Seeing the demon licking her blood on his spear, she knew she was in trouble. Everything turned into a silent slow-motion movie as she fought to look around at the fighting going on. Through echoes, she could hear Alex screaming out, "MY QUEEN!" just as she saw him.

Feeling pleased, wearing a lazy smile on her face, she saw Alex was alive. Holding her neck, her body got heavy. She crashed to the edge of the branch before the demon, laughing, kicked her off.

Time had stopped for her. Feeling weightless, she looked to the sky one last time as her vision started fading faster and faster! Sassy hit a tree limb, then hit the ground, lying limp in a growing puddle of warmth around her head. They killed her. Her lifeless body lay on the ground as evil creatures began creating a circle around her, celebrating their win and protecting their prize.

Horns were blown all around, alerting the war was over! Evil had won. Cheers of roars and screeches filled the air. They picked up her body and carried it down a trail toward the waterfalls. There, at the beginning of a cave, he stood.

Standing on a rock above the crowd was a massive being with a red cape blowing in the wind behind him. Part human form, but not. Way bigger, with claws for hands and feet. They handed her body off to him.

He held her body in the soldier's position, looking around and laughing in a deep, creepy tone resounding across the hoard of evil beings. The crowd praised him as he stood above the hoard of demons gathered. He raised her body above his head, her limp body hanging across his arms. Wrapped around his right claw was the necklace.

"WE FINALLY HAVE WHAT WE NEED!" he screamed over the crowd. Laughing his evil, deep, creepy laugh, he screamed out to the crowd, "THE WHITE QUEEN IS DEAD! HA! HA! HA! THE WHITE QUEEN IS DEAD!"

After some time flaunting her body, this leader turned and entered the dark cave behind the falls and took her body and the necklace with him. Glowing, red lightning bolts rocketed across the skies, switching its color and replacing it with a depressing, dark-gray color, adding a chill to the air. The dying process had begun. Faermorreya experienced the worst thing that could ever happen. Now the nature realm was under control of evil. Any surviving fairies and guardians of the woods went into hiding until they could make it back to the old wise tree alive.

TWELVE

In Celestrian, at the Grand Cathedral, meetings and discussions were in full swing, seeking answers on what to do with Michael and his disobedience against orders, leaving the monastery.

"Michael has never disobeyed an order. He does not have free will. What was he thinking?"

An Elder appeared to take control of the chattering. "Michael is an Archangel, a warrior of Heaven, not to mentioned loved dearly by all realms. We will hear him out on his decision to leave the monastery. We must know the reason for his actions."

Another Elder spoke out. "Aree and Michael are soulmates. I understand why he would panic from overhearing a private conversation between Elders, especially when he only received opinions in a discussion. He made a rash decision without facts. We need to decide what he should know."

Pausing for a second, the Elder continued, "A watcher delivered the news to us earlier that the White Queen is dead. The one hope we had on sealing the veil is now gone. What happens to Aree is to be seen now. Her story could die forever, lost in Faermorreya, or her earthly powers will keep her alive and she will reunite with Michael."

"Keep her in your prayers" was mumbled across the room.

"When are we meeting with Michael? He is going to demand answers. Compassion is what Michael is going to need. We need to get Gabriel and Raphael to explain the issues we are experiencing with Aree. The bond between brothers will make it easier for Michael to understand and accept. We will send a message to the brothers with the utmost importance."

***

A beautiful, white dove flew and delivered a scroll tied with a gold ribbon through the window of Raphael's apothecary deep in the woods. He knew exactly where it had come from. Standing by a window reading and running his fingers through his hair, he started rubbing his red whiskers on his chin … as he pondered what he read. He laid the scroll down and continued working on a new, more potent flavor of elixir.

Raphael had invented the drink many moons ago. He tried over and over until one night he had the right fermented figs and grapes with a small amount of Absinthe for the euphoria effect and VOILA! It was the favorite drink of the Heavens, maybe throughout the realms.

"This new one I will call Ambrosia," he spoke as he spun a sample around in a small glass, looking at its clarity before drinking it.

Replacing the tops on multiple jugs full of different herbs and turning to blow out the fire heating oils, he picked up and rolled the scroll back up and shoved it into his pants under his belt, preparing to leave his apothecary for the day.

He flew to his personal quarters in the east wing sharing a floor with Gabriel. Before he met up with Gabriel, he needed to be cleaned up. He pushed open the immense bronze doors, which caused a strong breeze to move through the room, moving sheer green curtains like waves on the ocean leading out to his balcony. His quarters dripped in bronze. There was a bronze railing on his balcony meeting the stone, African turquoise floor. Different medicinal plants and vines hung from the ceiling throughout his quarter. He had a fancy bottle collection he kept different medicine oils in. It had an earthly, Roman era decor to it. He could hear violins and harps playing in the distance. Closing his eyes and enjoying the harmony of both relaxed him. This was just what he needed after a day of scientific mixing of herbs and fresh oils.

***

A dove was in flight to Gabriel in the stables painting portraits of the stallions grazing in the meadows. He enjoyed cataloging all paintings of the stallions and Griffins as they grew. It gave him great peace to do this.

He had paintings lining the walls in the stables of the heavenly creatures. His favorite paintings involved the horses as colts jumping and playing in the meadows trying to figure out their wings.

The scroll fell to the ground next to him while he cleaned a paint brush. The Cathedral dove flew away as he looked up. Turning his attention down, he was curious as to what this could be. Removing the gold ribbon and unrolling the scroll, after reading it, he started packing up his paints, cleaned his brushes, and covered up wet paintings on easels. He headed back to his quarters in deep thought with some concerns. Rushing a little faster, he knew Raphael had received the news also and was probably waiting to talk with him.

It was cooler than usual that evening. Gabriel stood on his balcony with elixir in hand, staring at the celestial skies changing in different colors. Raphael helped himself in and walked up to Gabriel and startled him!

"Shit! Man!" Gabriel shouted.... "I didn't know you were here! Get yourself a mug out of the cabinet and meet me here!" Gabriel mumbled, irritated.

Raphael grabbed a mug, filled it up to the rim, and took a gulp, then sat down across from Gabriel. "You are a little jumpy this evening. This is a mess!" Shaking his head. "How are we going to explain this to Michael?"

Raphael continued, "From what I understand, Aree went to the earthly realm as Saslia Hudson, a.k.a. Sassy. The last and lost forest crystal found its way to her, and she figured out how to activate it. It transported her to Faermorreya, where she became the white queen and was in a battle with demons and killed by a wound to her neck. Am I correct?"

Gabriel just nodded yes, still in shock! Not knowing if Aree was gone forever, he held the rim of his mug to his lips. Standing up Gabriel spoke, "OK, Michael is on his way home because he overheard only bits and pieces of two Elders speaking in private about Aree's actions in Faermorreya and not knowing what to record in the House of Records?"

"My brother, that is what I believe to be true," Raphael agreed.

They both took long drinks before breaking the silence. Raphael spoke, "Let's tell him the truth, but not the part that will worry him. He doesn't need to know that the White Queen is dead. Michael cannot handle this news! Let's just reassure him she is doing exactly what we need her to do and that she is fine and well. We're hoping she completes her mission soon." Looking at each other, wanting to convince themselves this was the right thing to do, they toasted to an easy delivery to Michael. They sat and drank more, trying to numb that feeling of anxiety creeping up on them as time passed and grew closer to Michael's arrival.

Two moons rose in the north when Michael was close to the castle. Without being attacked by anyone, he was hit with some tremendous pain in his neck. Holding his hand over his neck, not knowing what went on, he almost fell off Nokomis from the dizzy sensation he felt. Holding on with all his might, Nokomis picked up the pace, knowing something was wrong with Michael. As they approached the water and its shoreline, the tower of the Archangels' castle was in sight.

Nokomis snorted and neighed louder and louder, trying to alert anyone around as they landed in the front gardens. Gabriel noticed and came running out to help Michael down. Looking worried and confused, not knowing what was wrong with Michael, he saw Michael was coherent. He unloaded his gear from Nokomis and sent him to the stables, but not before Michael reached for Nokomis to hug him around his neck. Nokomis tilted his head into Michael's hug. Whispering in Nokomis's ear, Michael promised to be nicer and not so demanding, then kissed his head. Nokomis lifted his head in approval and turned toward the stables for some nice rub downs on his legs, water, and some carrots with treats.

Gabriel helped Michael to his quarters. He watched Michael touch his neck every now and again, noticing he was a little dizzy as he unpacked, anxiously covering it up, wanting any information his brother might have about Aree. Gabriel saw the pain in his eyes and wondered what was going on. Raphael showed up to greet him and welcome

Michael home, but Gabriel interrupted, asking Michael about his neck. Michael couldn't hide the pain anymore. Facing his brothers, he explained the pain had come out of nowhere. He walked over to the full-length mirror and saw a black bruising had formed. Covering his neck fast, he didn't want his brothers to see the mark.

Michael changed the conversation, asking how thing were around there to take the focus off his neck. He continued to unpack, keeping his back to his brothers. Thinking over and over, We heal differently than humans. Our bodies do not keep battle scars. Confused where it came from, it burned and grew darker.

Rejoining his brothers in the living room, both were surprised by Michael's calm demeanor when he said, "So what do you two know about Aree?" After listening to what his brothers had to say, he smiled at them, hoping to convince them he believed them. Which Michael did, but he knew something was missing. There was something about Aree not being told to him, but WHY?

Fighting to hold back his anger and trying to look calm, Michael looked at both brothers, telling them he was tired from a long trip. "Let me catch up with you two later," he hollered as he turned to enter his bedroom. Gabriel, feeling pleased, opened Michael's front door to leave with Raphael close behind.

The next afternoon the singing bowls vibrated Michael's call on the F note. The Elders requested his presence. Knowing they didn't like to wait; he flew to the steps of the Cathedral. Slowing his breathing, putting away his wings, and wiping down his clothes, he ran his hands through his hair, trying to look as good as possible, covering his neck with his hair. A concerned feeling took over his body. The burning mark on his neck intensified as Michael adjusted his collar, hoping no Elders would see it. He entered the room in silence. He expected some greetings, but it was complete silence. A mist formed an Elder; he waved for Michael to take his seat on his throne. Another at the head of the table expanded, questioning Michael.

"WHY ARE YOU HERE?" Suddenly, feeling like a school child sitting in the principal's office waiting for a punishment, Michael wondered how severe his actions were. Sitting straight up with his hands at his sides, he began explaining how he overheard Elders and feared for Aree's safety, so he felt it was best if he returned.

The Elder at the head of the table grew larger, and his mist drifting around him grew. He shouted loud toward Michael in a stern voice, "WE DECIDE WHAT'S BEST FOR OUR REALM, NOT YOU!"

Another Elder spoke softly, saying, "You disobeyed your orders, Michael! You fail! Chaos is what you cause!"

Michael held his head down, disappointed in himself. He knew he had been wrong in leaving without permission, but something told him to do it. He knew in his heart he did the right thing, so why was he going to be punished? Didn't they feel the same way? Something is not right, Michael told himself.

An Elder approached holding his hand above Michael's head, saying, "Michael, your actions require consequences. As an archangel, you lost focus on your duties. You have put others' needs behind yours. Obeying all orders is what you are required to do. You are to report every dawn to the Cathedral and pray for forgiveness, and after that, you will have new orders of what is required of you."

Michael stood in silence, then reluctantly bowed in acceptance. He never had disappointed an Elder or any of his brothers. He walked to the door when one glided in a ring of smoke in front of Michael and looked at him quizzically, tilting his head to side to side, then questioned the mark on his neck. Michael nervously grabbed the collar of his shirt, pulling it tighter to his neck. Bothered by the feeling, hiding the mark was uncomfortable For Michael. It was something new, and he didn't understand why he felt pain and had a mark on his neck. Michael, looking around to make sure no one else listened, told the Elder what he had been doing when he felt it and the dizzy feelings he had afterward.

"At first, I thought it was a scratch and didn't know what caused it. I was in flight with Nokomis returning to Celestrian from the monastery."

The Elder listened closely to Michael, knowing that a knife killed the White Queen in her neck in the same place as Michael's mark on his neck. This caused much concern.

Walking down the corridor, Michael felt heaviness in his chest. Rubbing his hand across his pectoral muscles, this was new too. He was not familiar with all the heartache and pain experienced. Pushing his hair back off his forehead, he couldn't figure out why he experienced mortal emotions.

He had seen the emotions of pain and heartbreak in humans on earth. He never understood it. Ever since Aree had left, he had an incomplete sense of himself, a fear that joy has escaped him. He was in Heaven, and there was no heartbreak here! What was going on? Why hadn't he told them? Neither the Elders nor he had mentioned the name Alex. . . . The Elders were hiding something.

At the altar, kneeling, he prayed for understanding of all the crazy thoughts and emotions he experienced. After he tilted his head, seeing through blurry vision caused by tears he held back, he felt a warm breeze filled with jasmine blow by. It was Aree's favorite scent. It comforted him. He knew it was a sign everything would be OK. Cracking a slight smile, he rose. Feeling a little better, he headed out. Feeling the pleasant breeze, he took a deep breath in of the fresh air and told himself she was OK.

***

After the meeting with Michael, the Elders decided on an agreement about Aree. "We thought there would be no need to record the actions of Aree becoming the White Queen. It is a position given to a being through a magical crystal, so the time with the protector, Alex, assigned to the queen could have been another pure soul."

Another argued, "But the White Queen died from a spear striking her in the neck, and now Michael carries a mark in the same place. Their bond of love has connected him to all the different lives Aree has. They are so connected he might already know of her descending into

Faermorreya and transforming into the White Queen. We must hold her accountable of lust and any other sin she committed in Faermorreya."

A different Elder chimed in, "Michael should not know of this incident or hear of the queen's death. Especially since he knows nothing of why the mark formed on his neck. We are all in agreement he is to be told nothing more about Aree's mission. Elders will be called to meet when and if we have any news. Until we meet again about the subject, continue to pray for Aree."

***

Morning prayers felt longer today. No matter how hard Michael tried to stay focused on the job at hand, he couldn't stop feeling something just wasn't right. This feeling haunted him. He wondered how he could find out some news on Aree. Knowing the Elders no longer talked to him about her and there was no reassurance on her progress, he knew his brothers withheld information. Never had there been so many secrets regarding a mission to a different realm.

He had a desire to know the truth, no matter what happened. He made a choice to find the watcher who kept track of her. Michael risked punishment talking with a watcher. The watchers only report to the Elders. He was crossing a line for love.

The watchers lived near the outer banks of Heaven's realm on the lowest clouds. It lied way beyond the Ruby Top Mountains. Making his plan to go to the outer banks was a little tough to pull off. He couldn't let anyone know what he was doing, and he had to make sure no one noticed he was gone.

Michael had never kept secrets from his brothers. He also didn't understand why everyone hid secrets about his relationship with Aree. The more he thought about it, the more he convinced himself to do it now. He knew there would be talk if he left during the day. So he waited for the late-night hours. His plan was to sneak around the main entrance of the stables to get Nokomis. Silently, then, they would exit the stables and into the night sky. They would head to the outer banks of Heaven near the edge of the universe.

It was a very different place than Celestrian. There was not much landscape there, just hazy gray-colored skies and gray granite with sand everywhere. The watchers looked down into the edge of the Milky Way. This was how they kept track of all movements and business in the universe. They could even view into an earthling's life like watching a movie. The watchers were the only beings who could do this. They saw all dimensions in dark space; that was why everything was gray.

The watchers were shape-shifting cherubs reporting all goings on in the universe to Elders. They were about the size of a small child and gray capable of change into any form needed. Entering the earthly realm, they looked like bright balls of light moving across the sky. Some were white and others orange. Michael knew he was not supposed to ask a watcher for information, but he had no choice since everyone kept him in the dark about Aree's mission.

Later that night, when everyone slept, Michael crept out of the castle. The moons were extra bright, so he moved around in the shadows so no one could see him. Feeling safe in the open, Michael walked down the winding, gravel road past Aree's little garden area. He only glanced in its direction. He was so focused he didn't have time to sit and remember her now. All he wanted was the truth from someone who knew it.

He went back into the shadows as he climbed over the wooden fence to enter the stables from the pasture. Nokomis felt him around. He used his skill of unlocking his stall door with his lips and pushed his way out to the pasture. Michael heard Nokomis coming toward him. He squatted down near a tree and waited for Nokomis to walk across the pasture. As they united, he told his plan to Nokomis so they would be on the same page when they arrived in the outer banks.

Michael noticed the shooting stars overloading the galaxy like rockets as they flew over. The stars trailed like bottle rockets in a line of sparkles as they arched over them, lighting up the area briefly. Michael lay back on Nokomis's back, watching the celestial show. He had his arms crossed behind his head. He felt content for once and secure. The peaceful feelings let him gently close his eyes for a nap.

Nokomis grunted to wake Michael up as they flew into voided skies. The atmosphere felt different to Nokomis as he slowed his gait. Above the milky clouds, looking down, Michael saw the outer banks. This landscape was void of color, but we are safe, he told Nokomis.

Slowing down to a gallop, then into a trot, Nokomis landed with his hooves sinking deep in the gray sand. Smacking his hooves, he didn't enjoy feeling this ground. "It's OK, buddy; you're safe," Michael reassured him, patting the side of his neck. Nokomis moved his head and neck up and down, responding to Michael.

Irritated with the sand feeling, they walked through a clearing leading them to two gigantic stone statues of shape-shifting cherubs created to resemble the small, gray beings with a colossal head and huge black eyes. The size of these statues is ridiculous, Michael thought as they passed by.

In front of them, they saw small rocks forming a walking path over the sand leading to exposing lights from beyond. He dismounted and told Nokomis to stay there. Looking forward, he noticed a watcher sitting on top of a boulder.

Standing at the base of the boulder, Michael spoke up to the little guy. "Hello there! I am seeking a certain watcher that looks down on earth monitoring a special being."

The small being looked down at Michael with a smirk and replied, "I know what you seek, Sir Michael. You want information?"

Michael raised an eyebrow. He changed his tone. It irritated him. "Who am I seeking, and I command you to tell me!"

"Sir Michael, you seek information on the human soul; that is correct, isn't it?" Michael's patience ran thin. He forgot how watchers liked to talk in riddles.

Grinding his teeth, Michael hissed out, "Watcher, it is in your best interest to come down off this rock and tell me everything you know!"

Slowly, the watcher came down off his rock. "Follow me." He led Michael to a small village where he lived.

Looking around, there were thousands of watchers that all looked the same, little grey beings. Keeping a close eye on the one leading him was difficult. Michael struggled to not lose him in this crowd. Many watchers had never seen an archangel. They touched him and liked the shininess of his armor he had called forth before he had landed. They approached a little hut carved into a rock. The watcher turned and told Michael, "What you want is in there." He pointed to the door as he deliberately backed away.

Facing the little door, Michael bent over and knocked before he entered. There was an older-looking watcher with pale-green eyes sitting in the hut, sitting on a pillow in a ring of smoke coming from his long curly pipe. He was their leader.

"Welcome Prince, please take a seat. I understand you are seeking information about the nature-loving soul and her journey?"

Michael, looking at the watcher, still in shock he knew what he wanted, sat down the best he could and waited for the watcher to speak.

"First, let me introduce myself. My name is Finius. I am the leader of the watchers, and I am aware of all things going on in the universe. I was the one who sent the update on Aree's mission, but I am sure you know about her mission."

Michael, trying to look convincing, nodded yes.

Finius continued, "She received the black box and made it to the nature realm (Faermorreya) safely, and she was well on her mission. Her survival training went well. She became a warrior; quite impressive she was."

Michael was still in shock! Sitting there quietly taking in every word he heard, but he didn't catch on when Finius had said *she was*. He couldn't imagine Aree being a warrior.

"My Prince, are you OK? Did you not know this?"

Quietly Michael whispered, "I didn't know. Please, Finius, tell me more. Is she coming home soon? Is she back in the earthly realm?"

Thinking hard on what to say, Finius dumped his burning pipe into a metal spittoon. He wobbled to a table and picked up an opened a wooden box and took some moist-looking tobacco into his tiny little fingers and stuffed it into his pipe bowl. Looking at the bowl, he pushed the tobacco down with the tip of his tiny fingers, which Michael noticed were black. Reaching for a lit candle, he reignited his pipe. He started puffing on his pipe before taking a deep inhale; he closed his eyes for a brief second, then exhaled multiple rings of smoke circling around his head.

Turning his attention back to Michael, he continued to tell him about her being transformed from a human into the White Queen. The Queen of Faermorreya. He talked about her learning the ways of nature in Faermorreya and how loved and admired by all the creatures of this realm she was. "She had a protector named Alex that she became close to and very fond of."

"FOND OF! What does that mean?" Michael interrupted.

Finius stopped and looked at Michael for a minute, then said, "Don't worry about that. It doesn't matter anymore." Taking another inhale from his pipe and slowly exhaling more rings, Finius told Michael the truth. . . .

"Demons murdered the White Queen. They stabbed her in the neck during an ambush."

Reaching for his neck! "That is what this is!" Turning to Finius, Michael removed his hand and showed the mark on his neck and said, "Was she stabbed in this area?"

Finius was dumbfounded, placing his hand over his mouth in shock!!! He nodded yes to Michael. "I need to know she's not gone. Where is she now?" Michael cried out in demand.

Finius told Michael again demons had killed her, and then they paraded her lifeless body as they took her to their leader. Finius reached and touched Michael's hand and spoke, saddened, "She did the best she could. We almost got the name of the evil leader running the show in the nature realm. I am so sorry for your loss."

Michael barked back, "Loss? I have lost nothing! Aree is not gone, or she would be here with me, right? I can feel her; I know she lives!!! Something went wrong; where is she?"

"Sir Michael, we haven't seen or heard anything from Faermorreya. If you have time, I can check for an update."

Excited about this news, Michael replied, "YES, I HAVE NOTHING BUT TIME. PLEASE, FINIUS, I NEED TO KNOW!"

Finius took a deep puff on his pipe and then released the smoke while lifting his head to meet Michael's gaze. "The realm is suffering now, but I will check for you, Sir Michael."

"No Elder must know about this! We are breaking protocol talking now." Michael got up and thanked Finius for sharing information the Elders wouldn't tell him. He agreed to stay for a while, hoping for more news on Aree. He got up and left the hut of Finius.

After stretching his legs and arms, he returned and approached Nokomis anxiously. Sensing Michael's energy, Nokomis snorted in happiness and nudged him in support with his enormous head. "Well, my friend, we should know about Aree soon enough."

Michael smiled as he placed his arms around Nokomis's neck and placed their foreheads together. He felt relief raced over his body, but worry remained, knowing she was still alive somewhere lost between the two realms.

Time passed and not having patience had made it excruciating for him. Finally, he noticed Finius riding on a Dik Dik. He watched, keen for some good news, as the tiny dear, perfectly sized for the watchers and very agile, moved fast across the gray sand. Finius reached Michael, talking in between puffs on his pipe.

Michael turned and placed his hand on Finius's shoulder. "Slow down, I can't understand!" Finius took control of his breath and spoke.

"She is alive! She is alive!"

"I KNEW IT!" Michael screamed excitedly. "Tell me more."

Finius continued to tell Michael she was alive because Aree entered the realm as a human. The human remained alive in the nature realm. "There is more, Sir Michael. I feel you need to know." Michael stood frozen, feeling fear as he gave his full attention to Finius and noticing his little hands trembled. Something deeply troubled him.

Finius calmly continued to explain how Aree was in the lair of demons alone, without the forest crystal necklace to save the nature realm. Michael interrupted Finius anxiously. "Can she use her abilities to survive?"

Knowing he would get an answer he didn't want to hear, Finius took a melancholy sigh before saying, "Sir Michael, if Aree gets into trouble, she will die as a human in the wrong realm. If that was to happen, then she won't return to you, my lord."

Standing in shock and speechless, Michael nodded in appreciation at Finius as he turned around to mount onto Nokomis's back.

"Sir Michael, please be careful. I fear your actions may have dire consequences." Michael nudged Nokomis gently, and Nokomis knew it was time to go home. Finius, still sitting on his Dik Dik, jumped back as Nokomis started spreading his wings.

Michael turned and faced Finius. "Aree's soul means more to me than any consequences or punishment I could receive." Like a flash of light, they took to the skies, heading back to Celestrian.

As they flew, Michael's mind spun in every direction. Out loud he said, "Nokomis, I must protect Aree! I must save her!" Nokomis answered with many snorts and neighs. . . . As he rubbed Nokomis right between his ears, he thought to himself, No one must know my plan, this must be a secret, but I need cooperation from Gabriel.

THIRTEEN

Everything in the land has a melancholy feeling. The skies have darkened to a smoky gray and an eerie chill in the air mingled with a creepy haze replacing the once warm, comforting breezes. Faermorreya had changed now that evil had taken control. Silence was a sign of uncertainty. All the creatures of the nature realm had gone into hiding in fear of being captured and tortured. No flowers bloomed, their fairies hid, and the trees were an ashy color, dropping their leaves.

After the celebration ended, the evil beings stopped showing off the lifeless body of the White Queen. Deep inside their dark lair, screaming and cries of pain and sorrow came out like a megaphone. Trolls bullied and hit prisoners as they guided ungarsungars and fairies, wearing chains and shackles around their necks and ankles, in lines headed behind the waterfalls.

They tossed queen's body into a dirty, rusty, old metal tub sitting in a dark room overflowing with dead bodies. The strong smell of iron was in the air from all the bloody guts and bodily fluids thrown all over, covering the once dirt floor and walls. It was the smell that woke her. At first, she was confused, not knowing if she was alive, when heaviness on her face caused her to panic for clean air.

Demons celebrated their victory and laughed, enjoying themselves, watching the fear on the faces of prisoners as they pleaded for their lives as trolls hit with bull whips made from pussy willows. Each hit making contact removed chunks of flesh with every strike. The screaming cries and moans of pain were horrible to hear, but luckily it covered up any noise she made trying to get out of the pile of bodies, which was bigger than she had thought. Pushing her way up, causing dead bodies to roll onto the floor, she reached air, making it easier to calm down briefly.

Gathering her thoughts, she felt her face sliding off, which made her fanatically freak out, not understanding with all the muck and guts everywhere. Grabbing her face, she noticed she put her fingers deep into the skin she shredded. The skin of the queen fell off her human body. She struggled to move; the left-over skin of the queen was cold and slimy as it fell to the ground, making a sticky thud as it hit the floor.

She stopped moving and played dead when a huge troll came into the room looking through the dead bodies for fairy pieces to eat. It eased her mind, knowing what he looked for was not her human body. Lying limp on the ground with her face in the slimy, black mud and bodily fluids, her eyes burned from the ammonia and blurred as she tried to focus on the troll so close. Struggling to see clearly, she could make out an octopus skin made into a cloak he thoughtfully laid down on a rock. She had a flashback of seeing pixies training with invisible cloaks made from octopus skin.

All the dead body parts occupied the troll, flipping bodies and sucking on any bone to get the marrow. Watching, she decided it was her chance to make her move. She crawled over pieces of flesh and blood-soaked, coagulated mud puddles.. It was so hard for her not to throw up from the odor of feces mixed with blood clots and other fluids.

She made it over to where the cloak sat and threw it over her. Holding perfectly still, looking back, she saw the skin and body parts, even pieces of the head of the White Queen smashed and deformed, lying in the old, metal tub with parts of matted hair covered in green blood and black goo. Seeing that scared her even more.

Lying there on the ground, she made a break for safety. She needed to see if the cloak worked for her. With all her will and might, she stood straight up and walked into the middle of the room, praying the troll didn't see her. Feeling so weak, her knees shook as she tried to hold up like a statue. The nasty troll threw different body parts everywhere after he would pick a piece up, sniff it or chew on it. She could tell he became irritated not finding what he wanted to eat. He started swinging his arms angrily as he looked around the room on the floor.

The cloak worked! She now stood next to the knee of the troll, trying to walk over all the body pieces he threw everywhere.

Seeing a dark opening in a wall across the room, it looked like a tunnel, maybe an exit. She could hear the waterfalls, so slowly and meticulously she moved in its direction. Making her way through the dark tunnels lit by fire torches stuck in the walls, she passed so many abused ungars chained to walls and tortured. Her heart broke because she could not help them.

She heard a lot of ruckus coming her way when, out of the corner of her eye, she saw a small pack of evil witches following a larger beast approaching her. There was no place for her to go, so she pressed herself up against the rocky walls, hoping to blend in with the cloak. They didn't notice her as they passed by.

She could hear trolls working in a secluded corner off the end of the tunnel. She heard talking; *cloak* she could understand. That must be where they are making invisible cloaks, she thought.

Walking closer, she noticed they had invisible cloaks. She could see them mastering their skill by taking the skin of an octopus lizard and other elements of magic. As she listened closely, she heard demons promising the trolls all the fairies they could eat.

The group of witches and demons finally walked by her. One evil being stopped and sniffed the air right in front of her. It had leathery purple skin looking like it had been in the water too long, like a raisin, and the smell, WHAT A HORRIBLE STENCH! It made her eyes water. It had a huge, hairy, upward-turning nose on a tiny face with beady eyes, like a vampire bat face, with a hunched back.

Sassy frozen in place, feeling dripping sweat covered in mud and blood and pieces of body tissue still falling off her. She was so scared. The demon smelled the air and looking directly into her eyes.

He sees me!!"! she thought, causing her to panic just as a large club from an old tree branch hit the demon across his back. He released a scream in pain directly into her face as he got back in line. Her heart pounded so fast and loud. She trembled in fear, too scared to cry.

That was such a close call, she thought. Watching as they continued walking down the dark hallway away from her gave her the opportunity to make her move, escaping out of their lair of evil from behind the waterfalls. With the cloak still wrapped tight against her body, she nervously ran as fast as she could for the exit. Not turning around to see if she was followed, she sprinted as fast as she could, plunging into the water, not knowing how tall the falls were.

Falling and falling, then splashing deep underwater, she sank to the bottom. Making sure she was out of sight, she let go and removed the cloak and witnessed all the blood and mud wash off her human skin. Yes, it was her skin! She was human again!

For a moment, her heart was full of joy knowing she was alive and human. Slowly, she swam up to the top of the water, but only when she knew she was alone and it was safe. Pleased to make it to the bank of the river, she rested there, catching her breath. Looking around and not seeing anything familiar, Sassy felt safe enough to get out of the water. Now she was in the open with one big problem. She was nude. Naked in a realm she was not from. She kept the cloak over herself as she ran, following the river, hoping it led her back to the Wise Old Oak.

It was dark and getting colder. She was naked and alone and needed to find shelter. Searching for a hole or a den, she tried to find anything to keep her safe from the elements. Being back in human form, she turned to her ability to communicate with nature. Sassy found a place to meditate, trying to focus energy on any plant that would listen. She ran into a dead wall; disappointment set in; with Faermorreya dying, nothing responded to her energy.

Right before Sassy gave up, in the distance she saw a blackberry bush shaking its leaves a little. Smiling from ear to ear, she thought, Oh, thank you, Lord! Feeling blessed, she got to eat and rest. Approaching the bush, its branches moved, allowing her shelter and security at the base of the bush so she would be out of sight. She made a nice little bed up against the trunk of the bush. Sassy verbally thanked the blackberry bush; it replied by closing the branches and moving its leaves to cover and protect her from any outside dangers as the night set in.

Sassy felt some relief. She lay down on the cloak, looking up through the branches between the leaves. She could see the night sky, noticing it was not her normal night sky. Eating some blackberries, she lay there wondering what the hell she was doing there. Feeling lonely and currently really missing Archie, she wondered if she was ever going to see him again. Was he OK? What about Barney??? Oh, how she missed her life as a human on earth. She curled up in a naked little ball and cried herself to sleep.

Sassy woke to the smell of fresh blackberries. Having an appetite, she started indulging herself with berries again, realizing she needed to snap out of this self-pity party and fix things. She had caused this problem in this realm, and she needed to repair the damage. She finished stuffing herself with blackberries. The bush hit the dirt when she started folding the cloak. She watched, wondering what it tried to show her. She placed her hand around a branch and closed her eyes, concentrating on communicating.

Shocked at what it showed her, she started moving dirt around, looking for something. A brief glimpse of gold sparkling caught the corner of her eye under the dirt. Brushing away more dirt, exposing this tiny little clutter of small blue and gold stones, she dug them up and placed it in the palm of her left hand, giving it a small squeeze, hoping it would glow. Nothing. . . .

Right before she was going to rebury them, she glanced down at the dirt and saw a green crystal buried next to the others. It gave off a glow she knew well. Her heart pounded, hoping that what she thought she saw was real. Slowly, she moved the dirt to reveal a magical, small forest crystal! This was amazing!

Picking it up out of the dirt; the crystal immediately began releasing tiny, crawling swirls of the beautiful gold fairy dust. Right then, all was changing. Tears of joy ran down her face as she knew she still had the powers in her human form. Feeling energized from a rush of refreshing adrenaline, she began looking for the way to the Wise Old Oak.

Before starting her journey for the day, she took the time to make a satchel out of thin branches and leaves to hold the little crystal and some blackberries. The female fairies had taught her how to make things like this. She hugged the bush, feeling very blessed. Placing the satchel cross her body, she threw the cloak over her body and headed out, being led only by intuition given to her by a gut feeling.

Sassy walked with the cloak only covering her body. Her head and arms were not visible when she heard a high-pitch buzzing. Looking out from under the cloak, she saw a young pixie flying around. She could tell she was interested in her by the way she flew back and forth. With her friendly nature, she said, "Hey there!"

"How do you see me?"

Sassy asked her to stop and listen to her as she buzzed around closer. "I am Sassy or the White Queen. Can you help me, please?"

The fairy stopped flying around and just hovered, examining everything about Sassy. She was beautifully dressed in yellow, green, and black stripes, shifting her head back and forth. Sassy thought of nothing more to do, so she held out the crystal she found and placed it in her left hand, squeezing it until it started glowing. The little pixie's wings beat faster and faster, causing a glitter effect around her. She zipped around so fast that all Sassy could see was trailing lights.

Slowing down, she came closer, staring hard at Sassy. "YOU ARE HER!" Looking at the glowing crystal getting stronger, again she cried out, "YOU ARE HER! YOU ARE ALIVE!" in her squeaky little voice.

This caused Sassy to cry in happiness. "Please help me find Alex. He is my protector." The little pixie, still very curious about her, noticed her body.

She landed on the ground, approached Sassy, and seemed to be very interested in the human body. Touching her arms, she smiled with approval at the feel of her skin. She looked at Sassy like almost comparing the difference in their bodies. Stepping back, she looked at her, then politely, in a squeaky voice, offered some clothing and said she would take her to the tree. It was such a relief knowing she was going to see Alex again.

The little pixie reached for Sassy's hand, waving to following her to her home, which wasn't easy as a tiny human trying to get to the top of a tree. Sassy precisely climbed her way up. Way, way up! They reached the pixie's home. She landed at the base of a branch and moved a piece of bark on the tree to the left, and it opened the door to her home.

It was so cozy! It amazed Sassy at how beautiful her tiny home was. All the furniture was made into the walls of the tree. Nothing was on the floor except her bed. That was the shell of an almond. She offered Sassy a lily leaf to wrap around her body as she searched for something for her to wear. Sassy patiently sat on her bed, shocked over the softness of the leaf that she just fell asleep.

FOURTEEN

After waking up, Sassy felt completely refreshed with energy. The little pixie had set some clothes out for her. Sassy got dressed, and then they enjoyed fresh aloe juice before they started the day.

It was a long distance to the base of the rosebush. As they got closer, the air turned a little chillier. Sassy stood still and looked at the all the sadness that had taken over the land. As they arrived, Sassy was stunned at the sight in front of her. The Wise Old Oak had dropped leaves, and the face frowned in such sorrow. The tree of life was dying. There were no roses and no bees. The pond in front of the tree was an ugly, dark-brown color with no movement in its water. Sassy stood there, absorbing the pain of the land.

The pixie caused a scene trying to get noticed by Gladys, who showed up at the entrance on her own.

"What's going on here?" Gladys spoke.

The pixie pushed Sassy forward and said in her high-pitched voice, "I found the White Queen!"

Sassy felt so uncomfortable because no one recognized her in human form. So much time had passed, and they had only seen her in human for one day. The little pixie flew above, repeating herself, "The crystal glowed! The crystal glowed!"

Only once had there been a human queen in the nature realm before her. . . . She cautiously opened her satchel, pulling out the small green crystal as it started glowing. "Hah, where did you get this?" After looking at her body up and down . . . Gladys smiled. "Sassy?"

"Sassy?" A familiar voice came from behind her. It belonged to Alex. It looked like he returned from a scouting trip and had heard the commotion. Sassy turned to approach him, and he looked up at Gladys and asked if this was true.

Gladys smiled and replied to Alex, "Yes, it is her."

Sassy stood there waiting for him to do something. Maybe run to her and hold her tight. He did nothing! He walked up to her, looked deep into her eyes, and then said, "I don't know you; the queen is dead. I saw her dead body being carried off in the hands of demons." His eyes flickered a glowing orange.

Sassy could feel his pain and anger toward her. Alex accidentally startled her when he quickly leaned forward and, in an angry voice, said, "You have no business being here. This isn't your realm. Go home, human!" Giving her a disdainful look, he turned and walked away. Sassy stood there like a lost little girl, watching him walk away.

Gladys approached her and took her hand. "My child of earth, do not cry." Sassy laid her head on her shoulder and cried. She held her for a while before they entered the Wise Old Oak.

Entering the tree was different. There was a community still at work but at a slower pace. The quietness was the worst. "Gladys, what is going on?"

She responded in a sad tone. "Sassy, our world is mourning as creatures die. Nature dies with it now that evil has control. My dear, when we lost you as our queen, they took the forest crystal. We have no chance of surviving unless a miracle happens and we retrieve the crystal again. But sadly, we cannot recover from the loss of the guardians of the woods and fairies. We just don't have the warriors."

Sassy turned to her and told her of the crystal powers, how she had her own human powers and would use her abilities to work energy and communicate with the land. If she could get the crystal back, could this save the nature realm?

Gladys, smiling, spoke, "Yes."

There is a plan. I just need to get my strength up, and then I will return to the falls and retrieve the necklace. Alone.

Being inside her old chamber felt distant. The thought of never meeting her soulmate or her home made her heart ache. She just wanted this to be done so she may return home and find her soulmate. One more thing was what she needed to do. She must walk into the evil lair alone.... Laying down to rest, she did something that always worked before, even if it only made her feel better. She prayed. Sassy prayed for help, guidance, protection. She prayed for a loving life with her soulmate after this.

Two days passed, and it had been very uncomfortable. Alex avoided her every chance he got, and there was quiet chattering going on around the tree. Sassy stood on a balcony overlooking the land; feeling the pain this realm was going through weakened her. Her mind spun with all the what ifs.

"What if they attacked earth? Did I cause all this?"

It was time; she must go.

Grabbing her cloak and the crystal cluster, she headed to the room where the crystals remained protected from the red poison ivy. Slowly she carried the small forest crystal in the palm of her left hand as she raised her hand in front of the ivy. She waited. Seeing movement on the wall, the ivy crept away, exposing a small cubby hole awaiting her to place the small forest crystal in. She carefully placed the crystal in the hole. Aggressively, the ivy moved to cover the hole with huge, luscious leaves and vines. Sassy felt better knowing she had helped save this magical realm from evil destruction.

Quietly she left and decided it was best if no one knew. Being late in the evening, everyone should be sleeping. She made her way down to the rose bush entrance and started heading back to the waterfalls. Sassy, looking back at the tree, noticed the face on it caught her eye. It had a slight smile for her! The small crystal had given hope to the realm.

Seeing that just confirmed she was doing the right thing. With a quicker step, the tree disappeared in the distance. Hours had passed. She worked her way through the deep forest and reminisced back to old times with Archie at the shop. Oh, how she missed that enormous ball of gray fluff. She wondered how he was doing and if he was hanging out with Barney talking about her. She missed home and her earthly life.

Sassy was in deep thought, then noticed she approached the grassy knoll and the ink cap mushroom patch. Hiding in the tall grass, she watched some old ugly trolls in the distance digging in dirt around their mushroom homes. It looked like they argued with each other as they slung mud around the fungi patch. As she watched them, she saw they tried to catch mosquitos around the muddy waters.

"Yuck!" she thought to herself, mosquitos? She watched a troll catch one, ripping the legs off one by one and eating them like eating fried chicken legs. . . . Such disgusting beings, she thought.

Sassy stayed hidden in the grass. The trolls got tired; she watched as they went inside their mushrooms, giving her the opportunity to make her way to the back of the waterfalls. It was the moaning and screaming of pain coming from inside the lair guiding her now. She had seen no signs of demons outside the lair, which had her wondering if this was a good thing or if they were all gathered inside. There was no time like now to make her move to enter the lair. She took the cloak out and wrapped it around herself as she headed in.

Slowly, hit by an overwhelming wave of the same wretched stench, she stopped to rub some honeysuckle oil under her nose, trying not to gag. The ground was slippery, covered in mud and what seemed like more layers of bodily fluids. The mud was thicker than she remembered. Seeing lightstorchlights down a dark tunnel, she slowly passed some ungars. She stopped to check on them and noticed they were near death, hanging on to the thinnest thread of life left as they lay chained to walls soaked with blood and other fluids. Sassy's heart shattered in a million pieces. She could feel all their pain and hear all their sadden thoughts. This wasn't right. Hell didn't belong here in this realm. "Dear Lord, I beg you to please see and hear the torture evil beings have created in this magical place."

Sassy entered a huge, open cavern. In shock, she saw demons raping pixies chained to walls, beaten them down and handing them over to trolls feeding on them. She saw rejects of evil in different forms gathering in different groups. Some looked like burnt dogmen, hunchbacked, scary, black forms. Other shape shifters transformed from a mist to a solid form of pure evil. There were witches and demons involved in what looked like sexual favors, taking pleasure rolling in the body parts and fluids that soak the smelly mud. Sassy calmly and carefully snuck by their movements without being noticed while monitoring the commotion moving in her direction.

Looking closer, she could see it was the same leader that hit the gross demon with the club. Watching, she wondered, Who is he?"? He had the necklace wrapped in his claws the last time she had seen him; she could not see it now. She felt the need to get closer to him.

This beast stood on what looked like a stage made from stone surrounded by sharp, spiked boulders with dead bodies lying over them, painting the boulder with blood dripping down. He started raising his arms; with control, he calmed the crowd of evil beings gathered in front of him. Standing there under her cloak, she had a front-row seat to this inhumane beast. Studying every move he made, she noticed the necklace was not with him. He surveyed the crowd like he looked for something through his tiny, beady eyes glowing white.

He licked his lips with his split snake tongue slithering between his nasty, blackened, yellow fangs, too big for his face framed with horn-looking nubs. Walking back and forth, he stood around ten feet. Taller than the others she had seen, almost human form, but so muscular it looked like his scarred, blackened, reptilian skin was going to rip from his swelling muscles. He had huge, black, burnt-leather wings with long, yellow, dirty claws. He dragged them on the sides of the rocks, making a high-pitched screeching sound and shooting sparks of fire, making Sassy's skin crawled.

Stomping and flaying his claws, he spoke. A voice so deep it vibrated the ground. The crowd of demons and wicked beings pushed forward in excitement. Sassy was so worried she was going to get caught, she nervously pushed her way to the edge of a row. He started by laughing his evil laugh, enjoying all the torture and pain surrounding him. The beast spoke of pleasure in destroying the realm and all its protectors. He displayed his hate for flowers by killing its fairy in front of his minions! He showed them how to kill this realm.

It was so loud and hard for Sassy to hear everything. Between roars and howling, he screamed about his master and having control. He praised them for the good work. He will have control of the two realms having an open connection to Boonah. Planning on ruling and controlling the earth and Faermorreya? His confidence and arrogance radiated all around him.

The crowd cheered on, boosting his ego as he leaped off the huge rocks elevating him above everything. He walked closer and closer and passed right by Sassy without noticing her, terrifying her, making her feel like her heart was in her throat. It beat so loud she thought for sure some evil being could hear it. Sassy, frozen in complete fear, tried to calm herself down. She backed away from the hoard of demons surrounding her. The energy was so heavy it was almost too much for her to handle.

Watching as he walked through the crowd like a celebrity, beings bowed and worshipped him as he began turning down a different tunnel Sassy wasn't familiar with. "Shit!" She had to follow him! She was so scared she was going to get stuck in there. But something told her he would lead her to the necklace.

Shadow people, so black and dense, they had no faces but could talk. Sassy could hear them discuss the plans to destroy the earth, turning it blood red from all its victims. They sought to kill. Some would live and become slaves sent to Boonah in the realm of icy hell. There they would become prisoners for pleasure and torture, or they would work in the icy mines creating the new city of Agony. There, their master would reign over all.

Sassy listened, unable to believe what she heard. Instantly, a strong, protective energy overcame Sassy, like a mother protecting her child. She devoted herself to making sure this couldn't happen!

She quietly continued to listen to the shadow people everywhere, laughing and peeking out from behind the sheer red curtains covering cells they had recently put up as they chained individuals to the rocky walls, beaten so bad they were curled up in a corner waiting to die. Out of nowhere, a tiny little demon, like a possessed toddler that had frothing mucus dripping from its nose and mouth, jumped in her face and looked deep into her eyes. Its breath smelled of sulfur and rotten fish.

Sassy was harshly gasping for air when it screamed out, "I see her!" pointing and laughing at Sassy! It said that repeatedly over and over. Sassy hunched down, remaining perfectly still, and said nothing.

In an anxiety-driven panic, she spun around, scampering away. Luckily, it seemed like nobody listened to the little smelly demon. An older-looking old hag that looked just like the nasty little toddler picked up the little demon, handing it off to a much, much bigger hag. The little smelly guy quieted down as they placed it on a high rock. The old hag mumbled something to it in tongues. To Sassy, it sounded like he was being scolded. Feeling so relieved, Sassy turned and continued down that tunnel to follow the leader.

The mud felt thicker and tarry. She walked down a very dark and cold tunnel. There were cells everywhere. She saw sheer curtains billowing and turning the cells into a glowing shade of red from the flaming torches, the only form of light. There were so many of them the tunnel glowed blood red! Slowly she moved, looking behind the sheer curtains and seeing nothing but more stagnant, blood-soaked floors and chains. And then there he was.

At the very back of the tunnel, lounging on a chaise made from flagstone, he laid eating pieces of bloody, stringy flesh ripped up into tiny pieces. Sassy studied him, noticing he took pleasure in being entertained by hitting the weak bowing at his knees. As Sassy got closer, she realized there was no exit. She must backtrack to get out of here. This became a big worry for her, knowing there was only one exit!

The screams were so loud, followed by very distracting laughter. She couldn't get caught. Franticly, she needed to leave. Panic set in, followed by the feeling of being claustrophobic. Suddenly, she wanted out from under the cloak. Sassy turned to run out of there but stopped dead in her tracks when she saw it! There it was! The necklace levitated above a rock slab surrounded by laser beams of yellow lights in a plaid formation all around the necklace. Shit! She hadn't been expecting this! It was a protection shield.

She needed to calm herself down. She started breathing slowly and controlled. Feeling like she was in control, she concentrated all her attention on him. Watching the leader, he had waved in two guards to watch over the necklace until his return. Quickly he grabbed the horns on the head of one guard; he threatened their life if anything was to happen while he was gone. He pushed them both aside with a swing of his arm. Sassy just stood there in shock and scared, watching the leader storm out down the tunnel, kicking anything in his way.

He headed right for her as Sassy pushed herself up against the wall so he may pass by her. He suddenly stopped, smelling the air all around him. Slowly he turned in all directions, looking for something. He took another smell of the air, then stomped away. Sassy shook from head to toe. What did he smell?

Gathering her thoughts, she squatted down near a corner and watched the guards. They were trolls. Knowing they were not intelligent and easily distracted, she felt safe with the cloak. Knowing now she was in over her head, she needed to get out of here. This was her only chance.

FIFTEEN

Michael went down to the old fishing dock Aree loved so much. He stood there looking at his reflection in the water as it rippled away, remembering how they would just stare into each other's eyes as they slow danced under the stars. Closing his eyes for a moment, he could almost feel her there with him.

Looking around, he got up and walked up to their tree; he noticed the tree wasn't as bright as normal. Is our tree suffering like our love is? he thought. Michael looked around to make sure no one saw him, then he hugged the tree like Aree would do. And for the first time, he could feel the energy of love coming off the tree. He giggled a little and then hugged the tree again. It made him happy.

He sat down under their tree and contemplated how he was going to help her. It wasn't long before Gabriel noticed Michael and wanted to check up on his big brother. As he walked up to Michael, he called out to his brother first, "Would you like some company?"

Michael turned, not expecting to see anyone, but pleased when he noticed it was Gabriel. He was the only brother Michael could count on with this secret mission. Michael smiled and waved him over.

Joining his bother on the ground under Aree's tree, Michael told Gabriel how nice it was to see him. As they embraced, Gabriel glanced up and saw their names carved into the tree, then looked at Michael with some reassurance, but Michael started talking about Aree's situation and how if she died in the nature realm that she wouldn't come back.

"Gabriel, I know she lives because of the mark on my neck. I can feel her still. I need to make sure Aree gets the name of the demon leader running this nightmare and get her back to the earthly realm safely. She can't do this as a mortal. No mortal has ever gone up against a hoard of demons and survived. She needs me! Please brother, help me save her. . . .

"Only you who can control the weather on earth can hide my arrival. I need to enter the earthly realm so I can find how she entered the nature dimension."

Gabriel was in shock! Rubbing his chin, he stared at Michael, knowing he couldn't say no to him. Eventually, he spoke, "You know, brother, that I too love Aree like a sister. I would never want harm done to her or you. You are asking me to assist you. . . . I will. They can't punish both of us. Right??? This is an act of love for an earthling. Weren't we created to assist earthlings and guide them through danger? Right?"

Michael had a spark of hope in his eyes and a smile on his face. He was pleased and so delighted to hear the words *I will help* come from Gabriel. They both sat, discussing how this was going to play out. Michael, receiving Gabriel's good news to help, had received a burst of adrenaline. He stood up, patting Gabriel's shoulders. It was time for them to think of a plan to pull this off secretly and successfully.

Later that night, Michael met up with Gabriel to complete the plan. He had spent all afternoon thinking and plotting this mission and felt he had the best plan. He explained to Gabriel that the best way to enter the earthly realm was through a storm, a nasty one. The more chaos happening in the atmosphere, the easier it would be to travel through the different realms without notice from any evil ones.

Gabriel agreed and committed to causing a nasty storm in central Texas. A storm so loud with thunder, lightning, and hail, it would cause humans to remain in the homes, so they wouldn't have to worry about being seen or felt. Also, demons wouldn't be expecting this, so it should make for an easy arrival on earth. Gabriel turned to Michael.

"What are the plans once you arrive?" Michael looked at Gabriel with a serious, stony expression.

"I will enter the nature dimension the same way Aree did once I find out how she did it. Once I get to her, I plan on returning her to a safe place without her knowing who I am. If everything goes right, I should be able to assist her return to the earthly realm, and then I will return home."

"My brother, this has to work." Gabriel nodded his head yes to Michael. "We will execute the plan in three days."

Gabriel was a little nervous about Michael doing a secret mission. There were earthly demons that might sense his presence on earth. Even though most demons feared Michael, this was a gigantic risk for the earthly realm and its nature dimension and, of course, the heavenly realm.

Two days left, Gabriel headed to the Cathedral to view the earth. It was time to start the storm. After arriving, he hastened to the hallway where the crystals magnified the earth. He stood there looking at the beautiful green and blue globe. It had a special place in his heart too.

In the beginning, when the earth was new, he had many missions to the globe. Times on earth are very different now, he thought. Looking at the weather going on now across the continent of North America, he saw a storm coming out of the northwest that would arrive in the south. This storm had enough energy in it to hide Michael's arrival.

Swaying his hand over a certain area, he spun the rotation in the clouds in a direction toward central Texas. Pleased with the formation he saw, he mumbled out loud, "That should give the earthlings plenty of time to prepare and take cover."

"Prepare for what?" startled Gabriel as Raphael questioned him. He and some Elders walked up on him.

Quickly, Gabriel said, "Just sending the rain where needed. It is their rainy season, and, well, I thought I would give them rain for their crops."

Raphael didn't hesitate to ask, "Why do they need to prepare?"

Gabriel glared at him, saying, "It's the south of North America! They always have some little crazy weather there this time of year."

"Hmmm..." Raphael said under his breath as he looked at Gabriel quizzically.

Gabriel knew Raphael did not believe in his story would not let this go. He knew something was up. He turned to the Elders and said, "I need to see the formula I wrote that is being stored in the library," as he walked away from Gabriel, knowing they would follow since they knew where all of Raphael's recipes and notes were kept in the secret files. This would give Gabriel time to finish whatever he was up to.

Heading back to the castle, knowing Raphael was going to question what he had seen, he stopped by Michael's, letting him know. Knocking on Michael's door jogged the door open. Michael gleamed, full of excitement.

"Gabriel!!! I have my plan, and it is going to play out perfectly so no one will notice a thing! I'm going to get to her, remove her from danger, and then return, all in one earthly day. Has the storm started up yet?"

"Yes," Gabriel replied. He watched Michael, noticing how happy he was. It was the first time since Aree's departure from heaven that he had smiled so much. He decided to not say anything about Raphael's curiosity. "The storm has started; we will be ready to leave soon."

Looking around, Gabriel didn't see any armor out. "Are you wearing just plain clothing?" Looking and seeing only a black shirt and black jeans and boots, even a black, long trench coat. Before he could ask why, Michael explained how earthlings liked to wear the color.

"It's normal to wear all black there. If I get noticed, black will help to blend in. I'm carrying some blades hidden in my boots and strapped on back. I am not looking for a battle, so no armor. This is an in-and-out mission.". I am ready."

The sun had passed by the celestial rainbow, and the time had come for him to leave. Michael headed to the old fishing dock. There, he would meet Gabriel, and then they would head to the outer banks. Michael would fall to the earth at the same time the storm would be in Texas. He wouldn't be using his wings on his descent; free falling would be much faster, and the noise from the hail and thunder would cover up the sonic boom his landing would cause.

As they flew quietly high in the night sky, they arrived at the outer banks. Landing on the sandy soil, Gabriel walked to look over the edge into the dark abyss. There was a vast universe Michael must free fall through. As Gabriel looked over the edge, he was interested watching some watchers peering over the edge, monitoring different planets and beings not only on earth. It fascinated him. Michael went to find Finius. Since only watchers could see what was going on down on earth, they were going to need him to guide Michael to fall when the storm had reached the small town.

Finius sat in his little home smoking a pipe when Michael showed up on his doorstep. He was really shocked to see Michael again, wondering what he needs now. Inviting Michael in, he looked at him and asked him why he was back. Knowing there could be trouble giving him so much information on what's going on with Aree, Michael explained his plan to Finius. After some time, Finius, who still toked on his long wooden pipe blowing smoke rings, jumped to help, only because he had always had a warm spot in his heart for true love. He was a cherub.

Gabriel saw Michael returning with a watcher by his side. Gabriel had never met a watcher. Quietly he thought to himself what chubby little creatures they are, unaware that they could take a distinct form. As they got closer, Gabriel giggled to himself, wondering what their father was thinking when he created these little, fat, wobbly beings. He tried not to laugh, knowing he should not judge a book by its cover. So much imagination our father has, he thought as he cracked a brief grin.

Sticking out his hand, Finius met him with a handshake. "It is nice to meet you, Prince Gabriel."

"It's just Gabriel, no need to call me prince," Gabriel replied.

"OK, OK. Now that we know each other, can we get to the job at hand?" Michael spoke with an impatient voice. Finius looked at him, then started his way over to the edge. Looking over, he scratched his tiny head with his fat little fingers, looking at the planet earth. Michael paced back and forth, looking over now and then, but he saw nothing. Only watchers could see through the dark abyss.

Finius called out, "There. There she is!" Zooming in on a certain area, Finius saw the storm. "WOW! That's a doozy of a storm going on down there!"

Impatiently, Michael cried out, "Is it time?"

Quietly and calmly, Finius told him to wait but be ready. Gabriel walked over to Michael and laid his hand on his shoulder. Looking into his eyes, he said, "Please be careful and call me if you need anything or you find yourself in trouble. I am here for you, my brother; don't forget that."

Michael smiled at Gabriel and agreed, "You just keep things on the down low here. I will be back real soon," as they locked onto each other's forearms.

"Take your position, Michael. The time has come."

Michael walked over to the edge of the heavenly realm. Looking over, he saw nothing. He closed his eyes and stretched his arms straight out from his sides, not calling on his wings....

Finius called out, "NOW, MICHAEL! FALL NOW!!" Michael fell backward into a perfect reverse swan dive as he disappeared out of Gabriel's sight. Opening his eyes, he saw the portal to the earthly realm approaching with an amazing display of gas clouds swirling into a funnel.

He passed through the Milky Way into the earth's atmosphere. So many colors flashed by as the speed of his fall intensified. Gravity and Gabriel's storm pulled Michael into the center of a horrible hail and lightning storm with extremely powerful winds.

He wanted to extend his wings to slow down but knew he could not take the risk of being seen. The rain and hail felt like being pelted with paintballs, intensely stinging. He struggled to focus, knowing the ground came up fast. He saw her home when he hit the ground with such force it caused a quake, sounding like a tremendous explosion! Gabriel disintegrated the storm with no warning to Michael.

SIXTEEN

Kneeling on one knee and wiping the rain from his eyes, he surveyed the land in the front yard of Aree's earthly home. Quickly he took cover under the front porch, hoping no demons here on the earth saw or heard him enter the realm. Looking out across the land, he didn't see or smell or hear any demon movement. He saw a lot of leaves ripped from their branches, leaving some trees to look eerie and broken from his landing.

Feeling secure and unnoticed, Michael turned his focus on getting inside to dry off. Walking around on the porch looking in the windows, he found one unlocked. He pushed the windowpane up, causing enough noise to wake Archie. Crawling through, feeling like no one was there, he took off all his wet clothes and placed them on the coat rack standing near the front door. Standing nude with his hands over his crouch, shivering, it was going to take a few minutes for him to adjust to human form on earth.

He walked into the living room and saw a blanket on the top of a couch. Wrapping it around his body, he realized this was the closest he had been to her in a long time. Looking across the room, he saw a fireplace and tracked down some wood to warm up.

The room became brighter from the fire flames. Michael could see more of her cozy home. In so many ways, he imagined a life with her here on earth and in this home. He placed his wet clothing out on the brick bench in front of the fireplace. Realizing it was going to take some time until his clothes were dry, he started looking for some clothing he could wear. He found her bedroom and saw a white, fluffy robe hanging from a post on the corner of her bed. He dropped the blanket to the floor to put it on, frozen, standing nude.

"Her smell!" He took in a deep breath, smelling her scent on the robe. "It's her! It's her!" He held it to his face, absorbing the feeling of being close to her. Being wrapped in her scent reenergized his mission to get to her and save her and bring her back here alive. He was tying the belt around his waist when he heard something moaning from the corner of the bed. His instinct made him reach for his missing blade on his side.

Slowly, Michael approached the bed. He walked over and saw the noise came from under the blankets. Carefully he picked up some fluffy blankets, and there, lying cautiously, was Archie.

"WOW! You are a big cat!" Michael said with caution.

"Hello there! Easy buddy, I'm not here to cause any trouble." Michael smiled as he calmly reached his hand out in front of a set of massive fangs for Archie to smell. After a few sniffs, Archie allowed Michael to take a slow seat next to him on the bed.

Archie allowed some good petting from Michael. He then stood up and took a long stretch and yawn, exposing his long fangs before he started purring deeply, letting Michael know it was OK for him to be there.

Rubbing Archie's head, Michael felt comfort from him. "Man, you are a big boy!" Wondering if what he felt with Archie was the same feeling Aree got from animals, Michael lay down on the bed next to Archie and, wrapped up in Aree's robe, fell asleep.

Hours passed, and Michael woke to robins chirping out by the bird feeders and some deep meowing from Archie. Lying there, he had no clue what time it was or day. Time on earth was so much slower than heaven. All he knew was it must be in the morning. Hearing the birds reminded him of Aree sitting in the garden feeding birds and squirrels and other small animals in the morning. He understood her need for animal companionship.

Looking around, he decided today he would learn everything he could about Aree's life on earth and how she found her way to the nature dimension. Humans didn't have knowledge of the nature dimension; it was invisible to them.

As he sat down on her couch, still in her robe, he mediated, traveling back to when humans and its dimensions coincided peacefully with each other. There was much respect for each other in those times. They put drastic measures into place, closing the earth off from its dimensions, not allowing humans to communicate with magical beings. It was the only way to protect the dimensions of earth and earth from his fallen brother and his minions.

Opening his eyes, he slowly got up. Walking over to look out a window, he remembered there were entrances to Faermorreya everywhere. Now they were sealed shut and turned invisible. So how did she get there?

Most of the day, Michael looked for clues. He went through piles of paper and looked in every cabinet drawer he saw. He knew what he needed was right in front of him, but what was it?

Plopping down on her couch, he rubbed his eyes in frustration. He took a deep breath in and let it out. Aree had taught him to do this to calm himself down so he could refocus. Sitting there admiring her home décor, he spotted the box near the fireplace on the floor. Staring at it, he got a sense the box had to do with something. It just seemed out of place in there.

Walking over to the box, he studied everything around it and in the room. Being drawn to the shelf with books, he noticed books lying over and others standing next to bookends. The books were all about crystals. Looking on the floor, he noticed the box sat where someone could use it as a step to reach the bookshelf. He squatted down to get a good look at the old black box, then he picked it up.

Instantly shocked by thousands of tiny bolts, he dropped the box. He knew then the answers were with this box. His hands burned, and he tried to rub out the sensation. He shook his arms, trying to get the feeling back to normal. This was an ancient spell placed upon it. So ancient it was even before the pharaohs of Egypt. Knowing he couldn't touch it; he needed to look inside.

He stepped back and sat down on the couch, his mind spinning a hundred times a minute. Without notice, Archie monitored Michael's movements, understanding he looked for Sassy and what had happened. From observation, Archie felt impressed with Michael's discoveries but knew he needs to help him, or Sassy would never come back.

Later that evening, Archie was busy thinking of a way to get this immortal to understand him. Knowing Michael didn't talk to animals, he resorted to his old panther ways. First, though, Archie had to get in the right state of mind, so he went on the hunt for his huge fish toy stuffed with catnip. Finding it, he carried it in his mouth. With Michael in his sight, Archie tossed the fish in the air and then pounced on it. Taking in deep breaths, he enjoyed the feeling of being giddy and high. Lying in the middle of the floor with his fish, he noticed Michael watching him, so he stepped it up a notch and flipped the fish near Michael to see if he would play. It worked.

Michael giggled and tossed it back to Archie. Knowing he had Michael's attention, it was time to communicate with him. Archie ran around the room with his fish when he went to the double doors leading to the back porch. He sat down, dropped his fish, looked at Michael, and gave out a deep, panther, playful meow, pawing at the door! Michael looked at him and asked if he wanted to go out. Archie knew Michael was learning, so he mixed a purr and growl again.

Michael got up and walked over, grabbed the door handle, and opened the door. Archie did a happy skip and nudged Michael with his head. As the doors opened, there was an immediate hit with the smell of jasmine, lavender, and rosemary. It was an intoxicating mixture of euphoric smells all at once. Archie noticed the effect on Michael's senses.

As Archie walked to the old wooden porch, he looked back to see if Michael followed him. Meowing and looking at Michael made Michael realize Archie wanted him to follow. Intrigued with Archie, Michael smiled and said, "It's almost like you are talking to me, how funny!"

He stepped off the porch and straight out to a hidden little bench perfectly placed under a pergola covered with grapes and leafy vines. Michael loved the location and the planning that had gone into the construction. Admiring the beauty of the landscape, Michael had a new understanding on Aree's protective, loving drive for nature she would speak of.

Archie sat on the bench looking at Michael, wanting him to come and sit. He growled a purring sound again. Michael looked at Archie and asked him, "Do you want me to come over there?"

Archie's response was, "NEOWWW!"

"WHAT? Did you just say NOW?"

Again, Archie replied, "NEOWW!"

Laughing out loud and throwing his hand over his head, Michael felt flabbergasted!!! He walked over, rubbed Archie's head, and took a seat next to him.

They both looked into each other's eyes, and just then, a bond formed. Feeling the sun's warm glow touching their faces, Archie, who sat straight up, turned away from Michael and looked to the west. Michael, watching Archie, did the same thing, and then . . . there it was.

A glimpse of heaven caught in the sunset with only a single sun. Colors of pinks and peaches, yellow, and golds streaking across the blue sky illuminating every cloud it touched. Michael noticed how everything, the land, trees, flowers right before they closed their blooms for the day, had a blushing glow of love. My father's love.

Michael reached over, patted Archie, and thanked him for showing and sharing that moment with him, then said, "You are my friend. I think you can help me find her and bring her home. Do you know how she left?"

Archie blinked twice at Michael and purred as he rubbed his head against his hand, satisfied with how quick Michael learned. They sat there quietly watching the beautiful sunset transform the skies.

SEVENTEEN

The next morning, Michael awoke to the sounds of an old beat-up pickup truck pulling down the driveway, honking this ridiculous horn. It almost resembled a sick rooster with a sore throat. As the noise got louder, he rushed to put his clothes on and hide. Realizing that he couldn't hide under the bed, he had to climb out a window. Just as he heard the front door open, he headed out back, running to the barn.

"Sassy? You here? Sassy, it's Whitey!" Not hearing a response, he slowly shut the front door but slammed the screen door and walked around the outside of the house looking for her. He had no luck. Mr. Whitey started headed for the barn. As he walked, he noticed her truck was there. He looked around, seeing if she was outside repairing fencing or something. Nothing looked destroyed, but some trees in the front yard were stripped of their leaves and a huge opening was in the ground.

He made his way over to the trees when the dogs saw him. They ran across the land, both excited to see him. Wookie had disguised his white fur in mud, so he didn't look white anymore, and Scotty was only muddy up his paws. Both jumped up on Mr. Whitey.

"Gosh dang it! You dam mutts! Get down!" Now covered in mud all over his blue jeans, he tried to slap some mud off, shaking his head in disgust. "Dam dogs! You're no good!" he yelled at them as they jumped around, playing and chasing each other.

"Now, what happened here?" Looking at the spot where Michael had landed, it looked like an enormous crack in the ground exposing massive boulders. Mr. Whitey looked at the ground and the surrounding trees. He concluded a huge lightning bolt had hit the ground. Moving the dirt with the tip of his boot, he pushed some down the crack, standing there just staring at it.

Over in the barn, Michael watched Whitey through a small window, wondering who he was and why was he there. He noticed Whitey walking over to the barn and panicked. Shit! There were no empty stalls, just Barney watching Michael.

Hearing footsteps across the gravel driveway, Barney saw Whitey coming and turned his head to Michael and started moving his head around, then up and down, trying to point his nose upward to the roof. Stomping his hooves and snorting, Michael turned and watched Barney. Finally, Michael understood, so he looked up. He saw some rafters in a far corner of the barn near the ceiling. There were some pigeons roosting up there. Michael opened his wings and flew up to the rafters just as the barn door opened, and the pigeons took flight.

Sticking his head in, Whitey looked at Barney and blamed him for the noise. Looking around in the barn, Whitey gave Barney some treats and asked him if he knew where Sassy was. Rubbing his head between his eyes, Whitey laughed at the thought of Barney holding a full conversation with him. Maybe they would discuss high school football or gossip about the locals. He pictured Barney talking and smoking a big cigar.

Chuckling out loud, "How I wish that was true my friend," Whitey mumbled to himself as he exited the barn, shutting the door behind him.

He stopped and raised his nose upward to sniffing the air. "Roses??? Why do I smell roses?" Michael sat patiently watching Whitey go to his truck and get in just to fiddle with something, then he got back out and heads for the house. Taking in a deep breath in of irritation, Michael sat, waiting to hear Whitey's truck start up and leave.

Finally, he heard a rumble from the diesel engine. Checking to make sure the coast was clear, Michael looked out the window to see Whitey's truck disappearing down the road. Standing straight on his feet, he brushed pieces of hay off his clothing. Barney was in his stall watching

Michael when he reached out and began scratching a specific area by Barney's ear, thanking him for the help. Barney's eyes closed as he enjoyed the scratching. Michael gave him a good slap on his ass as he noticed a stall tag with the name Barney on it.

"Barney, huh? That's a good name. My name is Michael."

Walking around, he looked at the old farming tools hanging on the walls. In the back of the barn was a bar with different plant seeds in containers, jars of soil, and different gardening tools. There were drawings and plans written on the bar of gardening plans. She wrote this. He traced the writing and drawings with his finger. Touching everything, he began picturing himself working on a farm, covered in dirt, living a country life with Aree.

Later, he sat in her truck. It smelled of her. There was a crystal hanging on a string around the rear-view mirror. He pushed it and watched the different colors shine as it swayed back and forth. Holding on to the steering wheel, he pictured them together, cruising down the road, with him driving of course. He started opening the glove box and searching for something, anything. That's when he found a piece of paper caught between seats. Only two words, KONA TRIBE.

"This is it! I know it is!" Michael cried out in excitement.

Back in the house, Michael went into the bedroom. Sitting on the edge of the bed, he laid out his clues in order. He knew the old box had an ancient spell on it. It was not a normal item found in this era of time. Also, there was the piece of paper with the words Kona Tribe on it.

He got up and went to her bookshelf, checking to see if anything referenced the Kona Tribe. After not finding anything, he went back into the bedroom, looking through the suitcase on the floor. There was warm clothing rolled up inside and some bathroom products placed into plastic bags. Nothing was really sticking out. He stood and kicked the suitcase in anger when a small corner of a ticket holder fell out from the front zippered pouched. Reaching down, he picked it up and realized it was a receipt for an airline ticket to Alaska.

"Alaska?" Why was she going there? Looking at the receipt, the travel date was for a departure two days from now. Feeling more confused than ever, in frustration he blared out, "SHIT! I need a drink!" Looking up from the suitcase, his eyes caught the sight of Archie sitting on the bed watching him intently.

Archie jumped down and led Michael to the kitchen, where he found some ice-cold Bud Light beer in her refrigerator. Cracking a grin, he giggled at the thought of Aree drinking beer. She was more of a sweet elixir kind of girl. Grabbing a six-pack, he headed out the front door to clear his mind and enjoy the afternoon breeze. Archie wasn't far behind; it wasn't long before the dogs joined him.

Standing on the porch looking over the beautiful scenery of hills and pastures, he enjoyed the taste of his first beer. It was very peaceful, exactly what he needed to clear his thoughts and refocus on his clues to find Aree.

Taking a seat on the porch steps, he felt something familiar. Finally, he figured it out. It was this step. She sat there a lot. He could feel her energy. Closing his eyes and enjoying the moment of feeling close to her reenergized him positively. He smiled and relaxed a little more, staying there on the steps, drinking beer and enjoying watching the dogs play in the front yard with Archie lying next to him, cleaning his paws.

Everything seemed to be in perfect harmony, the color of the sky to the warm breezes making a low-tone whisper between the trees. It caught his attention; Aree had spoken of this low whisper between trees before. Never had he felt what he felt right then. It was magical! It was an invisible force of earth's energy. Its love, its peace, it was everywhere! It was in all animals and in the plants and trees and clouds in the sky. It connected her to it. This was what she felt all the time.

Michael understood Aree's gift to communicate with nature. Only she could understand this energy of nature. He had a newfound respect. He also had a new understanding of why the Elders had picked Aree for this mission to Faermorreya.

Reaching for his last beer, he popped off the bottle cap, shooting carbonation bubbles into his nose, tickling it and causing him to sneeze. Wiping his lips with the outside of his right hand, he wobbled to stand. A little headedlightheaded, he stood and walked out to the front yard to the trees. He remembered seeing Aree time after time place her hands flat against the tree. She would hug the tree and then smile from the energy she received from the trees through her hands. She would tell him it was like tiny vibrations she could feel radiating from the tree to her. This was how she communicated with trees. She could tell if the tree was happy or sick or even lonely.

Michael walked up to a gigantic oak and placed his hands flat on it. Not feeling anything at first, then he felt a slight vibration along with a view of gold dust everywhere. Immediately, he pulled his hands away. Shocked at what he had just experienced, he looked back at Archie on the front porch, who watched everything knowing somehow he needed to show the forest crystal to Michael since it had given him a sign. Gold dust. . . .

Back in the master bedroom, Michael lay on the bed, still fully clothed with his boots still on, snoring so loud it rattled the windows. Archie got irritated by the repetitive noise of Michael. He jumped on the bed, walked up to Michael's head not liking the odor of alcohol. He pounced on the pillows, forcing Michael to readjust his pillows and turn over on his side to stop snoring. Finally! Quietness.

Archie knew he was going to have to connect the crystal to Michael. He remembered her placing the crystal on the windowsill so the morning sunlight would send beams directly into the crystal, creating that reflection, the gold fairy dust looking like liquid with tiny ripples moving through it. The big problem was the crystal fell on the floor below the window. How was Archie going to get Michael to pick it up off the floor and place it on the windowsill in the perfect position? This was going to be difficult since he wasn't the best communicator, nothing like Sassy.

Around four in the morning, Michael woke, hating the way he felt, so he showered, made coffee, and lay out his clues again to find Aree.

Archie watched, impressed. Staring at the coffee table in the living room, he had his clues in order:

Ancient box with spell attached

Paper with Kona Tribe written on it

Airline ticket to Alaska and half packed suitcase

Vision of gold dust

Michael drank his coffee, realizing it was his third cup and the sun wasn't up yet. He got up and went to go outside to find a pleasant spot facing the east to meditate as the sun rose.

During his meditation, he received visions of the Kona Tribe beings of an ancient civilization. He also saw flashes of a war revolving around that tribe. Slowly opening his eyes, he received his clues just as he could feel the morning sun kiss. Feeling peaceful, he got up and went to the living room with all his clues laid out on the coffee table. Feeling so much better, he knew he now just needed to concentrate, and he would figure out how to get to Aree.

Archie lay at his feet, allowing Michael to rest his legs on his back. Michael closed his eyes and began replaying in his mind that horrible time. One of the few surviving the biblical flood was the Kona Tribe. They were beings that knew about the secret of Faermorreya. The Kona Tribe became earthly guardians. It was vital for the survival of both realms to keep their secret unknown. He recalled they had sealed the entrances to the dimensions until it chose a pure soul as a protector. Aree was that protector.

Slowly, Michael opened his eyes. Turning all his focus on the box, he knew the answer was in the box. Taking another look, Michael walked over and bent down, picking up the box, getting electrified the whole time he had contact with it.

Flipping it over with his foot, finally, the lid loosened up enough for him to open it. Not wanting to touch it again, he used a book and wedged it under the lid and popped it open. Hel fell back onto the couch as the box lid flew off. He dropped the book. Reaching down, he wanted to see if the electrical shock had disappeared once the lid was off, and it was gone.

Looking inside, he only found a black, old, silk scarf and an indentation pressed into the wood placed inside. He took a step back, placing his hands behind his head. "Now what?"

Pushing his hair off his forehead, he realized what occupied this box was a small object that opens the seal to the nature dimension. He rubbed the indentation to try to locate the object around the house. It drove him crazy knowing the answer was right under his nose, yet he didn't know what it is. Sitting down again, he thought and thought. "But what was the gold dust about?"

He went into her bedroom, standing against the door frame, looking around for anything. Pushing his hair back again and then rubbing his bare chest, he looked at Archie, who lay across the bed. "Archie, if you can help me, please help me find what I'm missing!"

Right then Archie stood up and did his long, slow stretch, leaning forward, and then an enormous yawn smacked his chops. With an excited skip, Archie walked over behind the suitcase. Looking at the ground, he started his deep meowing, purring sound. He would MEOW, then look at Michael. It took a couple of meows and head movements until Michael caught on and walked over and asked, "You got something?"

Archie pushed his nose under the zipper part of the suitcase until Michael reached down and moved the suitcase and VOILA! There, sitting on the floor, was a brilliant forest crystal. "What is this?" Michael mumbled, picking up the crystal in astonishment. "This is it! I know it is!" He turned it and looked at it from all angles.

Without warning, Archie startled him by jumping up and placing his huge paws on the windowsill sitting at chest level to Michael. Rubbing on the glass and making noises, Archie tried to show Michael where to sit it down. But he just wasn't looking or listening. The sun appeared through the top part of the window, and Archie had little time before it was too late.

Michael wasn't paying any attention to what he was doing. He was too busy examining the crystal up close. He mumbled out loud, "Gold dust." Archie hit the windowsill with his paw. Meowing over and over, Michael acknowledged him, "WHAT?" Archie then stretched a paw, showing his long claws near the dust ring from where Sassy placed the crystal before. Michael walked closer, and it worked.

"What is this?" He ran his fingers through the dust on the windowsill. He placed the crystal on the windowsill, and it matched the dust ring, but nothing happened. The sun beams were now gleaming through the middle half of the window, just about an inch from the top of the crystal spheres.

Archie bumped the crystal and pushed it into place so the sun hit it. Seconds away from showing Michael what Sassy saw, he grinned at Archie, still confused, and went to grab the crystal and received a slap on the hand by a big paw. Archie hissed an authority sound, forcing Michael to remove his hand just in time for the magic to happen.

Like a bolt of lightning, there appeared a glowing gold reflection of fairy dust illuminating the wall. "What is this?" Michael calmly spoke in awe of the beauty.

Archie didn't waste any time showing him how it worked by jumping down and standing underneath the reflection on the wall, then erecting his gorgeous, long tail straight up so the tip of it disappeared in the dust.

Michael stood there, speechless. Archie then moved his tail out of the dust, and it was visible again. As Michael watched on, Archie displayed the ability to make part of his tail disappeared and return by moving in and out of the dust beam from the crystal. Before it was too late, Michael approached cautiously, first just moving his arm in and out of the floating gold dust. He got comfortable about this crazy magical dust. It shortly faded away. Turning to see what happened, he noticed that the sun wasn't shining through the window anymore. Clouds had moved in.

Nodding his head excitedly, smiling, he scream out, "Woo-hoo!" He now knew this was the way to Aree; this was the entrance to Faermorreya.

Relief rushed over his body and excitement at the same time, giving him goose bumps all over his skin as he ran both hands through his unkempt hair. He rubbed his arms to get rid of the goose bumps covering them. With a smile from ear to ear and a gleam of hope in his eyes, he started dancing around the bedroom. Archie jumped back on the bed, watching every move he made, pleased with his accomplishment.

Michael took a seat on the edge of the bed breathing heavily; he reached to pet Archie. Michael looked at him in amazement. The intelligence and willingness of Archie to communicate overwhelmed him. He hugged him close to his chest.

"Thank you, my friend," He whispered into Archie's ears. "I guess you miss her too." Archie tucked his head under Michael's chin and started purring, feeling relieved this mortal understood and communicated.

Michael got up to leave the room, acknowledging the time on the clock sitting on the nightstand so he could plan tomorrow morning. Noticing the clutter on the nightstand, he picked up a couple of books and a beautiful picture of Aree sitting bareback on her horse. Holding it in his hands, he saw *Sassy & Barney* written on the top of the picture. So her name was Sassy here.... He envisioned that day.

Her hair blowing in the warm summer winds, her cowgirl hat, cutoff daisy dukes, a red polka-dot shirt with the first three buttons undone and tied at her waist, and cowboy boots on. "Man, she is beautiful." He placed it back down on the nightstand. There, next to it, was a picture of Archie with his name on the frame. It was a picture of him as a cub when Sassy had found him. He turned facing Archie on the bed, mumbling softly, "I am going to bring her home, Archie."

Throughout the day, he removed any evidence of him being in her house. Mr. Whitey was coming tomorrow to tend to the animals, and he was sure he would enter the home looking for a note from Aree.

Searching for a pad of paper and pen, he looked in every drawer in the kitchen and nothing. Finally, he found a pen and continued searching for a notepad. He found a used envelope and ripped off a piece. Stumped on what to write, he tried to figure out how Aree talked to him. Does she say sir? I know that's a word they use down here. Ahhh!!! Feeling really stressed out, he wrote:

Mr. Whitey Sir.

I will return in a few days,

You know what to do.

Thank you.

"Shit! What if she didn't tell him?" Trying to figure out if the note was required or not, he tapped his finger in synchronicity on the countertop. He just couldn't decide. "Oh well, this is good enough. It's straightforward and to the point; hopefully, he won't question the note." Michael placed it on the counter near the refrigerator. "Now I need to get rid of her suitcase."

Back in her bedroom, Michael threw her suitcase on the bed, unpacking it. Placing her clothes back on hangers and hanging them up in her closet, he smelled every piece at first, enjoying feeling close to her. He saw a royal-blue, silk scarf hanging on a hanger. It resembled a ribbon Aree had back at home that she used to put in her hair. Wrapping it around his hands, he then shoved it in his front jean pocket, keeping it as a souvenir.

Her closet was half empty, and Michael daydreamed of his clothing hanging on that side, imagining life as a human. He was even envisioning what they would look like as two old people sitting in rocking chairs on the front porch holding hands, watching their grandchildren playing in the front yard. How cool that would be. Both would be older and frail, but with a love making them feel like teenagers inside.

Back to reality, he hung up the last shirt and zipped up the suitcase, placing it in the back of the closet. The house looked wonderful. There was no sign of him being there or her disappearing.

"Mr. Whitey won't know a thing, Archie," Michael said as he scratched the sidebackside of Archie's ears, causing Archie to close his eyes and purr like a motorboat. "You know, my friend, you have helped me gain a new respect for animals. I never fully believed that Aree, I mean, Sassy, could communicate with all her fuzzy friends, but you have proved me wrong."

Archie meowed and looked Michael in his eyes, letting him know he heard him. He stretched himself out on his favorite white, furry blanket so Michael could rub his belly as he enjoyed his company. Archie closed his eyes for his one of many naps.

Michael walked around outside. He headed to the barn to visit with Barney. On his way, something distracted him. It was the smell of Texas Blue Bonnets blooming. Not knowing this smell he took in, he walked around until he knelt in a blue bonnet patch, realizing the fragrance came from this little flowering plant. Sitting down, he felt the soft leaves reminding him of velvet, and the unique stem had a blue and purple and white flower petals all over it. He lay down, surrounding himself with blue bonnet flowers, and was just being in the moment, feeling calm and peaceful. Placing his hands behind his head, crossing his ankles, he looked up at the sky and the clouds lazily passing by and realized he never looked up before like this. He thought of his father.

As he lay there, lost in thought, Barney startled him, walking up. Barney was unsure what he was doing on the ground. He bent his head down and pushed on Michael. It was his way of checking on him. Michael laughed and sat up, letting Barney know he was OK. Getting to his feet, he wondered if he could ride Barney.

Rubbing one of his favorite spots under his chin, Barney stretched his head out with his eyes closed and showed his teeth in pleasure. Michael reassured him things were good as he jumped up on Barney's back. Michael immediately thought of riding a young colt. Nokomis was massive compared to Barney.

Pleased there was no resistance or stress, Barney turned around and started a nice, slow gallop. He took Michael around the perimeter of the ranch, showing him everything. They ended their ride at the barn. Michael got off Barney and rubbed his butt. He walked in the barn looking for a brush for Barney.

He remembered good thoughts of being back at the stables in Celestrian. Michael always enjoyed brushing Nokomis's mane and tail, so he thought Barney could use a brushing. Finding what he needed, he walked back out to where Barney was and brushed his mane. After smoothing his hair, Barney's mane and tail looked like strands of gold tinsel in the sun. He placed the brush back in the barn and picked a couple of apples off the apple tree and gave them to Barney.

Before walking away, he turned to Barney, telling him, "I am going after Sassy." In acknowledgement, Barney moved his head up and down, letting Michael know he understood and approved.

Back in the house, he started the shower. The smell of horse was all over him, and he did not like it. Creatures back home smelled of roses, so he was eager to clean up. As the hot water steamed up the bathroom, Michael unbuttoned his shirt. In front of the mirror, he stood. He took off his shirt and then dropped his jeans to the floor. He looked at himself nude, standing there. Flexing his arms, then puffing out his chest, he felt his abs, his hands moving down to his penis, holding his jewels in his hand, he wondered if the earthling Sassy would like him. Noticing he got aroused quickly thinking of her, he felt the thickness of flesh and turned and got into the hot, steamy shower.

Taking a whiff of the soaps, he grabbed the one smelling of roses.. Using her scrubby to wash his body, he covered himself in a lot ofsoapy bubbles; he placed his arms stretched out against the wall in front of him. He let the water run down his back, washing off the soap as he dropped his head forward, enjoying feeling the warm water. The water was going down the drain, and he thought about tomorrow.

What was his plan when he arrived in Faermorreya? Archangels had never been called to help. It was not a territory they watched over. He knew the nature realm held all the magical creatures. Fairies and ungarsungars had always maintained the peace there on their own. So he wonders how bad the battle was and if she was safe.

His shower was so hot it fully steamed the bathroom up with a dense fog; he searched to turn off the water. Shaking off the excess water on his legs, he exited the shower, feeling around for the only purple towel he saw. Finding it, he wrapped it around his hips, then used a smaller lavender-colored towel to dry his chest and huge arms off. The steam dissipated, letting him see. He was not surprised about the colors of her towels. It was her favorite color.... When he was done, he folded the towels and placed them back from where he got them. Throwing her robe back on again, he went to relax in the living room.

He plopped down on the sofa, placing his feet up on the coffee table, then grabbed the television remote to figure out how it worked. He had seen these before and knew it controlled the big screen on the wall. After a while he figured it. He sees a picture of space on TV. It caught his attention. It was the starting of *Star Wars*.

Michael knew all about humans pretending when making movies that played on the screen, but they blew him away with *Star Wars*! It intrigued him with the fighting between good and evil. It reminded him of the similarities he once faced.

Sitting on the couch, he couldn't figure out why demons were still there in Faermorreya. Also, what did it have to do with Sassy? What was she walking into alone?

Turning off the television, Michael walked into the kitchen and opened the refrigerator, looking for something to eat. He settled on roasted turkey lunchmeat and slices of White American Cheese. After finding a bread box, he made a huge sandwich. He pulled a Coke out of a refrigerator. Pulling the tab off sent small fizzy bubbles out, tickling his nose.

Shocked by the carbonation, he kept forgetting this happened when he opened cans; he poured it in a glass and enjoyed the taste. "Now, this is something Raphael needs to create in heaven," he said between gulps.

Without knowing it, he drank the whole Coke in two huge gulps, giving him cravings to get another.

It was late in the evening. Michael went outside to see the full moon lighting up the night sky. Looking up in amazement, the night glow came from one small moon so far away. As he looked at the sky from the front porch, through the Milky Way, deep in the stars, he saw asteroids fly by. Also, he could see many stars and planets that he knew. Looking onward, he admired the darkness of space against the celestial bodies. The creation was so beautiful. They looked so tiny. He wondered if Finius watched him.

"Hmmmm, what is going on back home? Have the Elders realized I am gone? Is there going to be a punishment for helping Aree?"

It wouldn't matter now. Michael could worry about this all night, but he needed sleep and to focus in the morning. Taking one more deep breath of the cool night's air, he leaned against the porch post. He closed his eyes and caught himself smiling at how calm and peaceful he felt. Even the unfamiliar smells soothed him.

Opening the front door and locking it behind him, he looked around the foyer at the coat rack by the front door. He took in everything he could. Picking up pictures of her set on a desk, her leather couch with a white, fuzzy blanket laid out on top, her kitchen. He made it to the master bedroom. Dropping her robe from his naked body, he crawled into the bed, smashing a pillow on his face, smelling her all over it. He closed his eyes, envisioning laying here next to her, cuddled up with her head on his chest and his arms around her. Their legs entwined together, both in the same breathing rhythm as they fell asleep. He fell asleep.

The morning came fast, which was fine with him. He felt anxiety getting the day going. There was a slight vibration noise next to him. Pushing the covers back, he saw Archie. Standing and stretching out his long, furry legs he took an enormous yawn, and during it he said "MEOOWW," asking for some scratching on his head. Michael knew what he needed and gave Archie a nice rub and scratch behind his ears.

"Good morning, buddy! It's the big day, my friend." Archie cleaned himself, then stopped, giving Michael another MEOW! showing Michael he could understand him, then nudged him to get out of bed. "OK, OK!" Michael giggled, looking at Archie.

After doing his bathroom routine, he got fully dressed in black with his coat, made the bed, and fed Archie and gave him some clean water. Everything looked wonderful. Archie jumped up on the bed and walked over to Michael sitting on the edge of the bed, looking at the wall, just waiting. Archie bumped Michael with his head down a few times.

Michael could hear Sassy saying, "They hit each other with their heads. It is a sign of acceptance into their pride." Petting Archie, Michael acknowledged him. "Wish me luck, my friend."

Archie blinked twice. "I will."

EIGHTEEN

Three guards stood next to the lasers surrounding the necklace. Sassy needed to leave this area. She needed to have a better plan. She turned and started making her way back out of the tunnel to the center of the lair. Walking over all the filth and waste, dead bodies of fairies and ungars and other creatures, her heart was so heavy seeing some in chains, with chunks of flesh missing. This was Hell. . . . She struggled to keep the cloak over her body as she tried to keep from slipping in the bloody mud.

She followed the dim fire torches lighting up the tunnel. Voices were getting louder and louder. She noticed a horde of demons and gremlins covering the entrance. There was no way she could squeeze by without being noticed or losing the invisible cloak. Sassy was in a panic, spinning around until she saw a little hole in the wall surrounded by rocks she could fit in to stay hidden until she could leave.

Feeling a little better about being hidden, she took the time to study everything she could see. Through the flickering of fire torches, she saw goblins around a fire with a witch's brewing kettle. It boiled over, causing a toxic-looking, yellow-green foam to rise out of the brew's steam. Standing close to a pile of dried Thornapples, the goblins broke off the spikes and dipped the tips in the foam. They were nasty little creatures with three heads, each having pointed ears with big teeth dripping nasty orange saliva.

She thought it looked like they argued, hitting each other with long, powerful arms. They were everywhere! Near the pile of Thornapples, climbing on the rocks and hanging from the ceiling, they seemed to stay out of the way in fear of getting hurt from bigger beings.

Across the tunnel she saw a fullhandful of trolls handing out weapons. It looked like a pile of iron netting and swords of Obsidian sharper than steel. She noticed ogres made blow guns from what she thought looked like cattails. Between the screaming of pain, bloody mud, and the sight of demons and trolls working, it was too much chaos!

In her peripheral vision were the waving, red, sheer curtains. Sassy had herself in the middle of a nightmare and didn't know how to escape.

They gathered the growing horde of demons of all shapes and sizes into a larger group. She couldn't make out what they talked about. All the yelling and screaming was just too loud. She sat in the bloody body fluid mixed with mud, cold and hiding for hours, struggling to keep her mind sharp and sane.

They got into formation. A loud, deep voice permeated the whole lair, echoing down tunnels, making her blood run cold. It was him laughing between yelling or roars. Dressed in black and red armor with a plate on his chest . . . "Shit!" Sassy was so far away she couldn't see what it was.

Gathering the nerve to get closer, she saw so many evil entities moving in a vast corridor. Their leader preached from there. Something was going to happen; they were planning something. Moving closer to the crowd, she tried to see the plate on his chest when at once they all started swaying their arms in excitement.

Demons carried weapons; they held them above their heads. Looking around, there were so many red eyes. It was like they caught her in a room of red lasers. This was just too much. So she moved closer slowly. The leader got up on a platform, walking and jumping from piled rocks putting him above the crowd.

He stood there looking out over all his minions. Maybe he looked for something. Standing still, he spread his leathery wings out and placed his arms above his head as he let out the most spine-chilling roar. It rattled Sassy's bones in her body and horrified her. He quieted down when he had everyone's attention, including hers.

Lowering his arms, she saw maybe an *S* on his armor? Wanting to get closer, she worked her way through the crowd slowly. Staying low to the ground made it easier for her to hold on to the cloak and remain hidden. The stench of rotten eggs and body odor!!! It took everything in her not to get sick!

She found an opened area and went there so she could stand up and see what was going on around her. She noticed behind her was a wall of evil beings that she must get through to escape. She was in front of the crowd and scared to death, trying to figure out how she could get out of this alive.

She glanced up at the leader as he spoke tongues to the crowd. His tiny white eyes pierced right through her soul. She couldn't tell if he looked at her. Whatever he said upset the crowd gathering. The red eyes in the room grew more intense, looking like flames of fire. Other beings got upset or excited, breathing heavy with growls and swelling muscles cracking bones as they transformed their bodies, causing sparks of red and orange energy emitting off their backs like bottle rockets taking off.

Sassy focused on the leader, who stood in the middle of his jagged rocks. When he jumped down and out into the crowd, he caused a wave in the crowd as they did whatever they could to stay out of his way. His huge claws on his feet were like spikes sinking into the mud with every step he took. His face became easier to see.

Standing there completely frozen from his hypnotizing, white eyes, coming closer and closer, she tried to close her eyes just knowing they had caught her, but she couldn't even blink! She shook so badly she didn't know if the cloak was still covering her or not. Evil beings tried to scatter away when he grabbed a big, hairy creature by its face with his claw-like hands, lifting him in the air. Slamming him down right in front of her, shaking the ground, he beat this hairy being down to the ground and screamed at him in tongues. The creature looked like he pled for his life.

Sassy was only feet away, moving back as she watched in horror at the worst kind of torture. All she could hear were squeals of pain in between bones cracking and the ripping of flesh. By the time the beating was over, there was a limp body on the ground, drenched in its own blood. The leader held high in the air the face of the hairy being he had ripped from its head. That gave Sassy the chance to see what was on his chest as he showed off his prize. Waving the face and flinging blood from soft tissue, hanging like cooked spaghetti, the leader dripped in the creature's blood.

Sassy took a chance and saw his chest plate. The name *SARTAEL* was engraved on it. That must be the leader's name, which she was sure was important. They were all praising him for what he had done. She wasn't sure what to do. . . .

At once there was the sound of Shofar horns blowing, causing every evil being to turn and face the entrance to the cave. Excitement was what they felt, gearing up for battle. Sassy turned to watch the leader with a handful of followers turn their attention to entering the cave, as they started moving in that direction.

Many creatures started charging the entrance. Sounds of roars and horns and steel clashing on steel. There was a battle going on outside by the Falls. A familiar sound played out, and Sassy knew it was Alex and the guardians of the woods who brought an army of Stone warriors. For a brief second, she had hope. She felt like she was going to get out of here alive.

Sassy tried to make her way through the black mud, and doing everything to get to Alex was her new focus. She struggled to keep covered with the cloak, wanting nothing more than to be by his side and safe. She thought, "He came for me!"

Outside, the huge trolls were in a panic seeing the Stone army. They feared stone warriors in every way. They yelped in fear and tried to hide, throwing their weapons on the ground and surrendering.

Chaotic fighting exploded everywhere. The magical stone warriors had special powers, with oversized noses they could use as weapons when needed. They blew up their noses, then shot out a toxic mucus paralyzing a troll when it gets on their flesh, turning them into granite.

Hearing all the animalistic screams coming from different directions made it difficult for Sassy to make her move to escape this hellhole. She closed her eyes to let her gut decide which direction to run when a warm, gentle touch on the upper part of her arm and a beautiful, deep, calm voice, a male voice, whispered in her ear causing all other noises to disappear.

"You must come with me before he sees you; you must come now!" Pulling her into his chest, this strange being wrapped his black coat around her, causing Sassy to drop the invisible cloak. He pushed them through the fighting like they glided on ice. He swooped her up into his arms, forcing her to be face to face with her rescuer.

***

"I know you!" Sassy was in shock!

Astounded at the speed they moved across the ground, she heard wings, wings, being ruffled open. They took to the sky, forcing her to bury her face into his chest, feeling his warm, soft skin, secure in his arms. She could feel the wind under her, and her feet were off the ground. They were flying.

Glancing back at the faded battle going on down below, there he was, walking out of the lair with a red cape over his shoulders, causing him to stick out like a sore thumb. She could hear his evil laugh echoing across the land.

Looking up, he aimed a spear gun in their direction. "I hate the smell of roses!" he huffed. He pivoted to the gremlins around him. He snagged one up and demanded to know who the earthling was! A small, little, smelly demon came out of hiding from behind an enormous boulder. "Master! Master, I know!"

He turned to see this minor demon with a green, stinky mist around him. Curiosity got the best of him, so pointing his finger, he called the little demon closer.

"My little friend, what do you know?"

The demon watched Sartael, begging him not to hit him. Approaching cautiously with his head down, standing at his master's feet, scared to death and shaking, he looked up and said, "I screamed out her name! Aree was wearing a cloaking cape and listening to your speech. I saw through the cape and was yelling her name! See? Here is her cloak." Shaking uncontrollably, the little creature told him no one would listen to him as he held up Sassy's cloak she had dropped.

He continued looking down on the little demon and gently picked him up and asked him face to face, "You can see through cloaking capes?"

Nodding, he said, "Yes, master." Cracking an evil smile, he placed the little demon on the ground.

"You will be useful to me." Patting him on his head, he said to him, "You are going to be my servant, working with me and doing what I say. What is your name?"

Feeling proud, the smelly little one responded, "YES, SIR! My name is Motley." Looking at Motley smiling an evil smile, Sartael demanded him to bring some poison darts. Quickly returning with three darts, he handed them to his master.

Watching on proudly, his master looked to the skies and said, "Say goodbye to your Aree, Michael!"

Sassy tightly clenched herself to his body. Something felt familiar. She turned her head, looking down; the ground slipped farther away when a quick burning sensation hit her shoulder with force as it pushed her into his body, and another quick burning feeling hit her right thigh. She could feel he struggled to fly with all her movement when another sharp, burning sensation hit her in the back. It caused him to yell out in pain! Sassy watched as he looked back to see what had hit them.

Michael focused his eyes on a figure on the ground holding a spear gun. He knew those white eyes. They belonged to Sartael, one of Lucifer's leaders, Michael's worst enemy. Sassy felt his flesh swell up, expanding his muscles in rage, angry noises from his deep voice. She could tell he wanted to a fight.

Michael had unfinished business and would love to destroy Sartael for good. Knowing he harmed Aree just took this battle to a personal level.

He flew them to a height above the clouds and in a more controlled flying patterned when he said to her, "Aree, stay with me!" She felt dizzy and started losing consciousness. He began speaking to her. "We are soulmates. We share an untouchable love. Please remember!" She felt as if she was under a spell listening to his voice. She closed her eyes. She felt like she was dreaming. Unaware, she loosened her grip around him. "Aree, my love, stay with me! Open your eyes for me now! Aree, I need you to stay awake! Stay with me! We will be home soon!"

Tightening his grip on her, something was wrong; he felt pain in his shoulder, leg, and back. Tears built in his eyes as beads of sweat covered his body. As he exerted so much energy, holding her and flying, he hadn't expected to be shot upon. Trying to tell himself he did the right thing got tougher as he became weaker. If he didn't get her to the earthy realm in time, would he lose her? He didn't know if she would return to him in Heaven.

Reaching dark matter, he couldn't see portals. He felt weak and forced to put all his strength into his wings to fly higher and higher. Tears burned down his cheeks as he clenched her limp body tighter to his chest. Sassy flung her head back with her hair blowing in the wind. The warmth of his bare skin comforted her, a familiar security she knew. She felt no fear, just completely safe in his arms, which made it harder for her to stay awake.

He called out to her … "Aree, my love, please remember me. It's me, Michael! We are soulmates, bound together in Heaven. My love, please … Aree, it's Michael!"

Feeling like she was medicated, her eyes were so heavy. She knew they flew far away from that horrible place. She caught eye contact with Michael; Sassy smiled. Finally, she was with her soulmate from her dreams. She knew those gorgeous blue eyes. She felt his warm lips across her forehead, feeling blissful and secure right before everything went black.

NINETEEN

Down on the ground, far away from them, the battle was complete as the stone warriors took control of the cave. All around, demons were dead or turned to rock, then smashed into tiny piles of gravel. The surviving ones were doing everything they could to get away from the immense army dominating them. Two stone warriors walked out of the cave holding and waving the necklace. They were on their way to give it to Alex, who had stationed himself on a grassy knoll in the distance, observing the battle from the back of a war hummingbird. As the two stone warriors delivered it to Alex, he was at ease to have the necklace back.

He smiled, then said, "No prisoners of evil entities; kill them all." He wrapped the necklace in a piece of white cloth and placed it inside the front of his pants. Looking at the group of men of the woods mounted on the backs hummingbirds decked out in war armor, he said, "We have what we came for. It is time to return to the tree."

A slight pull on the reins, and the humming began. He turned and cried out to the stone warriors to "FINISH IT!" then he and the men of the woods were out of sight.

Alex arrived at the wise oak tree and rushing through the rose bush to get to Gladys deep in the tree. He breathed heavy when found Gladys in the Gold Room with her guards. She looked at recent records to see how much of their realm had been taken control of by demons. She stood and swayed elegantly as she approached him, placed her hand on his arm, and told him to take a deep breath and explain what had happened.

Alex followed her orders, then took a step back, reached down the front of his pants, and pulled out a cloth he held in his hands. Gladys watched every move he made, wondering what he had. Smiling, he unwrapped the necklace and held it out in front of Gladys. She gasped for air in excitement!

"Alex, you did it!"

The necklace reflected the beautiful gold lighting up the room. Before Gladys touched the necklace, they first took it to where the other Forest crystals lay. They approached an alter table near the crystals. Gladys turned and looked at Alex to place the necklace there. Alex laid down the cloth and opened it so the necklace lay exposed.

Gladys approached, picking up the necklace and holding it in her left palm. She raised her hand to the wall. After a second or two, the ivyivy covering the walls and protecting the crystals moved away, and a soft, green and gold glow grew in the cubbyholes where the crystals stayed. The necklace glowed and was being surrounded by streams of gold ribbon like mist moving into the air. Like a mini tornado.

They all watched in amazement as the necklace transformed back into its original crystal formation. When it was complete, the mist disappeared. The Forest crystal was ready to be placed in its own cubby next to the others. Gladys gently placed the crystal where it belonged. Just as she set it down and stepped away, the three now complete forest crystals throbbed like a heartbeat, with a glowing, dark green deep inside of each one. Almost like they communicated with each other.

Gladys and Alex watched, completely still, when unexpectedly there was a shockwave of white, brilliant light shaking the ground and racing across the land. It was like time had stopped and reset itself. As the shockwave crossed the land, everything woke up to new life. Grass turned from gray and dark brown to green and, dancing and waving in the now warm breeze, flowers bloomed and drenched the air with their sweet aromas; all the wonderful creatures of this realm came out of hiding.

Fairies and pixies danced in circles, and the different animals celebrated life. The singing of birds could be heard, and serenity stretched across the land. Even the Wise Old Oak burst with new leaves, wearing a smile of contentment for all to see. Love and peace would thrive in the healed land.

The shockwave continued rolling across the realm, causing much pain to any demon or evil being in its path. The light rolled over them and caused them to go up in flames, burning like acid had been thrown on their skin as the white light engulfed each one. They screamed in terror, feeling the pain as they turned from melting, burning flesh to ash that blew away in the wind, leaving no sign of evil.

Watching from a distance were trolls that didn't help the demons. They were safe and continued living in their mushroom houses. They looked on in terror, learning an important lesson. . . . The lair near the waterfall shattered and leveled. A mountain of red granite rocks stood in its place now. . . . Some evil ones escaped but forever lost their opportunity to control Faermorreya.

Gladys herself had gone through a change. She was no longer old with white hair. She had returned to her young, beautiful youth. All her strong powers she once possessed returned twice as strong. Gladys had returned to her royalty title as the Queen of Faermorreya. It was the first time in millennia that she again led the nature realm with love and compassion and peace for all. Feeling delighted, she turned and reached for Alex's hands.

"I want to know how this happened. Any sign of Sassy, the human?" Alex kissed the hands of his queen, admiring her beauty.

"Let's eat. I will tell you everything. I watched the battle from a distant, grassy knoll."

With full bellies of wine, berries, and nuts, they both sat in carved wooden chairs near a fire. The room was empty. All they could hear was the sparkling of the wood burning in the fireplace. Looking at the flames, Gladys, in a loving voice, spoke directly to Alex. "I know you loved the White Queen and that you had planned on being her king." Alex looked up and tried to interrupt her, but she continued. "Look at the flames, Alex."

"You see how one flame flickers and another flame follows. One leads the dance as the other follows the same steps. One flame is OK, but it can't do what two flames can. Two flames grow strong together, gaining strength and power from each other. Moving and swaying in motion, always in rhythm with each other. Sharing energy that balances each other, becomes each other, growing together as it expands together. Becoming two flames that become one raging fire.... Twin flames are what they are."

"She was not your twin flame. She is the soulmate of another flame. Try to understand what I am telling you. It was beautiful and necessary for her arrival and departure from our world. The crystal picked her to return our world back to the way it must be. Do not hold on to what could have been.".

"Your fire hasn't started yet. And when it does, you will feel the flame flicker, and your twin will feel the flicker, too. You will grow into a raging flame together."

After a bit of silence, Alex reached out to hold her hands. He looked at her and said, "Thank you. I didn't know how much I needed to hear that. I will work on it, I promise." Peace came over his face as they continued watching the flames in the fireplace. "Gladys, where is your twin flame?"

She turned and looked deep into his eyes then said, "I haven't had a flame ask me to dance!" Alex's eyes sparkled as he looked back at her.

Alex told her about the battle and how an Archangel showed up in perfect timing and took the human Sassy. Seeing the Archangel caused enough distraction that gave the stone warriors what they needed to retrieve the necklace and get control of the battle.

Gladys said, "What Sassy did was heroic.". The leader was planning an attack on us, and we didn't know that. He gathered all his minions right as we arrived. Our happiness and peace are because of her. I didn't see the Archangel up close. He was in the air holding the earthling close to his body until they left out of sight. I don't know if she was alive or not.

Gladys took a moment thinking hard ... then she said to Alex, "We will create a memorial in memory of the human woman, Sassy. She saved our world. Now she is with the angels in heaven."

TWENTY

Deep in the dark sky of Faermorreya, Michael felt very weak. With all his strength, he let out a scream. "GABRIEL! GABRIEL! I NEED YOU, BROTHER; HELP ME!"

Fighting for the strength to get Aree to the safety of the earthly realm, Michael was in a panic as he started asking his father for help. This was something he hadn't done in a long time. He knew he had broken the rules and disobeyed his orders, but love drove all his actions. Michael just could not resist helping her. They must understand!

"FATHER, PLEASE HEAR ME! HELP ME SAVE HER! PLEASE, FATHER, I NEED YOUR HELP!"

Just when he thought he would not make it, Nokomis let out a loud neigh, followed by some snorting, letting Michael know he was here for him! He neighed again, flapping his wings to slow down as he approached them. Tears of joy swelled in Michael's eyes in excitement as he saw Nokomis along with Gabriel on a stallion with him. Nokomis flew under Michael and let Michael basically fall on top of his back. As soon as Michael and Aree were safely on Nokomis, Gabriel motioned to fly and fly faster.

As the two stallions flew at lightning speed, they came out of the dark into in a portal of colors zipping by. Faster and faster they flew. They got close to entering the earthly realm. Gabriel became alert to the danger from demons living on the earth, knowing they could sense when archangels were around. Smelling odors of the heavenly flowers, the scent burned their nostrils. So he created a rainstorm, causing all kinds of noise and washing all that scent out of the air as they entered the earthly realm.

The rain came down in buckets as the heavenly stallions landed in the field near the barn. Michael jumped off Nokomis, holding Aree in his arms, he continued to whisper, "Come on, baby, we are home; please, Aree, honey, open your eyes." He rushed her through the front door.

Meantime, Gabriel took the stallions and hid them in the barn where Barney was in his stall. Barney watched through the window and saw them land with Sassy, so he showed no fear. The stallions towered over Barney in size. With their wings laid flat, Nokomis approached Barney with a smell of his head, then started looking around for the treats.

Gabriel left the barn and shut the doors behind him. Rushing to find Michael, he entered the house through the front door. Looking in different rooms, he found him in her bedroom with Aree lying on the bed, not moving.

Gabriel stood at the foot of the bed soaked from rain. He wiped his face when he noticed Michael's shoulder had a black scar. "What happened to you? Michael, did they hurt you?"

Not listening, Michael ripped Aree's shirt off her shoulder, and there he saw a black wound with the tip of a thorn stuck in her skin. Pulling it out and smelling it, he knew this smell; it was oleander poison. They hit her with poison darts. Knowing where his pain was, he looked at her back and upper thigh and found more tips stuck in her skin.

Gabriel said, "They poisoned her with oleander! They hit her three times. What do I do?" Standing there, he shook his head back and forth.

Looking at Michael, he said, "I don't know who can survive oleander poisoning? If she recovers, it's going to take time for her to heal, brother, if she can." Feeling hopeless, Gabriel left the room, giving them privacy. He found a dish towel in the kitchen Fland dried off. He didn't know what was going to happen to Aree, but he couldn't seem to not think about the marks on Michael's body that didn't disappear. How was this happening? Was he feeling her physical pain? Was he poisoned too?

After a few hours, Gabriel checked in on Michael and saw him kneeling on the floor next to her bed with his head on her stomach. She hadn't moved. Gabriel walked over and touched Michael on the arm, trying not to startle him.

Michael lifted his head and turned to Gabriel, and in a low voice he mumbled, "Doesn't she look like an angel?"

She lay there still under white silk sheets and a comforter. Michael had tucked her in like a small child going to bed. Smiling, he told Michael, "It's time, my brother. We must return to heaven."

Waiting for a reply, finally, he said, "I know First, have you seen a huge gray panther around the house?"

Before Gabriel could answer, there was a loud, deep, mumbling growl coming from the closet. Out walked Archie, now knowing it was safe. He jumped on the bed and walked up to Aree's face. Looking at her, he bumped his head against her arm and looked at her, making purring sounds softly. Sensing something was wrong with Sassy, Archie looked up at Michael.

Michael looked at Archie and said to him, "She is going to be OK. Don't worry, my friend." He walked around the bed and rubbed Archie's back. "I brought her home like I said I would, buddy," he told Archie, who was still next to Aree.

Michael grabbed Archie's favorite white fuzzy blanket and laid it next to Aree's side so Archie could cuddle up to her. He even fluffed it. Gabriel watched this in shock! He could not believe what he saw! A big cat talked to Michael.

Michael turned to Gabriel and said, "You keep that quiet!"

Gabriel threw his arms in the air and responded, "I don't know what you are talking about," then giggled under his breath. As he pushed Gabriel out of the bedroom, Michael gave him a stern look.

Michael walked back around the bed and bent over and kissed her softly on the lips, then her checks, her forehead, and one more time on her lips, remembering feeling her. "My friend, look out for her and keep her safe. I love her."

Archie sat straight up, looking deep into Michael's eyes!"! Michael walked out on that note, looking at Gabriel, who was on the couch, surprised because he heard his brother and a big cat talking! Michael smacked him on his shoulder, smiling, and said, "Let's go." Aree was safely home, and Archie would look after her until Mr. Whitey found her tomorrow.

Gabriel was just dumbfounded. He would have thought Michael knew everyone in her life. Standing on the porch looking at the rain coming down, Michael took a deep breath in and exhaled in relief. He patted Gabriel on the shoulder for thanks. They started walking out to the barn to get the stallions. Gabriel saw Michael had a blue scarf in his hands, smelling it before shoving it in his front pocket of his jeans.

Michael saw his brother watching and said, "It's a souvenir."

They threw the big barn doors open, only to see the stallions were buddies with Barney and his treat bag. Nokomis had made himself right at home, munching on sweet alfalfa bales stacked in the back of the barn.

Michael walked over and said goodbye to Barney. Barney stomped a hoof and moved his head in agreement. Again, Gabriel saw his brother communicating with animals. He was shocked he was doing it! Michael again said in a stern voice, "Don't say a thing!"

Gabriel responded quickly, "OK, OK!" as they led the stallions out of the barn.

As they waited for loud thunder and lightning to take to the skies, the goofy dogs raced across the land, thinking there were intruders on the premises. Lightning strikes created a loud rolling thunder, enough to cover their tracks. The stallions spread out their wings, and with a gallop and one huge flap, they took to the skies just in time as the dogs closed in on them. Barking over and over at the sky, they felt proud of themselves for chasing off strangers. They played, celebrating their good work, until a flash of lightning followed by a creeping clash of thunder sent them running for cover under the front porch.

The sky was full of very thick dark-gray clouds.. Speeding through the clouds and avoiding lightning bolts, the stallions soared with mighty wings and started running as they climbed higher and higher into the earth's stratosphere. Here was where the portal to the heavenly realm appeared. Nokomis seemed to know where to go, so he led the way to a portal passing through a black hole, which would keep them safe and out of sight from evil eyes. At least that was what they thought. But a black shadow phantom, an evil entity, witnessed them flying by.

The stallions were in a state of slow motion as they flew through a kaleidoscope of colors and patterns. They lay their wings flat, leaving trails of light streaming from the point of their wings as the portal moved and changed. It then shot them through the black hole faster than the speed of light. Feeling the pressure on their bodies as they passed through time itself, a sudden, sharp turn slung them toward a tiny white light that grew and grew as they got closer. It was home.

Michael felt anxiety as he looked over at Gabriel. One minute later, Gabriel looked over at Michael as he yelled, "We are almost home!"

TWENTY-ONE

As the stallions flapped their wings in sync with one another, gracefully they flew over the Outer Banks. Quizzical cherubs flew nearby, observing the brothers who had made it home. Soaring by, glancing down from Nokomis, Michael noticed Finius near a crowd of watchers from his smoke rings rising above his head.

Finius enjoyed his pipe as he sat on top of a rock overlooking his village. He waved to the archangels, pleased to see they'd returned. Michael raised his arm straight in the air, making a tight fist. He would have stopped to thank him properly but knew he had some explaining to do to some Elders. He cried out for help to Gabriel, alerting every one of his absences. If they hadn't known of his disobeying then, they sure did now.

Crossing over the mountains and near the crystal spires of the Cathedral, peeking through the cloud bank above it, there were sounds of harps, flutes, and violins playing beautiful music. The closer they approached the warmer and more loving the air felt. It amazed Michael every time he experienced this warm feeling and the refreshing smell of roses drenching the air with a welcoming vibe.

They had their castle in view, along with the stables off to the right side. Leaning forward, he directed Nokomis to go to the castle. The stallions gracefully landed in a gallop; then when they came to a stop, they knelt forward on one knee so Gabriel and Michael could dismount. On the ground, Michael rubbed Nokomis behind his ear just before he held Aree's scarf as he carefully slid off Nokomis, thanking him for the rescue. Nokomis stood tall and looked so majestic in his war armor covering parts of this massive, muscular frame. He held his head high as he motioned to the other stallion just in time to feel Gabriel slap its ass to walk to the stables.

Michael looked at Gabriel, not wanting to talk about it. Gabriel saw it in his eyes. He also noticed the black mark on his shoulder had become worse. Before Michael could speak, Gabriel said, "Let's get cleaned up and rest, and then tomorrow we will talk."

Michael smiled, knowing Gabriel understood. As they were about to split up to retire in their own quarters, Gabriel shouted out, "It is good to have you home, my brother!" Michael cracked a quick grin under soaked hair stuck to his face and shut the door.

Hearing the door click shut, he looked around on the inside, then he slid down the door to the floor, placing his fingers though his wet hair, matting it down. He covered his face with his huge palms, crying, sobbing like a baby. There were so many questions racing through his mind: Did I do the right thing? Is she going to die and come home? What is happening on earth?"?

Lifting his head up, his sadness quickly turned to anger. Clenching his jaw and forming fists, he placed one hand over his other hand, squeezing so tightly he had white knuckles and swollen biceps to match. He had never felt this rage so focused on another being before. His eyes showed a glowing neon-blue color as he lifted his head, staring out to the balcony.

"Why was Sartael in the nature realm? He was last spotted on Boonah, in the darkness and cold. It's the farthest realm. The atmosphere radiates a piercing, cold pain that no being can run from."

Undressing and struggling to remove wet jeans, Michael didn't know what to feel at that moment. He walked into the bathroom, turning the shower on. He stood nude in front of a mirror, and for the first time he saw the blackened scares forming on his body. His mind took him back to Sassy. He pushed on a scar on his thigh.

"Ouch!" A sharp pain radiated. He realized that since he could feel her pain, she must be still alive.

He stepped into the shower. He placed his arms on the wall in front of him and leaning his head down, letting the hot water run all over him, outlining every muscle drenching his tan and beautiful body. He washed away his sad feeling and fatigue. Looking through the steam in the air, he noticed his fingers looking like raisins. He got out and wrapped a towel around his waist, then fell on the bed. Seconds later, he was asleep.

It was morning. Gabriel had orders to bring Michael to the Elders. Feeling unsure of what was going to happen to his brother, he knocked on Michael's door, calling his name. Michael opened the door fully dressed and ready for his explanation to the Elders.

Both brothers seemed to take on a slower walking pace as they came up to the stables. The road seemed rockier than usual. Michael kicked stones aside on the way to the Cathedral. Today, the same stones looked brighter to him as his nerves got the best of him. He sweated profusely and kept rubbing his hands together, then placed them in his front pockets. He developed a routine of this over and over.

Gabriel reached out and grabbed Michael's arm to stop him. They shared some small talk. Gabriel knew just standing side by side with his brother was what Michael needed right now, not questions. He was going to answering plenty of questions soon enough.

Reaching the steps of the Cathedral, Michael felt like all eyes were on him, even though it was a very ordinary day. He noticed the birds flying and humming beautiful tunes. He could feel the dominate energy of love and happiness. Pausing still for a moment, he turned, holding on to the railing overlooking down around Celestrian.

Gabriel whispered, "Everyone is busy, tending to their own," helping Michael realize he was just panicked and maybe his absence wasn't noticed by all. They resumed ascending the steps. As they entered, he stopped at the altar and knelt, paying his respects. Michael lowered his head and prayed.

It wasn't long when Michael turned and looked at Gabriel, then took a deep breath and said, "Let's do it!" Gabriel, with a proud grin, placed a firm grip on his brother's shoulder and nodded agreement.

They walked down the corridor, seeming as if it was longer than before. In the distance, approaching fast, were the massive doors. Michael placed his hands upon the doors nervously and pushed them opened. Quietness ran through the room as all eyes looked at Michael standing in the doorway. They gathered all around the table. One reached out his smoky ,misty hand, waving Michael and Gabriel to approach. They both took their seats in their proper thrones as the meeting began.

An Elder rose as smoke dominated his space and grew in height. Through the mist, a pointy, long, white, boney index finger appeared aimed at Michael and with a voice of authority said, "YOU, ARCHANGEL MICHAEL! YOU HAVE DISOBEYED HEAVENLY ORDERS NOT TO ENTER EARTH WITH A MISSION YOU ARE NOT ASSIGNED ON!

"WE ARE AWARE OF ALL ACTIONS YOU HAVE DONE, AND THE DANGER YOU PUT YOURSELF IN! WE HAVE DECIDED YOUR PUNISHMENT FOR YOUR DISOBEDIENCE!"

Another Elder stood, saying in a louder voice, "GABRIEL, STAND BEFORE YOUR ELDERS! YOU HAVE RESPONDED TO A CALL FOR HELP, AND AFTER MANY TALKS, WE HAVE DECIDED THAT YOU DID WHAT WAS NEEDED IN A TIME OF CRISIS! BUT YOU DID PLACE HEAVENLY STALLIONS IN DANGER OF BEING SEEN IN THE EARTHLY REALM. FOR THAT ACTION, WE HAVE DISCUSSED THE MATTER AND CAME TO AGREEMENT THAT MICHAEL PUT YOU IN THIS POSITION.

"SO, WITH THAT, YOU ARE EXCUSED WITH NO PUNISHMENT BUT MUCH GRATITUDE FOR A QUICK RESPONSE TO SAVE YOUR BROTHER. YOUR ACTION OF LOVE FOR YOUR BROTHER WAS A SACRIFICE. YOU WILL NOT BE PUNISHED FOR THIS."

The room hummed with gratitude toward Gabriel. He stood, not feeling worthy of any. Glancing through his peripheral vision in Michael's direction, he witnessed a slight grin appear then disappear as fast as it had appeared. Gabriel wanted to say something to the Elders in

Michael's defense but knew it would only cause more problems for him. A debate over actions with an Elder, especially in a situation like this one, was a huge NO-NO. He felt sorrow for his brother. Keeping his chin up, he continued to stand at attention, showing no emotions, like a stone statue, as he waited.

Thick mist moved from the far side of the table, creeping closer to the brothers. Elders' forms appeared in view from the depth of the mist to assist Gabriel to the double doors. They would proceed forward in private.

Back at the table, all Elders were seated, placing all their attention on Michael. There was silence across the room. One by one, a smoky figure turned to face Michael. He could feel the tension rising through their bright, glowing, purple eyes turning huge, ready to give him his punishment. Again, an Elder spoke in a loud, deep tone.

"ARCHANGEL MICHAEL, THE LEADER OF THE HEAVENLY HOSTS, YOU ARE BEING PUNISHED FOR THE DISOBEDIENCE OF ORDERS GIVEN TO YOU! AS WE STAND HERE, YOU ARE HEREBY BEING INFORMED OF YOUR INTERFERENCE IN AREE'S MISSION. YOU ALSO ENTERED THE NATURE REALM WITHOUT PERMISSION! The leader of the watchers gave you information about the matters of the earth. YOU PUT YOUR EGO WITH YOUR FEELINGS FIRST, A RULE THAT SHOULD NEVER BE DISOBEYED!

"AREE COMPLETED HER MISSION. THE FOREST CRYSTAL HAS BEEN RETURNED, AND THE VEIL IS SEALED SHUT, PROTECTING BOTH REALMS. AREE ALSO WENT A STEP FURTHER BY FINDING THE LEADER'S NAME AS WE REQUESTED. YOU CHANGED THE OUTCOME OF AREE'S RETURN. PUTTING HER LIFE IN DANGER; FOR THIS, YOUR PUNISHMENT BEGINS.

"SHE WILL HEAL FROM HER INJURIES AND LIVE A LONG LIFE ON EARTH! MICHAEL, TO SHOW YOU HOW SERIOUS YOUR CRIME IS, YOU ARE DENIED THE RIGHT TO FLY! YOUR WINGS WILL BE CALLED BACK SO YOU MAY NOT LEAVE THE HEAVENLY REALM!"

Michael cried out, "NOO! Please, I beg you!" Pushing his throne back, he dropped to his knees, begging for forgiveness. Lowering his head into his lap, pieces of his hair stuck to his face in the path of were his tears flowed. He collapsed on the floor, begging for forgiveness. "I beg of you! Please, I will do anything! Please don't take my wings; anything else but this! Please don't do this! She was going to die in the hands of SARTAEL!"

"THE PUNISHMENT STANDS! SOON YOU WILL RETURN TO YOUR QUARTERS! PREPARE YOURSELF; YOUR PUNISHMENT TAKES EFFECT IMMEDIATELY!"

It was like an invisible force catching him off guard, punching Michael in the stomach. It pressed and forced him to the ground. He was suspended in midair, followed by a violent smashed to his knees as he was held hunched over with his arms pulled and wrapped around his midsection. Violently, his shirt ripped open on his back, exposing his shoulder blades down to his lower back.

Michael breathed heavily, scared of what was coming next. Surrounded by Elders in this room created a soundproof barrier against Michael's screams as his bones snapped like cracked baseball bats, powerful blows forcing him to wrench his back, pulling his shoulder blades together as he felt the excruciating pain of his skin being torn open, then singed by an invisible fire, fusing of bone together where his wings would appear....

Michael collapsed, spread out on the floor, barely breathing and drenched in perspiration from the severe torture of the removal of his wings. He was nothing without his wings. This was just as devastating as losing Aree. Never had they handed out a punishment so severe. This was new punishment territory for all.

The Elders quietly watched Michael until he regained the strength to stand and pick himself up off the floor. Some Elders had a view of two black marks on Michael's body from where the poison darts had hit Aree. Concerned with what they saw, they had not known of multiple wound sites on Michael.

Slowly getting his bearing straight, he gave it everything he had to stand on legs so weak and trembling from pain his attempt failed. His head felt heavy, like a fifty-pound bowling ball, as he tried lifting it up to glance around at the floor, only being able to see surrounding smoky mist. The Elders present were speechless.

Michael tried to cover himself up with what they had left of his shirt, struggling with eye and hand coordination by the shaking of his arms and fingers, battling the lingering pain he felt radiating from where his wings would once appear. Soaked in sweat from the shock his body had just went through, he could taste sugar as perspiration ran down his cheek to the corner of his mouth. He struggled to hold his head up.

He never looked into the eyes of the Elders. With any dignity he had, he dragged himself out the heavy doors. Michael walked at a turtle's pace. Nothing existed around him. He didn't hear a sound as he walked through the Cathedral, exiting the front doors.

Gabriel, who hid in the distance behind a gargoyle statue, prayed they went easy on Michael. But after seeing his state of being, he knew to give his brother space. Watching him from a distance, it flabbergasted Gabriel, seeing Michael's shirt ripped and bloody all over his back. He could see Michael's weakness from pain and feeling humiliated. Slowly, he descended the steps, looking as if he was in a daze with tunnel vision. It emotionally cut him off from everything around him and everyone he passed, knowing they whispered when they noticed his backside.

When he reached the bottom of the steps, he stopped and dangled his foot with a slight shake until his shoe fell off. He did the same with his other foot. Dropping his shoes in the dirt, he stepped down into the rich, dark soil and stood there for a minute, wiggling his toes in the emerald-green grass.

It intrigued Gabriel, wondering what the heck Michael thought or did. Watching on, Michael, without warning, took off like a bat out of hell, running faster and faster until he was out of sight. Gabriel watched on, then he went and picked up Michael's shoes.

Later that day, back at his quarters, he found Gabriel and Raphael waiting. Gabriel immediately started rambling on, apologizing over and over. Michael held up his hand to stop Gabriel in midsentence.

"Don't apologize; it's my fault," Michael spoke in a soft, broken voice. Raphael walked over to hug his brother when Michael pulled away, not letting Raphael touch him.

"Are you OK, my brother?" Raphael spoke in a very concerned tone.

Michael looked up into their eyes as tears swelled up, and all he could get out was, "She's gone forever."

"WHAT!" both brothers said simultaneously. Michael carefully sat on the couch, being careful not to hit his back. "They took her away. She is going to heal and stay in the earthly realm having a long life." He took a long pause. All choked up, he managed, "They took my wings too. . . ."

Gabriel winced. "How could they do that to you?"

Looking deep into the eyes of his brothers, feeling tormented and needing empathy, Michael turned around, exposing his horrific scars where his wings had once appeared.

Gabriel trembled with goose bumps of the thought of ever losing his wings. It would be like cutting his legs off. He couldn't look anymore. Raphael touched Michael's scars as he bowed his head in prayer.

A white, thin, light-like string left Raphael's palms and entered Michael's shoulder blades. After some prayers of healing, he took his hands off Michael. He transferred healing and positive energy through the palms of his hands, and he demanded Michael look into his eyes. "You will survive this, and I'm sure this is not permanent. You are an archangel; you are a leader, a warrior! We make mistakes, but we learn; we improve and move forward with no shame. This is not a judgment on you; it's a judgment on actions."

Being a little frustrated, Raphael grabbed Michael's hands and squeezed them tighter. "You must reflect on this without your ego, Michael! Listen, the Elders want you to learn a lesson. You will show them respect and honor their decisions. You understand me!"

Squeezing and shaking Michael's hands even tighter, staring into Raphael's eyes for a second, he nodded yes. Yanking his hands away from Raphael defiantly "You are right. What would I do if you weren't here to keep me in check?" Michael spit out sarcastically.

Raphael, playing around, slapped Michael's hair on his head as he walked into the kitchen, looking around.

Michael, still hurting and humiliated, said, "My brothers, I love and need your support through this, but right now, I just need to be alone to let everything settle in."

Raphael, as he reentered the room, responded, "We understand. Just know we are here for you."

They all stood in a circle, gripping each other's forearms. "Michael. If you need us . . ."

"I know; I will reach out," Michael reassured them.

Walking them out and being a little pushy, he shut the door. Looking around at the house, it was just Aree everywhere. His heart ached, breaking again, standing there slumped over and sad. He went to the bedroom and fell on the bed. All his senses were heightening with the smell of her all over the white, fuzzy, fur blankets and the pillows. He drowned in her memory and cried himself to sleep.

Not knowing what day it was, feeling the loss was unbearable. He couldn't seem to get out of bed. He got up and tries to eat, but then saw her in the kitchen and lost he's appetite and crawled back into bed. Never had he been like this. There was a time before he ever knew Aree. He believed feelings and love were just for humans, a crazy notion. Archangels were unbreakable, with no weakness. WOW! How he was wrong!

Along the fence line of Aree's Gardens, the three brothers had some time to themselves to discuss Michael. "Michael is giving up. This is a major concern for all in the heavenly realm. He doesn't talk or show that amazing drive of his to protect or lead. I noticed his hygiene isn't the best. He stopped caring for himself. He has grown a long, unkempt beard; he even removed his braids. It is perfect for his alternative lifestyle. I had a glimpse of him on his balcony, looked like he turned himself into a hermit, wearing Aree's old bathing robe. Also, there is no contact with others. I am scared for him, Raphael. What if things don't change? What if he doesn't get his wings back?"

"OUCH!" Gabriel's attention shifted when a splinter from picking bark off a small twig was now wedged far under his right thumbnail. "DANG! How the heck am I going to get this out from under my nail? It hurts like hell!"

They stopped so Gabriel could tend to his thumb, and it reminded Raphael of how he fiddled with things when he got nervous, and now he had a throbbing nailthumbnail that took the spotlight off his concerns for Michael. "Can we continue, please?" Raphael became impatient. Uriel told Gabriel to just listen while he tried to get that splinter out!

"Michael, born of light, has developed skills and feeling we thought humans only had. He has created a bond, like nothing we have ever seen before. The love they share must be alive! Michael still carries her scars! Aree and Michael have become like one soul. No matter how much space is between them, they stay connected. How is it possible that he can feel her pain and wear her scars too?"

Gabriel gasped, just flabbergasted. "What do you mean, Raphael? Please explain this!" Before Raphael could continue, Uriel spoke as they walked up to Aree's gardens.

"Are you saying Michael's heavenly light is fading?"

Raphael responded quickly, "YES! I think he is trying to die." The silence seemed to last forever. . . .

Then Uriel spoke. "I did not know that Michael was suffering so much. Being punished for love doesn't feel right. I will meet with the Elders to plead his case and his actions. For now, do what you normally do during the day. Try not to bother Michael. He doesn't need more stress. We will pull together to fight for Michael and Aree. The more we pray, the more they will hear our prayers! We must have faith if we are going to save Michael!"

TWENTY-TWO

Sassy still felt weak from recovering from the oleander poisoning. Time had passed, and along with it, she, as a person, had changed. Remembering her time in Faermorreya, she looked through the window near the front door, thinking of the fairies and the tiny size she had been. The entire experience in Faermorreya had given her a different outlook about nature. Suddenly everything was very delicate to her. She now knew fairies were real; there was a living creature helping each and every plant or tree to the tiny moss on the ground to survive in her world. It had matured her and her love for the earth while strengthening her bond with nature.

The icy roads and conditions outside made it easy for her to decide not to open earthly Creations. The morning was quiet, like the calm before the storm. A winter morning with the smell of snow hanging heavy in the air, it was a perfect morning for the smell of a crackling, cozy fire.

She gathered wood and stacked it in the fireplace, sparking a splendid memory of a time when her father would have a huge fire in the fireplace that would shoot flames out, just safe enough not to burn their home down. She could hear him calling out, "Sassy, go get me some wood. I need more wood!" Her mother would yell at him to be careful!

Outside, the woodpile would have a layer of ice pinning them together from all the sleet freezing on the wood. Ahh, good times . . . That beautiful memory made her realize she was lonely and ready to make fresh memories with the same old smells. She really wished she had a companion, someone who could help bring in the icy logs for a change.

After creating the fire and making the house warm and cozy, she grabbed Archie's favorite white, fuzzy blanket. Archie joined Sassy on her couch, snuggling up to her, knowing she felt lonely. Sassy shared stories of Faermorreya with Archie and how her protector showed up and brought her home. She only had bits and pieces she could remember.

Archie licked his paw and purred, for he already knew who it was who brought her home. "Living a life with him would be perfect," she told Archie. Envisioning him with a couple of kids, she wished out loud to pull him into reality as she slid off her house slippers. She wanted to find him, and not only in her dreams, as she mumbles, "This big house gets lonely in the winter."

The Dark Mountains in British Columbia, Canada, were the subject of a National Geographic show. She wasn't really listening to the show, but something about those dark, cold mountains looked familiar, which was crazy since she had never been there or ever thought of these mountain ranges. The more she watched, the more she felt like she had been there. Maybe she dreamed of a place resembling them.... Sassy thought of the waterfalls. And who saved her from that demon leader?

Scratching Archie's belly, Sassy looked at the coffee table and saw her journal. She sat there staring at it, having mixed feelings about her journal. Or you could say her book of "HIM." Sassy wished he would return. She didn't know where he had come from or even how he got her back to her house. His voice haunted her. Who was he? She heard his voice in her head, "I love you!" He had called her a different name she couldn't remember.

Reaching for her journal, rereading all her notes of him, now and then she would remember something, so she had been keeping a running journal with the goal of finding him. Flipping pages, she saw one that read "REMEMBER ME!" Something he said over and over. She saw where she wrote of the warmth of his body as he held her tight. Also, the sound of wings flapping?

"Wings?" Wonder what that meant? Why did she write this? She turned to Archie, asking him, "Do you know why I would write this?"

Through his long yawn he said, "Yahoww."

She scratched his chin. "You do?"

Again, she got a "Yahoww!" in return.

Looking at Archie, Sassy wondered if he knew who the mystery man was. She thought to herself, "I need to make plans and find this guy. Maybe I should hire a private investigator to find him." She threw the journal back on the table and grabbed the remote to find something to distract herself from the thoughts of him.

She must have fallen asleep for a little while. It was the wind blowing that awoke her. The dark-gray skies and snow covered the back porch windowsill as she sat up. She hastily got up and opened the door and called for the dogs, who came running full speed, excited to be in the house, out of the cold.

Wookie slid across the ice near the back door, falling on his butt. He couldn't get into the house fast enough. Scotty came in and snagged a spot right in front of the fireplace, claiming it, being on his best behavior, showing her he could be an indoor dog.

They both were so loyal, and this was such a treat for them, being allowed in the house. On the top of the couch, Archie lay irritated with all the heavy breathing and wagging of tails that all at once took over the house. He had such a snobbish personality sometimes.

Wookie found Archie's food bowls and cleaned them out with his enormous tongue, splashing water on the floor all around Archie's feeding station. This just seemed to piss Archie off even more. He jumped down and went over to where Wookie was near his food bowls and slapped him on his nose, making Wookie yelp and run under the kitchen table! He then turned and walked with his tail straight up into the master bedroom and jumped on the bed, claiming it for himself. Sassy gave up on trying to make them all get along. They each had a place in her home, and they knew it.

Sassy cleaned up the mess Wookie had made and moved Archie's food bowls onto the counter. She knew it would make him feel better. Returning, she sat back down on the couch as "HE" returned to her thoughts. She was on the verge of driving herself crazy if she didn't get this man off her mind. She decided she needed to throw herself into work. She hadn't been to the shop in a while. If she stayed busy, maybe he wouldn't dominant her thoughts.

Later that night, Sassy awoke abruptly in a cold sweat with her heart racing. The feeling of fear overcame her body as she pulled the surrounding blankets tight. Trying to control her breathing, the feeling of danger was almost overwhelming. Quickly, she felt the need to close her eyes and started praying. This time, though, she prayed to angels for protection.

Her breathing calmed down; that overwhelming, scary feeling subsided. She had controlled her fear enough to push the blankets off and get her bearings straight. Sitting up, she convinced herself it was a dream, a nightmare!

"Those eyes! Those white eyes! Evil runs through those eyes with the ability to burn scars on my soul after I locked eyes with him."

Also, his laughter! Creepier than any Halloween laugh she had ever heard. It was deep, scratchy, guttural, roaring laughter. She didn't recall the beast, just its laugh and those white eyes.

Getting up, she put on her robe to go get a drink of water. The house felt a little different, which heightened her senses. In the kitchen, she took a glass out of the cupboard; she got a drink of water. Placing the glass in the sink, she went back to her room. She took off the robe and crawled back into bed, hoping to fall asleep peacefully.

As she lay there, still weirded out a bit, she started envisioning a place she had created in her head when she was a little girl. Whenever she got scared or had bad dreams, she would go to this place in her mind, and any ill feeling she would experience would disappear. This was her tiny piece of Heaven. It was beautiful, with enormous trees and hills covered in green grass with wildflowers and the smell of jasmine in the air. Nature's beauty mesmerized her. She was safe in this place.

Sassy saw herself lying on a branch up in a massive tree, a special tree of colors. Looking up through the branches, she saw leaves of different colors. It was magical. As she saw herself there, she felt safe, so comfortable she fell asleep peacefully. It worked for her every time, even this time.

She was in a deep sleep; she witnessed visions of a faraway place where there was barely any air, a barren, desert landscape. It was a constant 120 degrees of boiling heat sweeping out and around a valley, hidden near deep caves with active tar pits. Again, she awoke. Opening her eyes, she was shaken! She couldn't remember much. Reaching for a pen and her dream diary, she wrote all she could remember. . . .

The area had no life and was far off the human grid.

Something was there waiting, and it was not good.

The ground was hot.

Confused, Sassy's gut feeling told her to beware. It was a warning vision. Unsure what this meant, she closed her dream diary and lay it on the nightstand with the pen. Lying back, she pulled her covers up to her chin, staying that way until morning.

***

Deep in the deserts of Death Valley, Sartael waited. After he barely survived his escape from Faermorreya, he had been waiting for word on Sassy's location on earth. He had been there waiting day after day, month after month sitting on an old piece of wood, staring at the tar bubbles. He watched them swell and pop, creating sounds like farts, releasing sulfur gases sucking the oxygen out of the air.

A shadow entity flew in and landed to inform him Michael and Gabriel were in the earthly realm with a woman. After he received this news, he immediately sent scouts out to find her. Until he heard about her location, he stayed there day after day, waiting. His hatred for Michael and Sassy built. He had plenty of time to come up with his scheme to destroy Sassy. Smiling his evil grin, he relished the day when he would destroy her.

"Michael will lose everything. He will no longer know what it is like to be loved anymore. He will be lonely, forever knowing what it feels like to not have anyone! Michael's suffering will give me such pleasures!" he cried out. Bending his black, reptilian, muscular legs, he released his claws' grip on a dead, old, mesquite branch where he stayed perched. Stretching out his leathery wings, he took to the skies, laughing out loud in pleasure, thinking of the day Sassy would die.

TWENTY-THREE

A few days passed. Sassy enjoyed her coffee and glanced out a front window in the dining room. Shining brightly of peach and yellow, the sun shot streaks through the winter clouds, just enough to melt the icy roads. Snow still covered the land and ice on the tree branches, glistening and twinkling in the sun like twinkling Christmas lights. If Thomas Kinkade saw this, he would paint it. Thinking of that, she went to get her camera and took some beautiful pictures of the landscape. She thought of having them blown up for a wall picture to hang near the fireplace.

Reviewing the pictures, the dogs harassed, wanting out. The dogs' whining ended the moment they knew it was time to go out and play. Sassy opened the door as Wookie pushed his way around her to get out first. He almost knocked her over. The air was crisp and cool, making his breath visible. Wookie tried to catch his breath as he jumped around in the snow, covering himself, making him look nice and clean again. Scotty wasn't far behind him. Sassy wasted no time shutting the door, feeling chilly, then went into the bathroom to start a hot bath.

Waiting for the water to warm up, she collected some candles, clean towels, and that journal. Adding bubbles to the water, she then wrapped her crazy red hair up into a bun. Testing the water, it felt perfect. She dropped her robe and climb into the tub, causing it to overflow with bubbles. Ahhh ... what a perfect way to start the day, all warm and relaxed as the water pierced every nerve in her body, causing a wonderful, blissful feeling. After a minute or two of complete relaxation, she dried off her hands so she could review her journal for the hundredth time. Hoping one time she would remember something new, anything!

Flipping pages, reading what she had written, what he had said to her. The most important one was when he said he loved her and to remember. "SHIT! REMEMBER WHAT? I have never been in love before. What does this mean?"

She threw the journal onto the floor and removed the bun from her hair, then sunk down under the water. Staying waterunderwater for as long as she could, it reminded her of being in the gold fairy dust from the crystal. She enjoyed the faint hum coming from being under the water. Sassy also loved feeling weightlessness, envisioning floating in gold.

Her eyes were closed underwater when a flash of a memory passed in front of them. She sat up abruptly, splashing water everywhere! "WE WERE FLYING! HE HAS WINGS! I REMEMBER HIM HOLDING ME AS WE FLEW FASTER AND FASTER! OMG! THE WINGS ARE HIS!" She reached for a towel to wipe the bubbles off her face, then stumbled getting out of the tub. Her hair was soaking wet, dripping down her back as she wrapped a towel around her body. She quickly ran to find a pen so she can write this down before she forgot. Smiling from ear to ear, she now knew she had memories to remember. "He is an angel!" This put her in a blissful mood, preparing her for the day.

Driving and being a little daring with the ice, she could see the town ahead. It seemed to be busy. People ere out and about. This made her happy she chose to open the shop today. Reaching over, she gave Archie a little pat on the head. "It's going to be a good day, Archie!" She drove around back to the park. Archie was eager for her to open the door but not happy about the slushy ice under his paws. Seeing more near the door easily put him in a bad mood.

Sassy pushed open the shop door and was delighted with the smells that hit her right when she entered. Taking a deep breath, smiling, thinking it was another wonderful gift today. She had missed this place.

Turning on the oven to warm the room, she waited for the front heaters to kick on so she could turn the open sign around and open the front doors. She started gathering fresh flowers she had dried from the last season so she can make some new candles today.

Sassy felt good and happy about the upcoming season. Christmas was coming up soon, and she really needed to get the Christmas scents ready and make up some holiday gift baskets, including candles and crystals. "Hey, Archie! Should we get the Christmas lights out and decorate the front windows? It feels like it's time." She heard nothing from him, so she turned to see what he was doing.

He was up on a top shelf cleaning his wet paws and belly, still in a bad mood from the slushy ice. He ignored her. Knowing what to do when he was acting pissy, she looked at him and said, "I will take the silence as a yes! Your mood will change when you see the twinkling little lights." He gave her a dirty look and gave her some abrupt noises as he continued warming up his paws!

The shop was still getting warm. Wrapping a scarf tighter around her neck before she opened the shop, she put her coat on and walked around downtown to see if any other shop owners had decorated for the holidays. There was a chill in the air. Something she had never felt before. It blew right through her clothing, down to the bone.

Hurrying along the icy sidewalk, she noticed the salon had a local tree service placing lights on their windows and building. The wreaths were up on the lampposts. Festivities were in the air.

Walking up on Tony's Deli gave her a craving for a hot ham and cheese sandwich. She grabbed the door to push it open, but at the same time, someone was on the other side. With the extra pressure, the person fell backward and landed on the floor covered in condiments.

"OH MY GOD! I am so sorry; I didn't realize," she said to a man sitting on the ground.

"Sassy, hello! Please come in out of the cold!" came from behind the counter.

"Tony! I am so sorry for causing this sloppy mess. Let me help clean it up!" Sassy looked down to see if she had hurt the stranger. She saw him wiping Toni's famous baked macaroni and cheese and BBQ sauce off his face and shirt. She tried to help him up when Toni started yelling at the guy to clean it up as he remade the macaroni and cheese. Sassy saw the mop bucket across the room, so she hurried over to it. Laying her coat down in a booth and removing the scarf, she grabbed the bucket and returned to the mess of melted cheese dripping everywhere.

First, she bent over to apologize when he caught eye contact with her. She stood there looking at him. He waved his hand in front of her face, pulling her out of the trance, causing her to blink multiple times and back to reality.

He asked her, "Do all redheads blush as easy as you do?" Sassy felt so stupid. She talked but didn't even hear her own voice.

"Please, forgive me. I didn't see you."

Pushing his cheese-covered hair back from his eyes, he said, "Are you psychic?"

Looking at him quizzically, she said, "No."

"Then how could you have seen what was on the other side of the door?" he replied.

Sassy stepped back as he got off the floor. He stood about six-foot-three. He faced a booth, so she watched as he removed his shirt and used it to clean cheese and BBQ sauce off the bench near the door.

Sassy couldn't help but notice his very sexy back with a pleasant form and muscles. Perfect physique. She had always admired a man with back muscles. She hadn't seen a man's body in years! There was this electric feeling running through her veins.

He turned around, looking at her, showing her a crooked grin. He said, "AHH... mam, do you feel OK? You are blushing now!" Sassy looked away and started cleaning up the floor.

Toni screamed out to the stranger, telling him to go look in the back for a shirt to put on and then deliver the food over to the school. "Take it to the teacher's lounge. They are having a retiring party for Mr. Johnson.

Also, rinse the cheese out of your hair!" The stranger smiled while looking at her. Sassy told him she would finish cleaning up, not to worry about it. She ended her talk with a lingering smile. Lowering her head, she started mopping, hearing him walk away.

"Man! I'm a dork! He called me MAM! I must look old. Oh, shit!" She remembered she hadn't styled her hair or put any makeup on! "What is wrong with me?" she thought as she continued to mop until he left.

Making sure everything was shiny and clean, she put the mop bucket back where she found it. Wrapping the scarf around her neck, then putting on her coat, Toni spoke from behind the counter where he made his famous sandwiches.

"You are just what I needed to see on this bitter day. Your beauty warms my heart, my dear Sassy! What do I owe for this lovely surprise visit?"

Please Lord, make Toni stay on that side of the counter, Sassy said in her mind.... She smiled and remembered, "I came in for a hot ham and cheese."

Toni had a way of making her feel uncomfortable, his eyes looking at every part of her. "OH, my lovey Sassy, give me a moment, and I will prepare a masterpiece of a sandwich for you!"

She smiled and said, "Thank you, Toni."

She made her way to the soda machine, pleased to see grape soda there, one of her favorite sodas. She topped off her drink with the small crunchy ice she called Sonic ice. Sticking a straw in the lid on the cup, she took a seat in a very squishy booth next to a window. After she settled in, she felt like a child at a gigantic table. What waited patiently, enjoying her grape soda.

Looking around, the decor was something out of Philadelphia. Pictures of William Penn and shots of the Ben Franklin Bridge in huge black-and-white photos hung between windows with team flags of the Eagles or Flyers stapled around the deli, was well as an old metal street sign reading South Street.

Toni always told a story about that sign; Sassy thought it was his old childhood street.

She was looking at all the beer signs in the neon team signs when her sandwich was ready. With her drink, she walked over to pick it up and pay. Toni had her sandwich in hand, smiling, showing his huge front teeth behind that huge, wooly mustache. Sassy dreaded his approach. Reaching out to hand her sandwich to her, he swiftly grabbed her hand.

"Sassy, you should know by now that I will never charge you for food." He stroked her hand in a gross, creepy way. Toni lifted her hand as if he was going to kiss it, saying to her, "You're special to me!"

Sassy pretended to trip so she could rip her hand back with the sandwich. She stepped back, thanking him, then turned and pulled open the door with no regards to anyone on the other side. She had to get out of there.

Back at the shop, Archie changed his mood when he smelled food. Funny how that happened, the power of food. She unwrapped it, torn off a good chunk for Archie. It was delicious! He might be a creepy, old, greasy bald man, but he was a master at food.

After lunch, she kept the shop closed so she could decorate with no distractions. She had Cinnamon simmering on the stovetop in the back room, releasing a festive smell making its way to the front of the shop. This spice helped boost her creativity with decorations, and this year she leaned toward a more Nostalgia Christmas theme.

Maybe it would spark old, wonderful memories for customers when they came into the shop. She knew exactly where her wreaths and décor were stored. She stood on a chair, pulling boxes off a wooden shelf. The dust on this shelf was so thick it caused her to sneeze, almost sending her to the floor as she rocked the chair on two legs. Slowly, she got down and went to get the ladder stored outside near the back door in the storage bin.

Outside, she stomped on the ice to break it up around the storage bin. It had gotten thicker here, so Sassy jumped on it like a small child playing in a water puddle. Jumping harder and harder, she suddenly got that feeling someone watched her. She stopped moving, convinced that someone was there, and cautiously turning around. There he was, leaning against a dumpster.

Looking like an angel, with the sunlight behind him. He looked so handsome wearing snakeskin cowboy boots with a tight pair of jeans hugging his body in the right places. Wow, he is hot! she thought to herself. He had a green, white, and black flannel on with a Carhart jacket and a black cowboy hat that had wet spots all over it glistening in the sun.

Sassy noticed he was laughing at her. It triggered her.... "What the hell are you laughing at?" she yelled in his direction.

He replied, "Is it safe to come over there? You will not knock me down or anything?" She huffed under her breath and waved him over.

When he was close enough, he asked for a redo for their meeting. Sassy giggled and agreed. His hand was out like he wanted to shake hands. So they did. He spoke first. "My name is Garrett Miller. It is nice to meet you."

Smiling back, she said, "Hello, my name is Sassy. I own this shop, just in case you thought I was breaking in or something."

Through a small laugh, he responded, "Well, I was curious. May I ask, what were you doing?"

Hitting the ice again, Sassy said, "I am trying to break up the ice so I can get into my storage bin. As you can see, the ice is thicker here, so that is why I was jumping on it," she mumbled....

"May I help you?" Garrett asked.

Feeling nervous, all she could say was "Sure." She took two steps back, giving him room. "So I see you have different clothes on?" She rolled her eyes, not understanding why she had just said that....

He turned and smiled at her. "The others need to be cleaned."

He placed his fingers on the edge of the storage door, and with one sturdy pry on the door, it popped open. Without looking at her, he asked, "Are you wanting the ladder in here?"

"Ah, yes! That's all I need from in there." He laid the ladder on the ground as he shut the storage door, making sure it sealed shut and locked.

He turned toward the ladder, and with one arm, he picked up the ladder, then looked at her smiling. "Where are we going?"

Sassy stumbled on a piece of ice but didn't fall. Thank God! She led him into the backdoor of her shop and suggested he place the ladder against the wall near the shelf so she could get her decorations down. Gently he put it in its place, then asked if she needed the only box on the shelf. She nodded yes.

He climbed up the ladder and reached for the box. His extended arm was so muscular he could balance the box in his hand as he climbed back down. Sassy couldn't help herself, thinking how sexy he was with a fine ass too! She stared at his ass as long as she could without him catching her.

Placing the box on her worktable in front of them, he took a few steps back and placed his fingertips in his front pockets as he began looking around. Sassy watched him, trying to take in everything about him.

He smelled different herbs and flowers, touching the leaves on the ivy, even picking up a candle mold, trying to figure out what she used it for. His looks were very quizzical, almost like he was seeing things for the first time. She thought it was cute, the way he would curl his lips and crinkle up his nose when he smelled something that wasn't pleasing to him.

"Garrett. Is that right?"

He pivoted to face her smiling and said, "That's the name they gave me!" placing his fingers back in his front pockets.

They stood in weird silence until she offered him some hot chocolate. It heated on the stove. He refused some, continuing to look around like a detective. She interrupted his investigation by telling him, "If you walk through that doorway over there, you will find the shop if you are looking for something, maybe special for someone?"

He approached the door, then turned, saying, "I am alone. I have no living family members. No one special either."

"OH" was all she could get out. "I too have no family left here on earth either," she spoke.

He walked closer, asking her, "You said not on earth, so are they on a different planet?" as he giggled.

Sassy poured herself a cup of hot chocolate and replied, "NO! They are in Heaven!"

She took a drink, watching him. His energy changed when she said that. She thought for a moment she saw a black aura around him.

"I am sorry; I feel like I hit a sore spot."

Garrett started walking to the back door leading outside, then stopped and turned toward her. "I apologize. My feelings of loved ones differ from yours. Anyway, it was nice to meet you, Sassy. I need to go."

Before he shut the door, she said, "Thank you for your help!" She saw him wave an arm in the air, acknowledging he heard her.

Well, she thought that was strange! Not every day a gorgeous-looking single man showed up in town. He was good looking. The complete experience uplifted her mood. She just knew this was going to be a good day! Turning the radio up loud, she enjoyed the privacy as she danced through the shop decorating. She placed tinsel in the front window surrounded by lights. She hung a wreath on the front door, one that her mother had made. It still looked brand new and very festive. Unfortunately, Sassy hadn't inherited that crafting skill, or she would make a wreath to sell at the shop this time of year. Her skills showed in her beautiful candles. Luckily, she got some candles made today that she would place in the front window tomorrow.

Looking past all the Christmas décor in the front window, she noticed how dark it was outside. The sun had gone away, and it looked like another snowstorm might be brewing. So it was time to lock up and start heading home before the roads iced over again.

"Archie, where are you? It's time to go home?" he moaned from the back room. She went to get him and noticed the oven was still on.

"OH SHIT! Again, you save my ass." She turned it off. "Archie, come on."

After loading up in the truck, Sassy slowly drove down the streets with ice-covered windows with visible spots through the fog. The truck's defroster/heater couldn't work quick enough for her.

***

Hiding behind a snowbank outside of town, behind the line of visibility in a snow-covered, wooded lot, Garrett stood there in the freezing weather, waiting . . . waiting to see Sassy as she drove by in her truck. Talking to himself under his breath, hissing, "This is going to be easier than I thought. . . ." Hissing again. "It's time, Michael, for you to feel pain and suffer as I destroy her." His eyes glowed a vibrant white as they transformed into his evil eyes; he hissed and licked his lips with his split tongue. Watching her drive out of sight, he waited, then turned and walked through the snow and sleet to the rocky hillsides just outside of town.

TWENTY-FOUR

The fate of Michael weighed heavily on everyone's mind.... The feeling around Celestrian was to no longer to punish him for being disobedient but, for the sake of love, save him.

Gabriel witnessed on from his balcony. Off in the far distance he could see a purple glow coming from the northwest side of the Cathedral. He knew the Elders had gathered in numbers and were meeting about Michael. It seemed like days that the glow had been there. No one knew what was being said. They must wait. This was one thing Gabriel struggled with.

Going into his kitchen, he filled a mug with Raphael's new elixir. He didn't wait for it to breathe before he slammed the whole mug. He refilled his mug again, knowing he couldn't get drunk, but boy, he wanted to. Pacing the floor, glancing over at the glow far away, he placed the mug down and headed for the door to go check on Michael.

Banging hard! Gabriel hoped he opened the door. Banging again and harder, then he knocked softly. There was no response. He placed his ear against the door, hoping to hear something, anything, but nothing.

Leaning his head on the door, he yelled out, "Michael! Please, man, open the door!" There was nothing. "Michael, if you can hear me, we need you! We love you, and we are fighting for you! Please, Michael, don't give up!" After waiting a minute or two, feeling disappointed, he turned and walked away.

Michael stood on the inside of the room listening to everything his brother had said. He knew Gabriel meant well. It was just so hard to be around others or even think about his duties as an archangel.

He went into his bedroom and inspected himself. Placing his arms straight out to his sides, he saw how they had shrunk. Lifting his shirt, he saw ribs and bones instead of rock-hard abs. He turned around to see his back in the mirror. What he saw caused him to fall into a deep depression. No beautiful powerful wings, just a man's back, with marks from Sassy's scars.

"I am not an angel anymore. I'm broken and weak."

Turning to face the mirrors, he looked at his face with this long beard and mustache. His hair was untamed; he looked like a wild man. How much time had passed? Sassy's scars still marked his body. The only good thing was they had told him she lived. He wondered if she even remembered him at all. Walking around the house, he pulled the curtains closed on all his windows, then went back to bed.

***

Gabriel made his way to Raphael's apothecary in the woods. As he walked up to the door, he could smell a horrible stench coming out the windows. Cringing his nose, he knew Raphael was in the semi-dark room making some new concoctions. Gabriel held his hand over his nose, pushing the door open, then asked, "What is that horrible smell?"

Raphael turned from a table covered in tons of branches and herbs sorted into piles next to different small bottles with colored liquid in them. He wiped his hands off on his apron and welcomed his brother.

"What brings you here? You never visit me here."

Gabriel grinned, still holding his nose. "Now I remember why I don't come here!"

"AH, it's not that bad!" Raphael laughed.

Gabriel, gagging, said, "You're right; it's not that bad. It's horrible!"

Raphael still laughed at his brother when he handed him a small bottle that had Rose Oil written on it. "Here, take a small amount, and rub it on the tip of your nose. You will be fine then." Feeling hesitant to follow his directions, it shocked Gabriel that it worked! He had forgotten the intelligence Raphael had.

Replacing the small bottle down on the table, Gabriel started asking Raphael if he knew anything new. Raphael walked over to a window, pushed some small shades in a blue fabric he had made into curtains. Glancing out, he saw the glow coming from the Cathedral. He pulled the curtains closed, turning to Gabriel. "The Elders have been conversing for a long time. Soon we should know something. I wouldn't worry about it."

"How could you not be worried?" Gabriel snapped back.

Raphael broke small branches into piles when he said, "Some Elders will not give up on Michael. Try to relax, my brother. Stay positive, and we will know something soon. You could help me with grinding some leaves I need. It will take your mind off Michael." Gabriel joined in and helped grind some leaves.

Laughing and joking killed a lot of time. Neither one of them noticed the glow had faded. Flying through the window, hitting the blue curtains, was an owl delivering a small message on scrolls for both. On the departure of the owl, Gabriel had the curtains pulled back, assisting him.

He looked toward the Cathedral and with excitement cried out, *"IT'S OVER! THE MEETING IS OVER!"* He looked at Raphael, who read the scroll.

The news put a smile on his face as he looked at Gabriel and suggested they get cleaned up before they go to the Cathedral. Before the evening moons arrived high in the night sky, the Elders had requested their presence. Gabriel was happy to know the Elders had decided something. He rapidly helped Raphael clean up and blew out some of the many lit candles.

Back at the castle, they landed in the courtyard. Both agreed to meet soon and arrive together. Raphael called out to Gabriel, saying, "Gabriel, don't forget to use soap; you stink something fierce!"

Gabriel walked away laughing, "HA-HA, your sooo funny!" A thought went through his mind, wondering if the horrible smell lingered.

***

The suns set over the Ruby Mountains when Raphael met up with Gabriel. They both were nice and clean, smelling good. Dressed in linens, they both tried to look really relaxed but were full of anxiety on the inside. They left early, walking together at a smooth pace, passing the stables on their way to the Cathedral. They did much of the walk in silence. Nokomis and other stallions grazed in the field. Glancing over, Gabriel noticed it would be a beautiful painting.

Ahead, they could see the Cathedral's crystal peaks poking through the pastel-colored clouds reflecting the suns setting in the east. As they walked by Aree's Garden, the smell of jasmine appeared in the evening air.

Gabriel mentioned the smell reminded him of Aree.".

Raphael reached over and slightly squeezed Gabriel's shoulder, then said, "I know; it reminds me of her too." After a moment, Gabriel broke the silence by asking his brother if he thought she would ever return.

Raphael responded fast with an optimistic, "YES! We will all unite again; I know this, brother."

Paying respect at the altar, they both felt the tension thicken in the air. "Let's go," Raphael said in a whisper. They walked down the corridor with all eyes on them. "I feel as if everyone in the Celestrian is here at the Cathedral, knowing about Michael and Aree," Raphael mumbled to his brother.

In front of them, they noticed the doors to the Hall of Records were open, awaiting their arrival. Taking their appropriate thrones with their names at the table, some Elders seated near them greeted them.

The doors shut. From the farthest corner of this massive room, the moon beams radiated a warm, safe feeling felt by all in its presence. An Elder stood at the front of the table; his gown glowed in the purple mist surrounding him. He stretched out his arms, palms facing upward. He then placed his boney hands in the prayer formations. His hair glimmered a silver color, intensifying his purple eyes. He took his seat in front of them all, all eyes on him.

"I, too, know feeling love for humans. Many moons ago, I walked with them. I witness their different beliefs and struggles they go through. They are curious creatures that need love and guidance. Aree was human and showed human love to Michael. Even though they are both light-beings, Michael was never human. The bond they created became one light being that grew and came alive." He laid his hands down on the table. There was a long pause before he spoke again.

"As you all know, I spent many hours in deep conversation with my fellow Elders. We hurt watching Michael suffer. We did not plan this mission to cause pain between Michael and Aree.... We now know Sartael is behind the attacks. It's time to end this mission and release Michael from his torture."

He stood and bowed his head to everyone. "A new mission is in order to watch and record all movement of Sartael and his minions." He then turned around and left the room.

Gabriel stood, slamming his fists on the table as he leaned over to the Elders shouting, "OK, release Michael immediately!" Raphael grabbed his brother's arm; no one had ever barked at the Elders like that.

"Gabriel, calm down, hear them out," Raphael said in a firm, low voice, forcing him to change his attitude.

The Elders coming in and out of view from the surrounding mist spoke to each other in an ancient tongue, used before the Archangels. They both sat there patiently wait for the Elders to speak to them. Raphael noticed Gabriel picked at his fingernails under the table and bounced one leg fast. So he reached over, pinching the back of his arm.

Gabriel calmed down. Just when Raphael moved closer to Gabriel to whisper something in his ear, an Elder stretched up above all others, causing the rest of them to settle down. He turned to face the brothers and told them, "We agreed it to release Michael silently as he sleeps tonight. We must privately execute this. Tomorrow his wings will return. He will still be bound to Celestrian, fore we can't have him interfere with a safe return of Aree. We will reach out to you both if needed. This concludes this meeting."

He pushed back the chair and stood up and all of them were gone, nothing but bluish-purple mist dissipating. It always amazed Gabriel how fast Elders disappeared.

He turned and hugged Raphael as he laughed, saying, "I told you, brother; we will unite again!"

Gabriel smiled, replying, "Yeah, yeah, don't get a colossal head. This wasn't you're doing!"

They pushed the enormous doors opened when Raphael said, "Prayers, my brother. Prayers."

***

Later that night, Michael struggled to sleep. Tossing and turning, he finally got out of bed and went into the kitchen to get a drink of water. It was so refreshing going down his throat. It had been a long time since he had drunk or eaten anything. He refilled his mug, gulped it down, releasing a vast sigh of satisfaction.

He replaced the jug in the icebox when he noticed fresh fruits and a charcuterie board sitting on the shelf.. He had an urge for food. Seeing all his favorite cheeses and meats gave him a sense of peace.

The silk curtains hanging in front of the balcony swayed slightly in the night breeze. He went outside and enjoyed some food and drink. It was the first time being on the balcony since his departure. After enjoying some food, he stood in her old spot, looking at the Ruby Mountains in the distance. It was so quiet he could hear waves hitting the shoreline of their beach they had walked and played on. A tiny grin appeared on his face as he whispered in the night air, telling Aree he would always have this memory.

Getting lost in time, he reflected on their life together filling the hours, bringing the slight hint of the seventh sun rising soon. He really wanted to stay out there to watch the sunrise, but the night air had caused him to feel drowsy.

Pushing the curtains aside, he walked back to his bedroom when an unseen force hit him, elevating him in the air. The force was so intense he let out a cry but had no voice. Not being able to move and not being heard, he didn't know what was going on. A potent force enclosed around him, causing him to feel nausea and pass out.

A faint light started radiating around his neck and shoulder blades as his bones snapped and broke as they tipped apart. Hanging in midair in a bubble of white light, his body transformed back to his healthy-looking self. All his facial hair shrank back into his skin, giving him a flawless appearance. His hair became clean and braided just like he wore before. His arms puffed up as his muscles reemerged just as his chest filled in and stomach muscles returned, giving him a firm six pack, and the fine hairs on his legs returned with color as his thigh and calf muscles expanded in strength. It suspended him in midair, looking strong and healthy.

His angelic glow intensified just as his wings ripped their way out as his shoulder blades began splitting. Slowly, his wings unfolded and looked brand new. They were massive, with feathers fluffed just as strong as ever, as they extending straight out from his body. The glow from the bubble was so bright it lit up his entire living quarters, causing the light to be seen for miles. Suspended in midair, it glided him and placed him on his bed, still in a deep sleep. Michael had transformed into his radiant, almighty, angelic being. The punishment had ended.

***

The morning came soon; he woke up. Stretching his legs and arms, he felt different. He noticed he was naked. Shocked, with his eye wide open, he began moving erratically, feeling his body on the bed. He kicked the blankets to see his leg muscles in a dark tan shade and strong as ever. His abs were rock hard, and he flexed his arms, excited to see his enormous guns back. Quickly he jumped out of bed, looking at himself in the mirror. He was so confused but bursting with excitement. No way just eating that small amount of food had done this. Looking in the mirror and trying different poses, he admired his body.

A sense of anxiety overcame him when he thought of his wings. He closed his eyes and called upon them. Before he could finish his thought, his beautiful, powerful wings appeared stretched out, giving off their slight radiant glow. Amazed, he stood there staring at his majestic wings with all feathers accounted for. Running his hand across them, he noticed they were just as smooth as glass, yet sharp as razor blades. Michael looked complete, an Archangel again.

Thank you, Father, for not given up on me. Michael had a new outlook. No more feeling sorry for himself. Knowing that forgiveness handed was rare, he promised himself to never disobey orders again.

***

Raphael was with Gabriel as they made their way to Michael's quarters. Before they arrived, Raphael turned to Gabriel. "Let's act like we didn't know. I feel it's best that way, so act surprise."

Bang, bang, bang!

Gabriel couldn't wait to see his brother.

Bang, bang, bang!

Michael opened the door just as Gabriel got ready to bang on his door again. They stood here looking at each other before Michael reached out to hug both brothers. "I'm so sorry for my behavior. Please forgive me."

They released each other when Raphael said to Michael, "Stop, my brother, you never have to apologize to us. We owe you an apology for not being here or understanding your pain."

A big smile appeared on Michael's face as he waved his arms. "Please come in. There is much to catch up on."

They all hugged again. Inside, Michael offered an elixir to both brothers. "I would like to raise a mug to the brothers united again."

"CHEERS!" they said in synchrony.

"Michael, Raphael has created a new elixir. The best one yet!"

"Oh yeah? I can't wait to taste it!"

Raphael started blushing. He did that when receiving compliments. "I call it Myristica Mule, and Michael, I have a keg of it set aside just for you!" They cheered and drank and laughed together.

Feeling quite tipsy, they enjoyed each other's company, just like the old days. Raphael flexed his arms, comparing himself to Michael's. As he reached over, he put Michael in a headlock as they laughed and fell to the floor.

"Oh, how I have missed you, brother!" Raphael says.

Michael, standing now, reached out his hand and helped his brother off the floor. Gabriel, smiling from ear to ear, felt relaxed to see both getting along so well. Taking a seat, Michael asked about Nokomis. "How is he? I feel horrible. It has been so long since I saw him after he saved my ass and Sassy."

"SASSY, who is that?" Raphael blurted out!

Michael smiled and said, "It's Aree's earthly name."

"Well, well, that is just fitting for her!" Raphael laughed, causing them all to laugh.

Michael stood, stumbled a bit, and motioned for them to leave. He needed to see Nokomis. He needed to know that he had not forgotten him. They all agreed and went their separate ways with peace and love and feeling tipsy too.

***

The alfalfa fields were luscious and full, standing around three feet tall, looking like dancing feather dusters swaying to the rhythm of the breeze. A wonderful treat for the stallions, Nokomis grazed in the far back corner of the field when he lifted his head with a mouthful, munching alfalfa. He saw Michael at the fence across the field waving at him.

Instantly, Nokomis neighed in happiness to see him. He galloped across the field, neighing the entire way, then slowed down when he reached Michael; he lowered his head so he could hug him and rub his ear. Neighing and stomping his front hoof Michael had a comforting vibe inside and smiled, so happy to see him.

"Nokomis, my friend. Please forgive me. I'm back and stronger than ever. I will never abandon you again."

Nokomis understood and was joyful to see his master. He flapped his wings, causing the alfalfa to lie flat against the ground for a brief second, showing his master he wanted to fly. Michael climbed over the fence.

Nokomis knelt and lowered his head so Michael could mount, giving him a nice rub on his massive neck. Nokomis turned and took off running and kicking and rising on his back legs with wings held in an upright position in excitement. Like magic, they shot into the sky.

Flying through the golden clouds floating in a violet sky, they hovered for a moment, absorbing the sunbeams way above Celestrian. The air felt good and cool, moving through his hair and across his skin, giving him a slight case of goose bumps.

Leaning forward, Michael spoke in Nokomis' ear. "Show me what I have been missing!"

Nokomis with glowing gold eyes gained speed as they did all kinds of tricks and maneuvers. It almost looked like they pretended to be in battle. Michael stood on the arch of Nokomis's back. With perfect timing between wings, he fell off, taking to the skies with his own wings. He was free.

They soared in synchrony, feeling their strongest in the air. They were a force dominating the skies together. All afternoon, they strengthened their bond with each other. Michael felt some peace and joy for a while. He started thinking about who he was. Worthiness of his title. How his love for Aree made him weak. Realizing he was being greedy and petty by putting his needs first. He made a promise to Nokomis he would never stray from his duties or disobey an order. Rubbing Nokomis' neck, he cried out loud, "I'm back!" Feeling stronger than ever, he knew who he was and knew he must come up with a plan. He must destroy Sartael. . . .

TWENTY-FIVE

The snow had eased up and now everything was coated with a deep layer of white. The bare tree branches looked like icicle lights when hit by the sun as it tried to break free from the dark, dense clouds. Sassy stared out the window near the front door. It was so beautiful outside, but with an eerie darkness she could feel in her bones. It was like the calm before the storm. She tightened up her grip on her robe around her neck as she tried to understand this feeling.

She screamed, startled by Archie, who walked up on her and swished the inside of her leg with his long tail. Looking at her a little bothered because she scared him when she screamed, Archie stepped in front of her to see out the window. Sitting down, he started slapping his tail around. He was unsure about something. Sassy knew this by watching him. She glanced out the window one more time, looking for anything different, before she went to get dressed.

A couple of hours passed, and the day was just getting darker. Sassy leaned against a wall in the foyer near the front door, putting on her Muk Luks so she didn't slip on the ice. Barney needed to be checked on, and she needed to make sure the barn was nice and warm inside. As she wrapped a scarf around her neck, she noticed Archie still sitting in the same place in front of the window, now fogged up in parts from his breath. She walked over to opening the front door but stopped. Something told her to look out the window to make sure nothing was out there. Never had she done this or felt this way! She saw nothing different except there was no movement at all outside, not a creature in sight.

"Archie, my love, what are you looking at?" She couldn't see whatever he saw. Trying to get him to move away from the window caused him to swat his paw at her, smacking her. Pulling her hand away, she knew to leave him alone before he got irritated and showed his claws. So she stopped and opened the front door, pushing through a layer of snow and ice that had built up on the front porch and the base of the door, sealing it shut.

Once the door opened, the dogs made a break for it, almost knocking her down the porch steps.

"Shit, Wookie, slow down!" she yelled at him, irritated.

She stepped off the last step into the deep snow. Walking her way through the snow to the barn, she felt happy watching the dogs acting like puppies playing in the deep snow for the first time. Nothing ever seemed to bother them, not even four feet of packed snow.

Sassy reached the barn, struggling to open the latch to the barn doors frozen solid. After a little work, she broke it free from the grip of the ice and pulled the immense doors open. To her surprise, it was very warm in the barn. Barney was in his stall, just as happy as could be to see her.

In his younger years, they would saddle up and enjoy riding in the snow, but age had caused some of his joints to not move so comfortably as before. The last few winters he had enjoyed staying in the barn in the warmth from the hay bales surrounding the walls. Also, he had made some seasonal friends that also took shelter in the barn. A couple of wild raccoons hung out in between the bales of hay. Last year they had a litter of little coons in there. Also, in the upper loft there was a hoot owl that seemed to be friendly with the coons. They have peace this time of year and understand each other's needs for warmth. So Sassy allowed them to stay.

Barney was happy to see her and neighed for some treats, which he knew she had. As she dug in a burlap bag, she heard the clumsy noise of the dogs come busting through the door. They didn't seem to hear anything she said but yet they could hear Barney's treat bag.

Running and sliding into her from behind, Wookie quickly sat down, looking up at Sassy so she saw him. All she could do was laugh and give everyone some sugar cubes. As soon as she gave Wookie some sugar cubes, he took off so excitedly he ran out into the snow, tossing his treats in the air. Losing them in the snow, then finding them again, and tossing them up into the air. Sassy couldn't tell if it was a game he made up, or he had really lost his treats in the snow. Either way, he enjoyed himself. Scotty stayed in the barn lying on the floor, licking his treats slowly, savoring the flavor.

Sassy stayed out in the barn awhile, brushing Barney, then placing his blanket on him, comforting him before she started rubbing down his legs. Barney closed his eyes in enjoyment of the massage he got from Sassy.

It got colder, and she still needed to collect some firewood and stack it on the back porch. Gathering up her gloves, she noticed Wookie running down the driveway to the gate. She couldn't imagine anyone out driving in this weather. Locking up the barn and looking down the driveway, she didn't see anything, but Wookie barked and paced in front of the gate. Scotty joined him, and they caused a ruckus, growling and barking near the gate.

Sassy could see nothing through the winter fog. She suddenly got a chill up her back, causing her to run to the house for safety. She unknowingly covered her head as if something flew above her. Pushing open the front door and quickly shutting it behind her, there she leaned on the wall, breathing hard from the burning sensation the cold air in her lungs. Looking down, she noticed she trembled with fear. What was it that had sent her into flight mode? She looked down to her left, and there in front of the window was Archie, still staring and now watching the dogs.

The sudden feeling of fear intensified, causing her to lock the doors. She kicked off her Muk Luks and scurried around, checking the windows and all the doors, wanting the house locked up tight. After she locked the last window, it made her feel a little better, but she still needed to get some wood brought up to the house. Not knowing what to do, she made some hot chamomile tea to help her relax and calm down to think. The actions of the animals had her on edge. If it was something dangerous, they would be the first to know.

Sassy caught the news on TV talking about a blizzard. They had a terrible blizzard last year; the weatherman had blamed it on global warming. She turned the channel and ended up on PBS with a deacon on a show talking about the weather changing. "Its global warming! The end is coming! Armageddon!"

Laughing, she thought to herself, people think too much.". As she grabbed the remote, she turned the TV off. She had her own problems and really didn't want to hear about somebody else and their problems. She still had to get firewood.

Finding the nerve, she finished her tea and hurriedly threw on a coat and ran out to the woodpile out back. There were layers of sleet, snow, then sleet covering the woodpile. It was like each piece of wood was grouted together with ice. She had to take a shovel to hit it multiple times before breaking free some logs. Finally, she could get six pieces, which isn't enough if she were to lose electricity.

Her fingers tingled and burn from touching ice. She rubbed her fingertips when she had an overwhelming sense of danger and being watched. She started looking around but couldn't see much through the strange, cold fog lingering over everything. It was creepy. There wasn't a sound, a weird silence. She could hear the snow falling. It was that quiet. She didn't feel safe and felt exposed. Looking at the wood, it was going to have to do for now.

She brought all the pieces to the back porch and stacked them in a corner away from the weather in a simple spot near the French doors, so she only had to open the doors and grab what wood she needed.

Back in the house, Sassy wanted the dogs in for extra protection but noticed they were still down by the front gate. Sassy stirred the ashes and added a log on the fire, rubbing her hands together, thawing out her fingertips.

The evening was darker with an ominous feeling. Sassy went to call the dogs in before she got ready for bed. Of course, they made it difficult. They were still down at the gate.

"What in the heck are they watching? Wookie! Scotty! Come on, NOW!" Finally, after another blast of cold air in her lungs and yelling at them, they came inside from the cold. Both made a beeline to the fireplace; they lay down to dry out and warm up.

Sassy turned off the lamp next to the couch and turned off the outside Christmas lights. Glancing out the front window, when she turned the porch lights off, for a moment she thought she saw an orange glow like from a fire far away in the rocky hills. As she looked again, it was gone. Thinking, no one lives out there. It's rough terrain with no homes. It's too cold for a campfire. She wondered what she had seen.

Rechecking the locks again, she thought to herself as she walked to her bedroom, Is this what the animals see, noticing it seemed extra dark in the house. An unfamiliar feeling lingered.

TWENTY-SIX

The snow came down heavier as the wind's whistles had turned into a moaning howl. He flew over the town, hidden in the frosty, night air. Back at his cave, he shapeshifted into a dark, heavy, rolling fog; he crept over the land, headed straight for Sassy's home. Once near her property, he rolled under the front gate. He moved across the snow in a shadowy haze, crawling up into the trees in her front yard. On a top branch, he turned into the figure of a shadow man as he stayed fixated on her windows and door, seeking an entrance to invade her home.

The snow blew strong and howled as he crept his way up to her roof. Walking along the roof in the shape of a man in the blackest of black with glowing white eyes against the snow on the roof peak, he made his way to the fireplace and, turning into a bellowing cloud of smoke, he went down her chimney.

There was a slight flame flickering left on a burned-out piece of wood. Wrapping his black, long, slinky fingers on the edge of the brick below the flue, he lowered himself, peeking out to see what was around. He noticed the dogs sleeping about three feet from him. Turning himself back into smoke, he eased up the brick wall of her vast fireplace.

He floated as smoke to the ceiling, then turned back into a creepy shadow person, taking on the crawling position as he moved across her living room ceiling. The dogs didn't see or hear anything; they laid there on the floor deep in doggy dreamland, while he crawled across the ceiling above them, heading right for her bedroom.

Looking at her from the bedroom ceiling, he crawled over to the corner of the room and crept down the walls, crawling like an animal stalking its prey. As he reached the floor, he turned into the shadowy man and stood at the foot of her bed, looking at her. Studying her. He wanted nothing more than to rip her apart piece by piece. With every tear of her precious skin, he wanted it to torture the Archangel Michael! Anger grew as his hatred had his body turning to a boiling hot temperature.

He approached her side of the bed. Dragging the blanket and then exposing her body, he looked at her like a beast about to attack. He thought of raping her before killing her. He secretly always lusted after human women. She was beautiful and plump in the right places.

He ran a shadowy finger, leaving a red scratch mark along her ankle, up her leg to her hip, all the way to her pretty face. This caused a slight moan of pain from her. He leaned over her precious face, inhaling in her smell as he picked up her hair, moving it away from her face and ear.

He started speaking in tongues, whispering right into her ear. She reacted but did not wake up as he talked faster and faster in her ear, causing her to panic, frozen with fear. He expected her to open her eyes, locked under his spell, but she didn't. He let his long, curled tongue dripping with saliva reach out and rake across her lips. Still no reaction from her. As he continued to attempt putting her under his spell, he whispered to her, then looked at her, trying to figure out why her eyes didn't open.

Feeling his anger rising in him, he backed up to the foot of the bed, confused. "She should have opened her eyes."

In frustration and rage, he instantaneously grabbed her ankles, raking his claws deep across her lower legs. Ripping into her flesh, he saw blood running down from his claw marks, staining the sheets she lay on. She still could not move. He had her paralyzed with fear.

At once her eyes opened, and it startled him, making him stumble over her shoes on the floor, making a loud noise. As fast as a flash of light, he turned himself into black smoke, rising to the ceiling, then crawled fast to the chimney. The dogs jumped, being startled by the loud noise and his icy breeze as he moved in front of them and out of the house. He rolled across the land like a fast-moving fog bank; headed back to his rock cave he had discovered deep in the woods.

Back in his original evil form, Sartael sat, angry and confused. Why couldn't he put her under his spell? She meant nothing to him. How did she awake on her own and see him? What had happened?

Hours went by and, camouflaged, Sartael sat in the deep snow, still trying to figure out what had happened. He had started a small fire and looked for answers in the flames but saw nothing. Every time he thought about hurting her, his thoughts would change to visions of her lips and her body.

"What the hell is going on?" he screamed.

Jumping to his feet, he paced back and forth. He had to see her. But how? The town was closed due to snow on the roads, so he had to think of a way to see her. He walked to the cave opening. He looked in the far distance toward her home just as another gust of winter stirred up again, sending creepy, howling sounds across the lands.

***

Days passed, and he left the cave the same way, as a black, thick fog creeping across the ground during the peak of the night. He made his way back to her home and entering it through the fireplace as a shadow man, then crawling across the ceiling and down the walls. He stopped at the bedroom door this time, leaning on the doorframe, watching her sleep.

As the night went on, he walked over next to her, whispers in tongues again in her ear, causing her to moan in fear. She looked weaker every day. He looked at all the bruising and deep claw marks on her body he had caused from the previous nights. Touching her bruises, he felt an electrical shock in his chest, causing him to step back, putting his hand over his chest. He tried to rub out the pain and regroup.

"What is going on? What is this I feel?" Realizing he felt bad from hurting her, he had convinced himself nightmares were best to keep her weak. No more marking her body with scratches and bruising. Now he was not focused on hurting her.

He whispered tongue in her ear when the smell of her hair stopped him in mid-thought and caused a distraction for a moment. It confused him until he realized he enjoyed her smell, and he enjoyed the feel of her skin. She was so soft. Sartael had never noticed this before. He got aroused from looking at her through her tiny, silk gown.

He had her trembling with fear in her sleep. Knowing she was paralyzed, he leaned over her body, blowing a cool breeze on her nipples, watching them harden up, looking plump and luscious, like they wanted to be touched and kissed. Sartael could not resist. Positioning himself on top of her, he had all these thoughts of raping and killing her by squeezing her neck, alongside with tender lovemaking thoughts as he envisioned giving her much pleasure.

Paranoid, he stopped himself, realizing his thoughts of her had changed. Looking at her face, he pushed himself from her, watching a tear form and run down the side of her left cheek. Touching her cheek softly, catching her tear with his black shadow fingernail, it moved him witnessing this, realizing he didn't want to hurt her. His battle was with Michael, not Sassy. He recognized this feeling. He wanted to love her instead.

Just then, he had a sharp burning pain in his chest intensifying. He lost the ability to keep her paralyzed. Sassy awoke from fear abruptly, able to move, panicking. Struggling to see around the room from the tears built up in her eyes gave Sartael enough time to retreat to the shadows, climbing the walls out of sight, slithering back to his cave, clinching his chest.

Sassy was in horror at her exposed breasts and a moist liquid like drool around her. The horrible visions she had experienced while sleeping woke her up. She sat up, turned on the light, and wrapped her arms around her legs as she gathered herself.

For the past four days, she had been battling night terrors, seeing visions of angels fighting, the earth in flames, but it was the screeching growls haunting her. The visions were so vivid. As she went to get out of bed, she noticed more bruising on her legs and ankles.

"What is happening to me?" She cried out for Archie.

Archie entered the room, sensing evil immediately. His hair stood up on end. On high alert, he scanned the entire room. He jumped up on the bed to comfort Sassy and lay down next to her, taking the position like the sphinx guarding the Great Pyramids. Protecting Sassy was his primary job. He didn't sleep the rest of the night.

The next morning Sassy woke feeling a little better and rested, thanks to her protective, fuzzy friend. She gave him a big kiss and rubbed his ears.

It was around two p.m. when Sassy drove into town to check up on the shop and to see what was going on in town. Driving around, it looked like a ghost town. Most businesses were closed because of the weather. Looking between each windshield wiper swipe, she saw an OPEN sign at Toni's Deli. As she pulled up, putting the truck in park, she looked through the windshield to see if any other lights were on inside. She saw movement. She turned the truck off and headed inside.

To her surprise, there he was, sitting in a booth. She could finally see his hair color, which was a dark brown. He had it slicked back on top and shaved tightly on the side, was freshly shaved, and wore reading glasses as he flipped through the *Waco Tribune*. Just then, she touched her hair and pulled it down over parts of her face, hiding some bruising on her neck.

Garrett lifted his head, noticed her, and waved her in. She walked inside and over to him, smiling. He had been dominating her thoughts during the day.

"Hello, Sassy," he said in a friendly voice.

She replied with, "Hello to you, Garrett."

"Ahh, I see you remembered my name," he chuckled. "Please join me."

She agreed. Sitting down, Sassy removed her gloves when he reached over and gently caressed her hands to warm them. Immediately she yanked her hand back when he asked her, "What the hell happened; are you OK?"

Looking down, he saw bruises and deep scratches running around her wrist and forearm. He looked up at her, concerned. "Sassy, what's going on?"

She felt comfortable enough to tell him, so she explained the weird visions and night terrors she had experienced, not expecting him to believe her. "Ever since the snowstorm started, something has terrorized me in my sleep." Garrett kept holding her wrist with a delicate touch, glancing deep into her eyes. His eyes were the lightest blue she had ever seen, outlined with full lashes and arched eyebrows. Sassy knew right then she had a crush on him.

"Sassy, please hear me before you say no, OK?" Leaning across the table, she nodded OK.

Garrett told her about his experience with the supernatural in his past. How he had saved a couple attacked in their home and how he had cleaned their home and removed all negative beings.

"Are you saying I have a ghost in my home?" Sassy asked in a low voice.

Holding her wrist, he looked down, examining it one more time before letting go of her hand. "Sassy, I think you have a demon in your home causing harm to you. And if that's the case, it won't stop until you have it removed."

Speechless, she stared at him. . . . "Just think about what I said. I can help you in your home." Before she could answer, he changed the subject quickly, asking, "What are you doing out in the bad weather?"

"Oh, I wanted to see if any shops opened." She quickly asks him the same question.

He looked at her, then said, "I was hoping to see you. I really enjoyed talking with you, and well, there aren't many single people our age around here." They both started laughing, which alerted Toni, who again made a big deal about seeing Sassy.

"Hot ham and cheese coming right up with chips and a pickle on the side and a grape soda to go! Anything else for Miss Sassy!" Toni cried out before he started humming loudly some old Italian song.

After receiving her sandwich, they sat there in the corner booth, enjoying their lunch together. Sassy sucked down the last of her grape soda when Garrett got up and offered to walk her to the truck. He then went around to the passenger side and jumped in. He reached over and turned up the heat as their breath fogged up the windows.

Sassy rubbed her hands together when he asked, "What are you doing the rest of the day?"

She sat there and pondered her day, really wanting to spend it with him, then said, "I need to go by the shop and get a few things, then I was planning on heading home.

"Why? What are you doing?" she asked.

"Well, if it is OK with you, I would love to see your home. I mean to see if anything is there. I am intrigued, nothing more, I promise!" he said, crossing his finger in midair and showing her his crooked grin. She just couldn't resist him. So Sassy invited him home with her.

As they pulled into the driveway, Garrett commented on the beautiful, rustic ranch. "It must be nice to have all this."

Sassy slowed down, approaching the barn. "I guess so. My parents built everything you see. It was a working ranch when they were alive. Now it's just me, two dogs, a horse, and my grey panther named Archie."

"Wait a minute," Garrett spoke. "Did you say a panther?"

"Yep," she replied . . . not saying anything more. She wanted to see his expression when he met Archie.

Garrett sat there quietly; he did not know that a big cat was there. Cats were mystic creatures that could see and kill demons. This could be a problem. . . .

They both entered the side door near the garage into the mudroom and started removing their snow-covered shoes when Archie came around the corner of the couch. Leaning forward, stretching his legs and yawning, making sure he showed Garrett his big teeth while extending his claws as he arched his back.

"Ahhh, is that Archie?" Garrett said in a nervous tone.

Sassy giggled over his reaction and told him not to worry. Archie hadn't eaten anyone in a while. He stood there nervously, looking at Archie, not knowing what to do.

"Relax, Garrett, I raised Archie from a cub, technically he still is a kitten, just bigger than a normal cat. He is very obedient."

Archie walked over to smell Garrett, and upon smelling his pant leg, he started growling under his breath.

"Archie! Stop it! He is a guest in our home, now be nice!" Sassy barked at him.

Archie looked over at her and stopped. Turning away from Garrett, he jumped onto the back of the couch, keeping Garrett in his view. "I am so sorry, Garrett! Archie never acts like that. It has been just the two of us for a long time. He is very protective of me, especially when evil comes around.

"Come on. Let me show you my home." After the tour Sassy made some Hot Totty drinks for them.

Garrett relaxed around Archie, even though Archie would look at him, showing a side profile of his long fangs and his enormous jaw while giving him a quick growl. He thought he hid that from Sassy, but she saw all.

Garrett noticed the fire getting low. "Sassy, where do you keep your firewood?" She showed him her supply on the back porch.

He laughed at her. "Sweet Sassy, point me toward your woodpile. You have a woodpile, right?" he asked sarcastically.

She opened the back door and pointed him in the direction, then turned and went back into the house giggling. It felt good to laugh. Everything was easy with him; this was going well. It felt almost too good to be true.

Turning, she glanced out the curtain to see if he had made it back to the porch, but he walked back through the snow with a huge amount of wood in his arms, at least enough for a couple of days.

Sassy watched every move he made. His walk, the way he stacked wood, the strength in his hands holding the frozen logs, even the banging of his boots to knock the snow off. She watched him hop around on one foot while removing a boot from the other. It was the cutest thing ever. She could tell he felt comfortable with her. Maybe it was the start of something. . . .

They had topped off the remaining Bourbon she had by making more Hot Totties and finishing the last of the carrot cake she had bought from the bakery. As the fire got low and more like a pile of glowing ash, their faces recovered from all the laughing they were doing.

Sassy got tired, fighting to stay awake. She didn't want this night to end. Eventually, Garrett told her not to worry; he would protect her as she slept. Through weary eyes, Sassy gave him a smile. She believed him.

As the night carried on . . . she slept, and he protected her from himself. Sitting in a recliner that sits off to the left of the couch, so many thoughts ran through his mind. The pain in his chest became stronger. He knew he was developing feelings for her, even protective of her from himself. He told himself, There will be no more pain for her. I need to keep her believing that she needs me here to protect her from evil.". He spent most of the night thinking about how he was going to convince Sassy she needed him there to cleanse her home.

It finally dawned on him. He wanted to be here, with her, as her mate. He wanted Sassy to love him and to never remember Michael. He sat in the chair grinning, pleased with his new plan. He could destroy Michael by stealing his soulmate. . . .

TWENTY-SEVEN

Michael was furious at the marks on his body. He knew Sassy was being tormented by Sartael. How did he find her? How do they know who she is? Did Sartael orchestrate this order against Sassy? AAHH! He smashed a mug against the wall, splattering red elixir everywhere as it ran down the wall. He stood in the middle of the living room, puffing in a panting rage as his eyes glowed blue with intense rage.

Gabriel came busting through the doors, able to feel Michael's rage. "What is going on? What happened to your wrists and legs?"

Michael spun around, locking eyes with Gabriel, and said in a deep, scratchy voice. "They found her; Sassy is in severe danger."

"Michael, your neck!"

Michael fumed with rage. "I feel strongly that Sartael is behind the attack on her."

"SARTAEL! Did you really say his name? How would he know who Sassy is on earth?" Michael calmed down, pacing back and forth across the floor.

"Someone or something must have seen us with her when we returned her to earth. That is the only thing I can think of, brother," Michael said.

Gabriel, confused, rubbed his chin, replaying that evening in his mind. He stood and said, "OK, let's not focus on who and how but focus on getting her away from him and bringing her home."

Gabriel continued, saying how her safety was compromised. The mission was over. It was time she returned to heaven. "The Elders must see this and will understand, my brother!" Gabriel said, "Why don't we go together to the Cathedral and plead her case and show your marks. Maybe that will be enough for them to let us save her."

The thought of this calmed Michael down. They couldn't deny her safety. "Gabriel, please find Raphael, explain everything to him and leave out nothing. With the three of us, our chance is much higher on getting granted access to step in and save Sassy."

With a nod in agreement, Gabriel shut the door behind him, wasting no time on this matter.

After explaining everything to Raphael, he sat in silence. Raphael had hoped something like this would not happen. He got up and walked over to a table covered in papers and experiments and started working again. Gabriel watched, wondering what he was doing. He didn't say again.

Raphael pushed his hair off his forehead and looked at Gabriel with a concerning look, then spoke "If what you are saying is true, this could start a war again. Lucifer took Sartael and 199 angels and turned against us and our beliefs. It began a war I never want to experience again."

"Sartael and Michael have a huge history of once brothers to sworn enemies. The fallen ones should have learned then. But Sartael is different. His hatred runs as cold as Lucifer's. He would love to hurt and destroy Michael, and I guess he has found a way.".

"Go back to Michael and we will meet tomorrow. I must prepare my words for tomorrow. Michael has taken this to a personal level. It will help our cause if he is silent and shows self-control in front of the Elders. It's the only way. Michael must understand, and it's your job to make that happen."

Leaning forward in his chair rubbing his head, Gabriel responded, "Great, just what I wanted to do."

Gabriel got back home. He sat on his balcony, thinking about Michael. Out of the corner of his eyes, he saw Michael on the beach, standing still, looking out over the seas. Gabriel watched and wondered how his brother must feel. This entire mission had caused nothing but pain and sorrow for him. Now he wore her pain and was helpless in protecting her. This wasn't the way true love should be. A tear ran down his face as he continued to watch his brother, motionless, standing in the diamond sand on the shores of the sea.

***

The next day had come, and Michael didn't take the advice well. He looked at Gabriel, asking him, "How do I stay quiet? This is my love! I can't sit there like some kind of statue!"

Gabriel walked over to Michael and took his hands, looking at the bruises and scratches around his wrists. "I know, my brother. Please don't make this about you, Michael. You must do this! Raphael will do the talking and persuade the Elders to listen. You need to show them you are in control of your emotions. Show them you are better and that you learned your lesson!"

Michael looked at Gabriel and said, "Sometimes your compassion makes me sick. OK, I will show them self-control. I will show them anything if it helps Sassy return home." A big smile appeared on Gabriel's face, making Michael kind of grin too.

It wasn't much longer before Raphael showed up on the doorsteps of Michael's living chambers. He banged on the immense doors as he pushed his way through the doorway. Inside, he saw his brothers in a calm atmosphere, having light conversation.

"It warms my heart to see that we are all on the same page on approaching the Elders."

Michael stood and greeted his brother with a forearm grab. "Raphael, thank you for your help. I need you both more than ever right now." Raphael nodded at Michael. He knew Michael didn't like to look vulnerable in front of him. It had been like this always.

"Before we head out, I thought it would be more convincing if we had on our armor."

"REALLY!" Michael looked at Raphael with a quizzical look.

"Yes, I feel if they see warriors, and Michael calm, they will witness his growth and the severity of the situation."

Gabriel jumped up excitedly. "That's a good idea!"

One by one they called forth their heavenly armor. It had been a millennium since the three brothers had their armor on together, not fighting in a war. Each one admired the other, radiating pride and strength.

Michael excused himself for a minute as he walked into his bedroom, standing in front of the ceiling-to-floor mirror looking at himself. He intently inspected each inch of his armor, thanking each piece for protecting him when needed. He looked handsome and strong, giving himself affirmations of strength, power, and control.

Taking another look, he whispered under his breath, "I am coming for you, and I am going to destroy you, Sartael." He placed his helmet on his head and turned, walked out to his brothers, and said, "Let's do it; it's time to bring Sassy home!"

There was so much commotion going on when the Archangels walked down the corridor of the Cathedral, making their way to the Hall of Records. It wasn't normal to see them in their war armor, so the inhabitants of Celestrian looked at them in awe. They arrived to meet with the Elders. The room went quiet instantly. Some Elders were concerned seeing them in war armor when Gabriel turned and shut the doors. All three took their seats in their thrones at the table. Raphael spoke first to all attending. A lot of Elders coming in were confused by the Archangels in war armor. There was a lot of smoky mist in the air.

After Raphael had time to explain their reason, telling them how Sartael had sparked a personal war against Michael by hurting and wanting to kill Sassy, he turned to Michael and had him show his wrists to the Elders. Showing his wrists caused much concern for Sassy and for Michael.

An Elder asked Raphael, "If he feels her pain and wears her scars, does that mean if they kill her ... Michael dies too?"

Gabriel turned and looked at Michael with fear in his eyes, allowing Michael to see Gabriel rubbing his hands together under the table. He only did this when he was nervous. Michael caught Gabriel's eyes and gave him a stern look through the helmet.

Don't ruin this, Gab!"! Michael thought to himself. He knew the chance of him dying was never a thought or a worry. But it was.... Staying calm and not moving, Michael let Raphael plead their case. It was the hardest thing he ever had to do.

An Elder got up and moved around the table, closing in on Michael with bright purple eyes and a trail of smoke. He was so impressed with the discipline Michael displayed. He called Michael out.

"Michael, are we experiencing a changed, calmer, new you? Please speak for yourself!" The Elder turned his attention on Raphael.

The Elder searched for a flaw in their story, assuming this meeting was called to fill the needs of Michael. Calmly, Michael responded, "Yes," shocking the Elder.

The Elder returned to his seat when another spoke, "There is much to consider. Michael is too valuable to Heaven and the future of all the realms. We must protect him at all costs." The Elder rose and spoke directly at the Archangels in a firm manner. "Please leave us for now! We will resume this meeting after we have a direct order for you to put in motion!" The Elder slammed the gavel on the table, the sound ringing out across the room as an Elder stood. Instantly, they disappeared, leaving the brothers sitting in a thin cloud of smoke.

Gabriel removed his helmet and said, "We sure know how to clear a room," making light of the situation, which worked because Michael giggled.

"Now what do we do?" Gabriel asked Raphael, who had a much more serious look on his face.

"We wait! We wait for our orders, and then we proceed! Nothing less and nothing more. GOT IT!

"We did what we came to do. We pleaded our case to the Elders and now return to our quarters and wait." Raphael looked at both brothers, waiting to argue with one of them. In return, he got respect and loyalty.

Raphael had always been the calm negotiating type, whereas Michael was brute force.

As they placed their helmets on before leaving the Hall of Records, they knew it was best to stay hidden. Gossiping ears wanted to spread rumors across Celestrian. Even this heavenly City had residents who just couldn't help themselves. Gossiping was in their nature, and nothing was more interesting than seeing three archangels in war armor walking through the Cathedral.

Naturally, archangels had a much bigger and taller frame, and armor made from Angelic Steel laced with gold, the strongest steel in all realms. Nothing could penetrate it, and it couldn't burn. It was the most important protective asset to any archangel.

Each had huge chest plates and armor covering their arms and legs. Their helmets were intimidating, covering their entire face, but a *T* opening in the middle gave them full vision. And golden wing emblems had been pressed on the armor for each shoulder. Each archangel was present when their Angelic Steel armor formed to their body.

An archangel would finish up their training at the Monastery. Once they had proven the loyalty and obedience, one by one they would lie in a vast cauldron made of rose quartz as they poured the Angelic steel onto them in a cold form. The Cauldron top would close, sealing the archangel inside. Glowing a beautiful rose-gold color, the cauldron's top would slide back and inside. The archangel would rise out with the armor formed to his body. It became part of the Archangel's being. In time, they learned how to hide it and call upon their armor as needed. They formed the same steel for swords and their companion beast armor.

Descending the steps of the Cathedral, they walked in silence, walking in sync next to each other. They all noticed a tiny creature hiding under a step ahead of him. As they approached, it drew Michael's attention the most. He slowed down and stopped on a step and stood in front of the creature as it looked at him. It raised its little arms and hands and reached out to Michael. Michael quickly looked at his brothers, not knowing what to do.

The creature touched his armor on his leg, startling Michael as he looked down at the little guy again, seeing him still reaching up. Michael tilted his head back and forth, watching the small creature, confused about what this little guy wanted. So Michael wrapped his hands around the body of the small, little guy delicately and lifted him up to his face.

Raphael and Gabriel watched their brother as he held the small creature up near his face. Tiny little fingers came into view as he touched Michael's helmet. It cooed and made little noises while examining, interested in Michael's helmet.

He put his little fingers all over Michael's helmet when he pulled Michael's face closer, looking deep into the *T* where Michael's eyes were, and then he muttered, "Sassy?"

Flabbergasted, Michael said, "WHAT?"

A small heavenly creature had just picked Michael out in full armor. No one could do that! The little creature again said, "Sassy?" followed by gibberish sounds.

Raphael gasped loudly. "Michael, he knew who you were! And it said Sassy?"

Quickly and very concerned, he turned to Gabriel and demanded he get all the information on this small creature. "Michael, stay with him. No one knows who you are in armor. I need to ask a few questions; I will return soon!"

It wasn't long before Raphael returned, directing Michael to take the small guy somewhere away from prying eyes. "I could only find out it is a legendary angelic Iska. I want to know more about this Iska being and its connection to Aree, I mean, Sassy. Michael, I will find you soon."

Michael turned his attention back to the small creature. He thought it was cute as he cuddled him in his arms with no resistant. The Iska was happy, wiggling his fingers and toes and cooing with some giggles. Michael placed the little guy on his shoulder. He perched himself on Michael's shoulder comfortably; he put his tiny little hand on top of Michael's helmet. Letting out a big sigh and a roll of his eyes, Michael started walking out to the countryside.

As they walked a suitable distance from Celestrian, the little guy kicked his furry legs, enjoying his ride. Occasionally, he would tap his little fingernails on top of Michael's helmet, causing it to move and irritate Michael's face. As Michael adjusted his helmet, he got a glimpse of Sassy's favorite tree standing on top of a hill, like a beacon overlooking the land. He decided the tree was a good place to wait for Raphael, so they headed there. Michael pointed to the tree and said, "Look! It is a nice private place, and Raphael knows where it is and will find us to tell me what to do with you." The Iska's response seemed happy with the choice Michael made.

Making it to the tree, it excited the little guy over the many beautiful colored leaves falling on the ground. Michael gently and carefully grabbed the little guy off his shoulder and placed him on the ground. . . . Instantly the little one played in the leaves. Michael smiled, watching it, feeling some peace. He sat down at the base of the tree in Sassy's favorite spot. He noticed the tree had lost many leaves. Never had this tree been this bare.

It caused Michael to be concerned about Sassy and their love. He took off his helmet and sent his armor away. He twisted his head when he heard clapping. The little one clapped and laughed at Michael. "So you thought that was cool, huh?" Smiling at the little one, who now touched Michael's arms where the armor covered his skin, he studied it. It then climbed up the trunk to get to Michael's head. He was very much enjoying playing with Michael's hair.

After that, the little creature made its way back down to the ground and sat in Michael's lap, enjoying the feel of his shirt. It nestled right in, then fell asleep. As he slept, Michael looked at him. He had never seen an Iska. He looked closer at the little guy, petting its reddish orange fur with black tips on its ears and black fingernails and toenails. He softly touched its little hands, amazed at the size difference of his hand to the hand of the Iska. It had three fingers on each hand.

His ears would move up and down like he listened as he slept. He had a tiny little snout that wiggled as he slept. Michael enjoyed time with this innocent little guy. Something new for him. He never took much interest in the creatures Sassy cared for. But there was something about this little guy that gave a feeling of being close to Sassy again.

Michael wondered what things would be like if he took an interest in the creatures and nature Sassy so loved. Maybe he would've understood the bond she had with nature. He laid his hands on the tree, feeling the energy race through the tree into his palm. He apologized for not learning.

It wasn't long when in the distance Michael saw his brothers walking in his direction. They, too, had their armor put away. Michael raised his arm and waved at them, trying not to disturb the little one sleeping. As they approached, it shocked both to see Michael sitting on the ground with a little Iska sleeping in his lap.

"Please, be quiet," he whispered and made the motion by placing his finger up to his lips, shh. . . .

Raphael took a seat on a long, dark root from the tree extending across the ground. Gabriel did the same across from him. Michael looked up at Raphael and said, "WELL? Tell me."

"I know nothing of Iskas except that they are very rare and have some powers or something?" Gabriel whispered. Raphael smiled and continued to tell them both what he knew of the Iskas.

"The mythical creatures were around before the Elders. They have great powers. They have bionic eyes that they can focus to let them see in all dimensions. He has been watching Sassy! That's how he could see you when we had our armor on. They are loyal and attach themselves to a solo angelic being. Once they have found that special being, then they show and teach secrets of nature to them.

"They will protect and guide their chosen one forever. I think this little guy might have chosen Aree, I mean, Sassy?"

"What do I do with him?" Michael asked.

Gabriel, smiling, said, "We will find out when he wakes up."

With a big stretch and yawn, the Iska woke up, all refreshed and curious. It made its way to each brother, touching them and studying them. Then he went back to Michael and touched his hand. Closing his eyes, he lifted his head to the sky. Its hand had a glow radiating around it as it read Michael's energy. . . . He opened his huge yellow eyes, blinking twice, then mumbled, "Sassy." The Iska patted Michael's hand with a frown on its face.

It sensed the loneliness and the strong love connection Michael had for Sassy. Michael stood up with the little guy in his arms and turned to his brothers. "We must wait to hear from the Elders, so I am going to head home, and I am taking this little Iska with me. It is obvious he has a closeness to Sassy, just maybe he can help. I feel I am supposed to bring him home. Sassy always listened to her feelings. I think I will start listening to mine." Neither brother questioned Michael or his motive.

Raphael reached over and grabbed his brother's forearm. "I will return to your place when I know something from the Elders." Michael smiled in agreement.

Gabriel played with the little guy when he said, "I could get used to him being around. He is so cool and cute!"

Raphael flew his way to his hidden apothecary in the woods. Creating something would help ease his mind while they waited. Michael and Gabriel also took to the air, flying. That was the best way to keep the little one hidden.

Back at the castle, Michael took the little Iska on the balcony, watching as he displayed some of his powers. The Iska held his little arms in front of his tummy, wiggling his fingers, making the ivy Sassy had growing around the railing move and wiggle. Stunned, it impressed Michael. Even an archangel didn't possess power like that.

The Iska continued to play as Michael started thinking of Sassy. Looking down at the marks on his wrists, he said a slight pray for her safety. He replayed moments of them together on the beach or dancing on that old dock with their initials carved into it. Closing his eyes, he could hear her laughing, and it caused tears to form in his eyes. Before he could wipe his eyes, the Iska touched Michael's hand. After making sure it had Michael's full attention, it then closed its eyes.

He showed Michael in his mind Sassy and how it showed her magic. Michael witnessed Sassy moving things with her mind. She could speak to a flower, and it would open. There was so much he didn't know! She never told him. . . . He saw her playing with the Iska.

"Why didn't she tell me?" Then the Iska showed him a scene where she told him. He had acted interested but he hadn't listened to her. He really had no interest.

Michael felt shame. How could he act like that? Especially to his soul mate! Hanging his head low, he looked at the Iska as he removed his tiny hand away from Michael's, then looked deep into Michael's eyes.

Blinking its big yellow eyes and wiggling its little snout, it said, "Weegee!" and touched its belly.

Michael watched. "Your name is Weegee?"

It blinked twice and smiled. Michael knew then that Weegee was communicating. "Did Sassy give you that name?" Weegee blinks twice quickly and a giggle with a cheerful smile. "Well, my little friend, maybe you can help me protect Sassy. You are welcome to stay if you like." Weegee blinked twice and smiled, then went back to playing with the ivy.

***

A white owl flew through the window and delivered a scroll to Raphael. He stood there, nervous about unrolling it. He removed the blue silk ribbon from it. As the scroll unrolled, he reluctantly began reading it.

Raphael,

The Elders have taken much consideration in the request you presented to us. With much humility, we deny Michael to leave the heavenly realm. He is too vital to the survival of all the realms. We understand the urgency of this matter regarding Sassy's safety on the earth. This mission will only include you and Gabriel to save her from any evil being trying to steal her soul. We cannot allow any soldiers to assist you. Your confrontation with Sartael needs to be handled quickly, with no victims or evidence left behind. There will be no holy war on earth. We cannot stress this to you both enough. If you find yourself in a dangerous position with no chance of avoiding war, abort the mission.

We have spoken; this is the order.

Raphael calmly rolled it back up. He placed it on the table and rubbed his forehead in a concerning way. Taking a deep sigh, he sat down in a chair, thinking to himself how dangerous this could be. Wiping his mouth and pushing his hair back off his forehead, he stood. He took off his apron and laid it on the table. He double-checked, making sure the jars were closed tightly, blowing out all flames on the candles, then he pulled the blue curtain closed on his window. Grabbing the scroll and placing in his front pocket, he opened the front door and closed the door behind himself. He stretched his arms out and shook them for a moment. Instantly his beautiful huge wings appeared. He opened his feathers, which flared out as he shot straight up into the sky and out of sight in a flash of light, flying his way home.

Landing softly in front of the Archangels' Castle, he got himself ready to deliver the news like he said he would.

Looking up at Michael's balcony, he could hear him in there. Raphael stood there for a moment, praying. Knowing Michael would not like this news, Raphael didn't know how he was going to take it. Just right before he walked under the archway to enter the doors, Gabriel stopped him.

"Is the news good?" he asked.

Raphael took a long look at him with a blank face, then handed him the scroll to read. There was silence. Gabriel rolled it back up, looking at his brother for some reassurance Michael was going to be OK when he heard this.

"It is time, Gabriel; we must go tell him. We must explain this is the right way to save Sassy, for everyone's sake."

TWENTY-EIGHT

Garrett awoke intimidated by Archie, who sat in front of him growling in a low tone, meant just for him. He pulled his legs up slowly in the chair. "Easy boy, I'm not here to hurt you." Archie took a step closer and growled louder, showing his teeth and flexing the muscles in his shoulders around his thick neck. Garrett looked at him and whispered, "I am not what you think I am."

"What does he think you are?" Sassy said, standing in the bedroom doorway in her robe, looking at Garrett.

She then turned her focus on Archie. "Stop it; what is wrong with you? Garrett is a guest, and you need to stop this aggression!" Archie didn't even look at her; he just kept his eyes on Garrett as he walked into her bedroom. "I am sorry for Archie's behavior."

Garrett straightened out his pant legs when he mentioned to her, "Maybe you should consider a chain for him. He is a wild animal."

"No! No! He is not!" Irritated, she continued, "I have had him since birth. He has never acted like this before. He walks through town with me, and no one has ever had a problem with him. I think he is feeling a little jealous of you being around. I mean, I haven't had a man here … ever!"

Garrett looked at her with his crooked grin. "That's some interesting news! AH, Sassy, you are blushing again."

Quickly, she held up her empty coffee cup and asked, "You want any coffee?"

He sat in the recliner with no shirt on and his arms extended behind his head. After scratching his head, he smoothed his hair back in place. He felt very comfortable. Wanting her to notice him, he flexed, exposing to her all his muscles in his upper torso across his dark, hairy chest down to his happy trail stopping at his jeans, which she noticed had the first button undone. This left everything below his waist for her to imagine. She experienced a tingling sensation around her groin area looking at him.

Knowing she blushed now and feeling embarrassed, she turned to make some more coffee right when he responded, "Yes, I would love a cup of coffee."

Sassy got out the sugar and cream when Garrett entered the kitchen, leaning near the stove. She looked up, and he had his shirt on now. She handed him a cup and showed him where the sugar and creamer and milk were. He stirred his coffee as he came closer, standing right next to her. They both noticed they made or liked their coffee made the same way.... Crazy sign, Sassy thought!

Garrett stood close, looking at Sassy. He envisioned grabbing her, kissing her as he rubbed his hands all over her body. Feeling a growing bulge in his pants, he made his move to make that vision true. But she walked back into the living room, resuming her position on the couch. He had missed his moment to seduce her into submission. Frustrated, he offered to restart the fire from last night. They both could feel the sexual tension rising between them.

"A morning fire is a great way to start the day, don't you think?" She took a sip when he asked, so she nodded with smiling eyes. She adjusted her robe to cover her bruised and scratched legs when he returned from outside.

She studied every inch of him. She saw his breath in the cold air with his hair sticking out unkempt and his five o'clock shadow from the night before. An awesome fluttering feeling swept across her heart, catching her attention. She watched as he rubbed his hands together to warm them as he laid the wood in a teepee-style stack in the fireplace, then lit the fire. It didn't take long before Sassy could feel that warm, cozy feeling she craved in the home. Or it was just the heated sexual tension warming her up.

They both enjoyed delightful conversation and the coffee, along with laughing, just like last night. Things felt comfortable around him; nothing felt forced. She got up to get another cup of coffee when Garrett asked, "How did you sleep last night?"

For a split second, she realized she slept well. She even forgot about being attacked at night. "I slept so good! OMG! Garrett, I slept all night in peace. I don't know what you did, but it worked!" She paused. "Would you like another cup of coffee?"

"Ahhh. That would be three cups, so my answer is no to the coffee, but it warms my heart to know that my presence in your home protected you and that you slept well last night."

Instantly, after he said that, there was a horrible, sharp, burning pain that shot directly into Garrett's chest like a bullet. So hard it hit him back down into the chair as he gripped his chest. His eyes never left Sassy, watching every move she made and keeping sure she didn't see him in this excruciating pain. She had her back to him in the kitchen and stirred the creamer in her coffee as he fought to bury the pain with no physical expressions.

Coming back into the living room, she returned to the couch in the same spot as before. She noticed Garrett was flushed red and sweaty. "Are you feeling OK?"

Garrett finally could speak calmly and said, "I get flustered when I think of you being alone in this big house. Maybe I should stay to protect you here in your home for a little while."

Sassy looked at him with her head tilted a little and promptly said, "Is this real? You're willing to stay here to protect me? Wow, Garrett! Thank you. It is so nice to know someone cares for my well-being!"

Garrett got up and approached her, taking her hand, saying, "I don't need to lie to you. I feel something for you, and I know you feel something for me too."

Sassy smiled at him. "Okay. Stay with me, at least until the weather breaks. I will set up the spare room."

He reached for her hand and kissed it gently. "Anything for you, Sassy."

The day was going perfectly. Sassy made them a wonderful lunch and then picked up the house some. She had to chase Archie out of the spare bedroom so Garrett had a place to sleep instead of on the couch. He wasn't pleased. This was Sassy's room as a child, and it then turned into Archie's room. He already disliked Garrett; this wasn't going to help the matter.

Garrett helped in her daily chores any way he could. He cleared the porches of snow. Sassy saw him feeding the dogs, and it touched her heart dearly. Her dream man must be an animal lover. So far, Garrett checked off all the right boxes on her perfect mate list. For a moment, Sassy wondered if he was the one....

They got bored inside; Garrett noticed the weather had lightened up. After putting on a couple of layers of warm clothing, they headed outside. It was the calm in the middle of the blizzard, so they went outside to make some snowmen near the trees in the front yard.

It was still an eerie gray outside with no wind, and a soft snow fell. Sassy made it prettier and more festive by turning on the porch Christmas lights. Seeing the reflections of blue, red, green, and gold shining down on the snow-covered ground made Sassy feel like a giddy child.

Sensing he was doing everything right to win her heart, Garrett commented on the beautiful glow of colors, knowing saying stuff like this would help her fall in love with him. Deep down, he thought he couldn't stand all this loving romance crap. But it was not this way with her. He enjoyed seeing her smile and the lights were actually pretty. He just wanted her to fall in love with him quicker, faster than it was happening.

In the old day, he preferred an aggressive relationship where he could be himself, not caring about her or her feelings getting hurt. Raping and beating them, he would take any woman he wanted anytime, not wanting to please them. It was about fulfilling his needs and pleasures. Now times were different, and women seemed to control the earth. They were used to getting their way and being pleasured by man. Man has grown weak on the planet, he thought to himself disgustedly.

A sharp pain shot through Garrett's chest, bringing his attention back to Sassy. He got concerned about the reminding pain he received. It was a punishment.

Admiring the snowmen they built, Sassy threw the first snowball, hitting Garrett in his upper back. They began playing tag around the trees when the dogs joined in, playing around them. The dogs did not pick up on what Garrett was, and they didn't seem to be threatened by him. Sassy noticed the dogs taking a liking to Garrett, not like Archie, who wanted nothing to do with Garrett.

Sassy ran around in the snow, Garrett chased her, and when he caught her, they would fall in the deep snow. Lying next to her in the snow, looking deep into her eyes, something sparked. Before he started kissing and pulling her tight to him, Garrett felt a burning sensation moving up his body as he fought to ignore it, knowing what it was. As a fallen angel, he was being denied feeling and receiving love in any form. This was a punishment.

Realizing now that he wanted to be with her, and she wanted to be with him, he was going to fight through the pain he felt. After the kiss, they gazed into each other's eyes. Sassy wiggled away to start the chase game again. Garrett wasn't far behind her. Both felt passionate, like teenagers in love.

Running around, not realizing where she stepped and the snow so deep in some areas, she almost fell into the hole that had formed in the front yard! Garrett reached out and caught her and pulled her close to his body. They stood there a minute, locked in each other's arms, kissing with such passion. Sassy was falling in love with Garrett Miller. She enjoyed the feel of his breath on her face as she looked deep into his eyes.

She thought he was going to say something. Instead, he stood frozen as electrical pain raced throughout his body. Garrett held a stone look, doing everything not to let her know. After she figured out he wasn't going to say anything, she started blushing, pushing him off her to start the chase game again.

Turning, she stopped when she saw a hole and focused her attention on it. "Where the hell did this enormous hole come from?" Garrett stood a suitable distance from the hole. Sassy dusted snow off rocks she had never seen before. As she inspected the rocks closer, she said to Garrett, "It's almost like they petrified overnight."

Wookie saw her dusting off the rocks and helped by digging in the snow next to her. This got Scotty's attention, and he joined in. Sassy laughed because as she uncovered rocks from the snow the dogs recovered them as they dug and threw snow too. Wookie looked up at her for her approval. He had his nose covered in snow as his long tongue hung out as he panted, enjoying himself. Sassy smiled and gave him a pat on the head for approval. She enjoyed watching animals at play.

Garrett looked at the hole and immediately knew what it was. He had seen many landing marks from angels on the earth to know enough that Michael was here. It made him growl under his breath. Sassy was really interested in the hole, and Garrett got irritated being near it. Pulling her away from the hole and the trees, she laughed as he dragged her through the snow.

They walked on the ice-covered driveway, sometimes sliding in a race against each other. Catching their breath, they started walking at a slower pace.

Enjoying the time together, Sassy asked, "Can you tell me something about your past love life?" Garrett had little to say about love, so he redirected it back to her about her love history. Sassy stopped and looked into his eyes and asked, "Do you really want to know the truth? And you promise not to laugh?"

Garrett smiled. "I would never laugh at anything you said. I would never hurt your feelings." Sassy didn't know why, but she believed him. She reached for Garrett's hand as they made their way back to the house to thaw out. Spending hours outside playing in the snow had made icicles out of them.

Sassy felt love. She hoped Garrett felt the same way. He tended to the fire, and she ran into her bathroom. She put some lip gloss on and brushing her hair, leaving it down to frame her cheekbones. Feeling happy and a little sexy, Sassy changed her clothes into some comfy clothing.

In the kitchen, Sassy made a nice charcuterie plate with blocked cheese and sliced meats and crackers Toni had pushed on her. She also grabbed a nice vintage bottle of wine and two glasses and met him in the living room at the coffee table. "My parents were big wine drinkers and had a cellar built for their collections. Lucky for me, the cellar is full of vintage wines." Garrett smiled as he reached for the bottle to open it.

Sassy searched for a channel on the radio, listening for some soft music. She found one playing country Christmas music. Before settling down, she went to a hall closet and pulled out some faux fur blankets so they could get real cozy on the couch. She spread out the blankets over their laps before she snuggled up near him. Garrett knew this was the opportunity he needed to make his move on her. Seeing the blankets convinced him he could make his move.

After taking a few big gulps of wine, Sassy looked and felt tipsy. Garrett asked her to answer the question from earlier. "Tell me about your love life." Sassy finished her glass of wine, then hiccupped, followed by a giggle, then told him about "HIM" the one who loves her and wants her to remember him.

"I even have a journal full of notes I have written. Flashes of descriptions about him or when he comes and visits me."

Garrett's voice turned firm. "He comes and visits you?"

"No, not really. Not in physical form. I only have visions of him. Don't you think it's crazy?" she asked Garrett, who got heated on the inside. And it wasn't from the wine.

He knew Sassy talked about Michael. The more and more she spoke he saw a gleam of excitement in her eyes. He thought to himself, She wants him! This pissed him off, making his hatred for Michael grow even stronger.

Sassy felt fantastic by the time they finished the wine. She shared a story of what happened to her in Faermorreya. She talked about how this man saved her from this scary, evil being that was so scary.

"He was the most horrifying-looking creature, with these enormous claws for his feet and hands and these horns all around his face. He is a demon leader who thrives on seeing and causing pain. A creature who doesn't know love and had the most hideous white eyes and reptile skin with hideous wings!" Sassy reached over drunk and grabbed Garrett's hand. "But it was his eyes that haunt me the most! Pure evil runs through those white eyes."

Garrett tried to control his anger when he finally stopped her. He yanked his hand back from her drunken grip. "Okay, okay, this is a good story. You have a great imagination, Sassy, thinking up a place of fairies and evil beings. Maybe you should be a writer. I think we have had enough of this nonsense tonight, Sassy."

Garrett started laughing as he stood. It irritated him. He fought back his anger at the way she talked about him. Sassy rambled on about evil white eyes when Garrett turned to face her and screamed, "ENOUGH!"

He flipped the coffee table, sending it flying across the room as the wine bottle smashed on the floor along with the glasses, and cheese and meats went flying in all directions. He immediately turned his back to her screaming. "Leave me now!" echoed throughout the house in an evil voice.

Sassy stood there confused, then ran for the kitchen in complete shock and fear. She squatted down, hiding behind the counters near the stove. Garrett stood in front of the fireplace casting a massive shadow across the walls as he hunched over, breathing heavily and talking in a deep raspy voice that she knew she had heard before.

He could not stop his true appearance from being exposed. He was furious and burning with hatred. Managing a calm manor, Garrett spoke. "You will not speak of Michael the Archangel anymore! You belong to me now!"

Sassy found her voice and started screaming, "Get out of my house! Who are you?"

Through an evil laugh, he said, "I am yours, Sassy...."

Slowly peeking over the countertop to see him just as he was going through his transformation from a gorgeous young man to a disgusting, wretched demon. Sassy watched in shock! She heard his clothing tear and rip, slowly being replaced by black, burnt-looking flesh across his back that was more reptilian than human now. He turned his head, and their eyes locked; he still had the face of Garrett but piercing, horrible, white eyes filled with tears pouring down his face. She saw him for who he really was....

She covered her mouth as she gasped for air! "It's you! Your white eyes! How could this be? Why are you here? What do you want with me, Sartael? That is your name, isn't it?" His eyes grew in astonishment!

"How do you know my name?" In the back of his mind this explained why he could not control her. She knows my name; she was in the cave when I had on my armor!

"Sassy, I would have never hurt you if I knew you were in the cave that day. I would have made you a queen!"

Feeling angry, she snapped back from behind the kitchen countertops as she felt around for the cutting board for the huge cutting knife. "I was a queen! The White Queen! Remember holding me above your head, laughing and showing my lifeless body to your minions? That hairy beast you killed right in front of me! You are evil. Stay away from me!"

Sartael's anger had exposed his true evil form. He started to plea in a calmer, deeper voice. "My battle is with the Michael," he growled.

Sassy stood up and saw him fully transformed, with white eyes and a distinct voice. "Please, you love me, and I love you. Come with me and be my queen." He cracked a smile for a split second, then licked his lips with his long, split tongue. He thought he had a chance with her. She listened to his plea for her love, then screamed back.

"It's true! All my visions are real. Michael an Archangel is my soulmate; he is my lost love who loves me! Thank you, Sartael, for convincing me to believe in love. It exists!"

He exploded again, screaming along with a roar, raising his arms in the air as he moved closer to her quickly. "NO! YOU BELONG WITH ME NOW! MICHAEL WILL NEVER SEE YOU AGAIN! YOU AND YOUR SOUL BELONG IN BOOHAN. THERE YOU WILL REIGN AS MY QUEEN! WE WILL CREATE OUR OWN HELL TO REIGN OVER."

Within a second, he pinned her against the refrigerator with his massive body. Inches from her face, she could smell a horrible stench coming from him. He placed his rough, burnt, sandpaper palms around her tiny face as he tried being gentle touching her cheeks but couldn't resist the opportunity to sink his claws into her flesh, making blood race down her face as she screamed in pain. He just loved the puncture feeling as the tips of his claws sliced the flesh. Placing his face next to hers, he inhaled the odor of her blood, causing him to roll his evil eyes and his body to quiver with pleasure.

He promised everything she could ever desire. "Sassy, please trust me. I will never hurt you. Let me take you where there is no pain for you. You will never be alone again!"

He pulled her closer to him, wanting to embrace and reassure her he could give her love, the love she wanted. With his arm around her body, he squeezed her into his bare, nasty chest covered in burnt whiskers, smelling of sulfur and horrible body odor. He wrapped one arm around her as the other still held her face. Sassy noticed she had movement with her arms and knew this was her only chance....

With a sudden rush of adrenaline, a wicked smile appeared on Sassy's face. Unaware of her intensions, he returned a smile back as his slithering, split tongue reached out to lick some blood off her cheek. A second later, he experienced a sudden, excruciating pain as she thrust, twisted, and ripped a buried large kitchen knife deep into Sartael's back, right between his ragged wings.

He pulled away squealing ear-pitching screams as he fell to the ground, glaring his white eyes at her as blood boiled and bubbled as it exited his body and spilled onto the floor. Turning and reaching, he could not touch or find the knife. Screaming at the top of his lungs, "YOU BITCH! YOU ARE GONNA PAY FOR THIS!" His claws raked at his back, but still he couldn't touch the knife embedded deep in his disfigured back.

Lying on the floor, he screeched in high pitches, such unnatural sounds. Sassy took a chance and stepped around him, grabbing the butcher's knife on the counter and running for the back door in the mudroom. Sartael still tried to remove the knife and hissed loudly. She could feel the evil in him rising.

TWENTY-NINE

Being outside was deadly. The snow was deep, and the skies howled with evil. She struggled to see and get through the thick snow before making her way to the barn. Freezing her ass off with only house slippers and sweatpants and hoodie on, she shook uncontrollably. Finally getting inside, Sassy pulled the barn door shut, struggling to lock the doors with a huge beam she pulled down to latch so no one could open from the outside.

Across the snowy yard, there was a slight soft-white glow coming from the house. The cold weather had fogged up so much she couldn't see through the window clear enough to see outside. Looking around in the barn, not knowing what to do, she saw Scotty, who lay upside down in the hay covering the floor of the barn. He was happy just hanging in the warm barn chewing on hay. He looked up with such loving eyes. Sassy was heartwarmed to know the dogs were in there with Barney. She sat down between the dogs for warmth.

She started replaying everything about Garrett Miller. Why does Archie dislike him? The strange attacks on her while she slept. "Why? Why did he hurt me? What was he scaring me for? What did I ever do to him?" She finally figured it out that all those nights it was Sartael coming into her house!

The more she thought, the sadder she became. Knowing he caused all the evil things around her home, even the bruises and the deep gashes from claw marks all over her body. He tortured her and deceived her, then tried to love her, caused her to cry, she felt disgusted and ignorant for falling hard for Garrett Miller, a.k.a. Sartael, the demon leader.

A loud crashing noise hit the top of the barn outside. It startled Barney, making him nervous. He started stomping his front hooves violently. Looking at Sassy, he could feel her pain and knew trouble was afoot. Scotty found himself under the hay with Wookie right next to him. Sassy looked around and tried to see anything through the window. Was it Sartael? Was he alive? The only light in the barn came through the window from the outside mercury light. They all could hear footsteps walking around on top of the barn.

"What the fuck is going on?" She looked at Barney when again another round of footsteps ran across the top of the barn. The pitching screams echoing above them worried Sassy. She recognized the screeching sound but could not place it. Barney tried to reassure her but knew he was too old to protect her.

She was scared. Sartael wanted to torture her. Banshees flew above her again. Something heavy walked on a snow-covered barn roof. Wookie started whining and growling and Scotty too as both their eyes looked upward toward the rooftop. Sassy hid with the dogs, sharing the same bad feeling.

She looked around the barn for a weapon just as the mercury light went out, scaring the shit out of all of them! Sassy could hear her heartbeat so loud in her head. She couldn't think straight. There were screeching sounds and voices coming from the roof speaking in the same tongue language she had heard before in the cave in Faermorreya. Sassy stayed hidden with the dogs, hoping Sartael wouldn't crash through the door and find her.

Her eyes adjusted to the darkness, making her able to see Barney standing in the back of his stall, quiet and still. Squinting her eyes to focus, she remembered where she had a lantern placed in the barn and quietly moved to retrieve it. Thank God it still had kerosene in it. Now all she needed was to find the place she had stashed those matches.

She felt around near the window when out of the corner of her eye she saw a black shadow flying to the roof of the house from off the barn. There was still some walking around above them going on. Sassy tried to focus through a fogged-up window. She watched the beings on the roof of the house, trying to see what the hell they were doing. As she stared harder and harder, one turned and caught eye contact with her. Huge, red, glowing eyes on a black form wearing something that blew around in the wind. It looked like a solid-black, shredded sheet letting out a screeching noise. It was the same banshees from before that she had battled in Faermorreya!

They worked for him! She lay on the ground shaking, knowing it saw her. So afraid to move, she started crying and trembling, scared to death. Covering her face and trembling from the cold, her foot moved and hit the matches lying on the floor below the window.... Quickly, she thought of some way to protect them. The demons knew she was in here, so she grabbed the matches and lit the lantern. Sassy had four matches and had one burnout. Two went out from her constantly shaking with one left. Finally, she lit the lantern. She turned it on a low flame and sitting it down near the doors so it doesn't catch the barn on fire....

The scratching on the rooftop became louder and louder. Whatever was on top of the barn was trying to rip its way through the barn to her, trapping Barney and the dogs in the barn with no defense.

Quickly, she stacked some hay under where the creatures worked at tearing the roof apart. If she needed to, she would burn the hay bales for protection. The demons on the roof of the house were now back on the barn, helping the others rip the barn apart. Scared to death, Sassy prayed. First the Lord's Prayer, then she prayed to Michael the Archangel for help. She remembered her mother always told her the angels would always be there to help her, all she had to do was just ask for their help. Through her crying and tears, Sassy called out to the angels for help.

***

Michael heard her prayers. "She needs me!"

He stood in the courtyard of the Archangel Castle. This was where he must stay until they handled the mission regarding Sartael. He had showed the Elders he had learned self-control, but it was all an act; he battled with self-control. It made him irate! He steamed with anger that he focused on his worst enemy. His mind spun with different ways to kill Sartael! It made him squeeze all the blood out of his fists and turn his hands white with fury.

It took everything out of him not to respond to her prayers. He could feel Sassy getting weak. He touched his face, feeling the deep mark across his cheek. Feeling helpless, he ached, knowing she was in pain. The bond and love he had for her kept him focused, even though he wore the marks from her being tortured.

He had pressed down the beautiful green grass in the courtyard from walking back and forth, trying to maintain a calm behavior. Running his fingers through his hair, he felt helpless, struggling physically and mentally to keep his word and not disobey any orders from the Elders. This was a test he didn't know if he could pass. He would do everything they asked to please the Elders and have her returned. He kicked some rocks, seeking faith in his brothers' abilities to save her. Knowing his evil ways, Sartael was sneaky and conniving with the abilities to do massive damage when he was pushed into a corner. Michael was the only archangel who had ever gone face to face with him.

Remembering his newfound respect for nature, Michael went and fluffed the grass he had pressed down and trampled. He felt better as he looked at the grass standing up now again. Sassy would be proud, he thought, as he started pacing again, this time on the walkway, awaiting news.

THIRTY

The wood on the roof of the barn cracked and snapped. The flying black banshees ripped their way into the barn. In a panic, Sassy grabbed one of Barney's wool blankets stuffed with hay before she rolled it up and lit it on fire like a big cigarette. Stretching and reaching, she tried to burn their claws as they reached through the roof at her. Barney was nervous. She had lit a fire in the barn.

Sassy's actions caused him to kick the walls, trying to break out of the barn stall. The dogs barked and whined, making her realize she had done a bad thing. "This is going to kill us all!" Sassy called out as she lost control of the flames and sparks from the fire. Small little fires broke out in different places in the barn. She felt a burning sensation on her shoulder blade when she realized she was on fire. She panicked, trying to put the fire out on her upper back. She crashed on the floor to roll around.

The restriction effect of losing oxygen affected the dogs, Barney, and Sassy. It overcame the barn with smoke when Barney used all the strength he could and kicked at the doors. Just as he broke out some planks in the barn walls enough to escape, a banshee violently ripped Sassy from the barn straight up through the burning roof into the blinding snowstorm. Sassy let out a scream from pain, knowing it was her blood running down her arm as the banshee's sharp talons pierced deep into her arms. The banshee flew straight up in the cold, freezing air, causing her lungs to burn as she struggled to breathe.

The banshee flew fast and high, Sassy hanging there. She could see others flying around, chasing them. Using all her strength, she lifted her legs into her chest every time one flew by, trying to rip her apart, screaming in pain. They had flown higher and higher into the dark, howling winds. Looking down, she could see two demons collide in a fight. Then a massive hit sent her falling through the blustering winds. Screaming in pain from the ripping of her flesh on her arms, she opened her eyes as she fell past the jaws of two demons slicing each other open with razor sharp fangs as their screeching echoed across the sky. A banshee snatched her upright before she hit the treetops. This time, its claws ripped right through her abdomen.

She experienced so much agony she couldn't scream. The only warmth she felt was her own blood running down her arms and legs. Besides her extremities, her body was numb from the freezing cold weather. With no energy left to fight, Sassy lay limp in the claws of the banshee when it looked down at her, thinking she was dead. It let her go.

Again, Sassy fell when she turned her head just in time to see the barn explode in a burst of flames, shooting pieces of burning wood and fire high into the air. Sassy felt her heart break, for she knew Barney and the dogs were gone. Closing her eyes, feeling death was near, she waited for the last hit.

Unsure of what she experienced, she was being cradled in warm arms around her, noticing she wasn't falling anymore. Raphael had Sassy in his arms as they came to a soft landing. He smiled at her as he gently laid her down. Sassy could smell roses, comforting her. "You heard my prayers." The angels were here.

Lying on her back in the deep, blood-soaked snow, with her eyes closed, she felt snowflakes landing on her face. Everything played in slow motion, even a deep, comforting voice saying, "You're safe now, my dear." She became numb to the world and all its sounds. Raphael ripped off his armor cape and laid it on Sassy as he attended to her wounds. He screamed out, "Gabriel, secure the area!"

Sartael got his strength and tried to get up off the floor in the kitchen when he heard the deep, rumbling growl of a big cat approaching. He turned around to see Archie slowly creeping up on him. Archie looked like a rabid, angry, wild cat, showing his strength with muscles bulging all over his body and his gray fur standing straight up. He showed his sharp teeth as he licked his lips like a hungry beast getting ready to attack. Fearing for himself, Sartael backed himself against the wall. All he could do was watch and wait for Archie to attack.

Pouncing on his shoulder, sinking his massive fangs deep into his flesh, Archie scalped him with his sharp claws ripping across his head. Archie clawed at his face and neck, shredding his flesh from his body, turning his beautiful grey coat into a dark red. Sartael did everything he could. He hissed and swung at Archie, screaming in pain, but it did nothing.

Archie held up his paw and released his razor-sharp claws, showing them to Sartael before he raked them across his face and down his chest, causing huge, deep gashes to ooze his fiery blood. Archie stood right in front of him, watching with pleasure, enjoying the fear he saw. Sartael screamed from being tortured. Archie dragged out the attack, then he roared and pounced onto Sartael, sinking his fangs deep into any remaining flesh. Shaking and ripping pieces of stringy flesh from his shoulder blade.

Sartael let out a scream reaching the ears of flying black banshees that immediately turned to assist their leader. Following the sounds of his screams led them to the chimney. Flying down through the chimney, they saw their master on the floor, beaten and being torn apart by Archie. Sartael demanded they attack!

Two massive, shadowy demons flew at Archie, biting and tearing at Archie's flesh. He fought for his life, swinging his enormous claws at the banshees, hitting one and sending it crashing into the wall. The other one sunk his talons into Archie's back, forcing him to cry out in pain as it fought to pick him up and fly. It crashed through the chimney, sending brick flying across the land like a tremendous explosion going off as the banshee appeared in the night sky, holding Archie in its bloody talons, flying off into the dark winter skies. Sassy thought she heard Archie crying. The evil banshee screeched out before he dropped Archie to his death.

Sartael, who struggled to stay alive, demanded his minion bring Sassy to him. In a scared frantic mood, most demons fled, knowing now they were not supposed to kill her. Sartael grabbed one demon by its neck as it screamed in terror.

"Where is she?" It promised to take Sartael to her.

The demon broke through the front door, shattering the windows, causing the glass to blow outward, allowing Sartael to see the barn on fire. As he looked around for Sassy, a force sent him flying across the front yard into the deep snow. Gabriel had hit Sartael without him knowing. He approached, pinning him to a tree with the tip of his blade at his neck. Sartael quickly began to plea for forgiveness as he spit out boiling blood.

Archie had removed a massive amount of flesh from Sartael, and he lost lots of boiling blood. He felt drained and knew they had beaten him, so he tried to defend himself against Gabriel just as Gabriel raised his sword to decapitate him! Cowardly, he begged for his life as he turned his head and saw Sassy laying in the arms of Raphael.

With the sound of compassion in his voice, he called out, "Sassy!" This stopped Gabriel from mid-swing. Gabriel looked over at Raphael holding her. She never responded to him. He continued yelling for her.

Gabriel started laughing at Sartael. "Oh, my lost brother.... Have you forgotten? You will never feel love!"

Sartael growled at Gabriel, curling his lip and showing his split tongue. He said, "She loves me!"

Gabriel started laughing out loud at Sartael, thinking there was still a chance for them to be together. He called to her again. This time she heard him, opening her eyes and using all her strength to lift her head. Raphael assisted by holding her neck for support as she looked around, seeing the barn burning in a fire and the house's roof blown off. Tears soaked the sides of her face and hair. She knew her life was ending soon. He had killed her dear animals.

Sassy gasped for a breath of air in between spitting blood out. Looking at the beautiful angel holding her, he smiled and told her she was safe. She knew that to be true. She returned her focus to Sartael, who still lay on the ground at the base of the enormous oak tree. Gabriel had a blade on Sartael's throat, so he didn't move.

Sartael knew they had defeated him, but he let out a laugh. "Michael couldn't even come and save you! Ha, ha, ha!"

Hearing him taunt her gave her just enough anger to produce revenge adrenaline. She raised her left arm, with the help of Raphael, holding her arm up, pointing her fingers toward Sartael.

Glancing up at the beautiful angel, she whispered, "Thank you." This shocked Raphael!

Looking down, he said, "Aree?"

Sassy, still smiling, closed her eyes and started moving her fingers in the direction where Sartael lay.

Through the quiet night air, suddenly, small snapping sounds came from all around him. Having limited vision from the beating Archie had given him, he tried to figure out where the noise came from. He could feel the rumble on the ground and deep in his bones. The noise of breaking branches made it apparent the wood cracking was the tree pulled up its roots from deep under the ground, popping up through the snow. The unique crackling sound echoed across the property.

Gabriel withdrew his sword, moving away from Sartael. He watched the snow and dirt being thrown up into the air from the tree branches busting through the snow and crawling toward Sartael's body. Long, skinny roots moved across the ground in his direction like massive, crawling spiders. This terrified the hell out of Sartael. He began screaming in fear as roots started wrapping around him, piercing his reptilian flesh with sharp roots and branches. Never, ever, had he seen someone with the abilities to communicate with and control trees.

He hissed in fear and growled and yelped as he was being strangled and pinned to the trunk of the tree. Roots and branches twined all around him, pressing him against the tree tighter and tighter, snapping his wings like twigs as his arms and legs were being pulled around the tree. Screaming in horror, Sartael's fears rattled Gabriel. He had seen nothing like this before.

Sartael was bound to the tree. His flesh was being sucked into the bark of the tree, like he liquefied into the tree. He let out a last scream of complete horror, knowing the outcome was permanent.

He screams out, "This is not the end! I will find you and kill you all!" as he gasped for his last breath of air before a root wrapped around his neck and crushed his vocal cords, sending any boiling blood left in him out his mouth as he liquefied, disappearing deep into the trunk of the tree.

There was a moment of silence. Raphael watched in astonishment; he too had experienced nothing like what they had just witnessed done with a tree. It impressed him by how she froze Sartael in time, in a tree. A forever prison. Sartael was nothing but a stain running deep in the bark of an oak tree. Raphael understood now why the Elder chose Sassy for the mission they sent her on. He never knew nature's magic was still alive in the earthly realm.

All at once the tree roots returned underground, and all branched moved back into their positions. You wouldn't have known nothing happened here except the mark on the land and the lonely kitchen knife laying in the snow.

Raphael turned his attention to Sassy as Gabriel finished any demons still in the area, making sure none of them survived to speak of this moment. When he finished scouting the area, he rejoined his brother, who still tried to stop some of Sassy's bleeding. Raphael looked at Gabriel and said, "She did that! She trapped him!" as he moved some hair away from her cheeks, gently noticing the severe cut on her cheek.

Gabriel looked at her and then looked at his brother. "Is she going to make it?"

Raphael quietly told Gabriel, "It is in her hands if she lives or dies.". We will stay with her."

Michael lay on the grass in the courtyard, paralyzed in pain, covered in huge wounds that had caused him to grow extremely weak. He knew Sassy was dying; but he didn't know what was going on down on earth. Was she in the care of his brothers or in the hands of Sartael? He had one more chance; she was his soulmate, and he must remind her.

He lay there, crossing his arms across his heart, and with all his strength, he focused all his energy to communicate with Sassy. "Please, my love, hear me, remember me. Remember our love! Look at me, take my hand. It's time to come home!"

As Michael used all his strength to send his energy to her, he lay in the fetal position in the middle of the courtyard with a baby-blue glow surrounding his body as he transforms himself into a celestial being of light, radiating his energy telepathically to Sassy....

They felt the skies trembling. As the brothers looked up, they knew it was Michael crying out her name. "Sassy!" With such a passionate plea to save the powerful bond they shared, his cries rattled all the realms.

After the tremors in the sky stopped, Sassy lay on the ground with Gabriel and Raphael standing over her body. She opened her eyes to see a soft, beautiful, baby-blue glow giving a familiar, warm, fuzzy feeling of a wonderful, loving peace. She could see tiny snowflakes falling gracefully and slowly through the baby-blue light. The snowflakes landed on her eyelashes as she smiled, looking so content. Raphael and Gabriel watched her, knowing Michael had reached her.

She looked up, seeing visions of Scotty and Wookie healthy and playing in the prettiest green grass, and Barney was there too, grazing in a beautiful field of green. She also saw Archie looking so strong and proud, with a beautiful gray coat. Next, visions of her parents in flashbacks of her life with them. Smiling and feeling no pain, she reached for the beautiful, gold clouds forming a perfectly handsome angel. Standing on a cloud surrounded by a loving glow of pale blues, yellows, and peachy oranges, he smiled at her, and he extended his hand out for her to take. His eyes glowed the color of the bluest sapphires as he radiated pure love for her. His hair blew behind him as his armor shined brighter than any light she had ever seen.

She knew him. He showed her visions of their love. She saw them laughing and playing around a beautiful tree of many colors, and she saw them dancing on an old fishing dock with fireflies twinkling about. She also witnessed Gabriel and Raphael enjoying drinks with them. Suddenly, with all the strength left in her body, she took the hand of her true love, her twin flame. She had heard him calling to her. Sassy felt his warm touch as he took her hand, pulling her toward him. She finally was content finding him. All she ever wanted was to be with him and feel his love for her. He wrapped his arms around her as the clouds slowly closed in on them.

Both brothers struggled to see her like this. Raphael crossed her arms and placed them on her chest. Like a beautiful statue lying in the snow, she felt no pain. Gabriel and Raphael watched her.

"Look, she is with him. She is smiling so peacefully." She was finally going home.

Sassy suddenly whispered, "MICHAEL!" releasing her last exhale.

Raphael scooped her lifeless body out of the snow and turned to walk to where the barn stood burning. Gabriel said, "We must cover all tracks. Make sure we left nothing behind to cause concern for humans. People cared for her.".

"This will cause pain for a few but is better than causing pain for millions," Gabriel shared.

"She is home with Michael," Raphael said, then laid her body on the fire. Minutes later, Gabriel laid Archie's body there as well.

They stayed there long enough to make sure all evidence was burned and destroyed. Headed home, they took to the skies. Both brothers were on alert during their flight home, expecting some distractions, but it was a smooth return to the heavenly realm.

THIRTY-ONE

Michael stood over her, watching her sleep. He was so relieved to have her home and to have this nightmare over. Touching her arm softly caused Sassy to stir awake. Feeling the soft fur under her fingers brought back wonderful memories. She slowly opened her eyes, seeing her bed and her room and her lover standing next to the bed, smiling at her.

"Welcome home, my love," Michael leaned over and whispered in her ear before kissing her on her forehead. Closing his eyes, he enjoyed her scent as he sat down next to her.

Sassy was kind of in a shock; she remembered everything now. Her love she shared with Michael and her life on earth, Faermorreya, and dying! Sassy instantly sat up and cried out, "Sartael!" Michael took her in his arms, reassuring her and reminding her of her abilities.

"Honey, you took care of Sartael, permanently imprisoning him inside a tree. He will never hurt you again!" He cradled her. The thought of those horrible nights she experienced torture filled him with rage.

That quickly disappeared when he heard her say, "I love you, Michael." All his attention was back on her.

Gently and delicately, he massaged her back. He accidentally rubbed his hand over her right shoulder blade, finding a scar on her. "What is on your back?" Sassy looked at him, unsure of what was there. Michael slowly pushed her beautiful hair off her shoulder and looked at her back. He was stunned to see the mark of a flame on her shoulder blade.

"My love, you have a mark just like one I have."

"Michael, what are you talking about? Let me see!"

Michael stood next to the bed and started removing his shirt. It thrilled Sassy to be home seeing her beautiful love standing in front of her. He finally turned around and exposed his back to her. Sassy sat up in the bed, touching his back, outlining the mark.

"WOW! Does it hurt? It's a flame!" After studying her lover's mark, Sassy got out of bed and stood in front of the wall mirror, wanting to see her back for herself. Michael sat on the bed, watching her.

"We need to report to the Elders, Sassy. They want to talk to you. We need to get dressed and head to the Cathedral this morning." Sassy turned, not worried about that or her back, and ran into the arms of her true love, falling back on the bed. "I missed you so much!" She kissed him, wanting to stay in bed with him.

Then suddenly she heard the cutest little giggling. She froze and looked at Michael saying, "I know that sound!"

Sassy raced out onto the balcony and scooped up her little friend, who played with the ivy on the balcony railing again.... "Oh my gosh! Weegee, you are here?"

Michael joined them on the balcony, smiling, watching the loving reunion. Sassy cuddled up with Weegee, crying happy tears. "Michael, how did this happen?"

Michael walked over and took Weegee out of her hands and cuddled with him, saying, "Good morning, my little buddy." Weegee wiggled his snout back at Michael, who turned to face Sassy and told her that some changes had happened, and one of them was his newfound respect for animals and nature.

Sassy stood there crying. "I think I just fell in love with you all over again!" she spoke. He handed Weegee back to Sassy and reminded her of the schedule they must keep.

***

The day was beautiful. Sassy inhaled the rose smell and peacefulness of flying with Michael. He gently landed on the steps of the Cathedral. They ascended the steps quickly, keeping on schedule. They stood in front of the doors when Sassy pushed the doors open, catching Michael off guard.

The Elders were all gathered around the table awaiting their arrival. Many of them shined their violet eyes in Sassy's direction, who walked in showing confidence as she took a seat in a throne next to Michael. She placed her hands on the table and looked at the Elders, then said, "Good morning!"

It surprised some Elders with her boldness to speak before them. But they continued to welcome her home. "We are pleased to see you return and complete the mission we sent you on." An Elder stood speaking, "Aree, we have been told of your heroic abilities, and we thank you for saving Faermorreya from demons."

Sassy pushed her throne back and stood before the Elders. "Thank you, but please, my name is Sassy. I am not Aree anymore. Everything that I have learned and witnessed and lived has given me experiences beyond any imaginable. I have grown as a human soul, wiser and stronger. It's only right for me to remain Sassy. It's who I am now."

She sat back down and looked at Michael, who was proud of this new powerful individual she had become. The Elders decided in favor. Sassy held Michael's hand under the table, and she squeezed it, pleased with their answer. They thought they adjourned the meeting when suddenly an Elder stood quickly and shouted out to Sassy.

"Sassy, we have granted your wish in your name. We also are grateful for all your sacrifices.".

"There is much we learned while you were out of Celestrian and the heavenly realm. Michael experienced many human emotions and had marks on him matching the same ones you received in battle." Sassy squinted her eyebrows in shock and looked at Michael!

"Is this true? Did you experience all my pain?" Before Michael could answer her, an Elder spoke and required Sassy to explain any marks she had recently noticed on herself.

Michael abruptly spoke up. "She has a mark on her shoulder blade in the same place where my mark is from my actions having my wings removed."

"Your wings removed?" Sassy glared at Michael wondering what the heck happened here.

"May we see?" an Elder requested, with many more asking too. Both Michael and Sassy exposed their shoulders, showing the Elders their marks. There was a silence. Then one Elder said, "It is true. They both wear the same mark."

The Elder looked at Michael and then at Sassy before waving them to take their seats. . . . "This mission has taught all of us many lessons. This one is very important," pausing for a moment, "We have learned about a serious connection of love that is so powerful it alone will fight to stay alive. Michael and Sassy, you both wear a matching mark of a flame."

Another Elder called out, "They are twin flames!"

"They are the most powerful of pure-love companionship. A love like this outlasts time and different realms. It will bond you both together for eternity."

Sassy got lost in Michael's eyes. Holding hands, both knew they would be together forever no matter what came their way. She forgot for a moment they were still in the presence of Elders, when a different one spoke. "Is there any more we can do for you?"

Sassy wasn't expecting her wish to come true, but quietly requested, "I wish my animals were here." Listening to the rumbling voices saying no, no, she hung her head and looked at Michael, wanting to leave the room. Michael stood. "Is there anything needed from her?"

One responded, "No, you may leave!"

Sassy turned, holding Michael's hand, and left the room, shutting the doors behind them. Walking through the corridor, she felt melancholy. He missed her beautiful smile and pretty ocean-colored eyes gleaming with happiness. So when they made it outside, he swept her up in his arms, kissed her on her lips, and told her to hold on as they flew to their tree. Sassy's mood shifted quickly, and her eyes got huge. She was excited to see their tree of different colors in her view.

***

The explanation of what took place on earth shocked the Elders. They were not aware of the dangerous situation Sassy was in. There was much commotion around the table. Raphael told them about Sassy's ability to control nature and how she imprisoned Sartael in a tree.

As he continued, he reassured them Gabriel made sure there was no evidence left behind for evil to trace. The area was secured and all victims burned. Once he had the Elders pleased with the information he had provided, it was the best time to bring up other items.

Raphael explained the actions of Archie as a protector to Sassy and the important role he played since Sassy found him as a cub. An Elder spoke. "Raphael, are saying the cub assisted Sassy?"

"I am saying the cub did what we did not in controlling the situation." Raphael sat there looking at different Elders saying their piece to each other, then disappearing.

"We are requesting passage for the animal. He would be an asset for protection!" Raphael sensed the conversation with the Elders wasn't leaning in his favor. He stood, placing his hands down on the table, and spoke firmly, getting everyone's attention. "I would never make a request like this, but you sent her to do a job, and she would have never had completed it without the help of the animal. The animal offered his life for her! Isn't that enough?" He stood looking at the Elders before they disappeared, leaving others to speak.

Finally, a single Elder rose above his throne and was gracefully moving around the room. The Elder touched his beard and his violet eyes glowed. He turned facing Raphael who had taken his seat again, anxiously waiting.

"Raphael, you approach us with an unusual request. But with much thought I agree with your explanation. We sent her there without protection. The animal loved and gave its life for her of its own free will. With this, we cannot deny your request. Yes, we grant passage!" The gavel hit the table. Raphael gleamed with happiness. As he rose and bowed, thanking the Elders who again where disappearing as fast as they showed up, he couldn't wait to surprise Michael and Sassy.

Back at the castle, Gabriel was on his balcony painting when he saw Raphael flying home. He waved Raphael over. Placing his paintbrush down, he couldn't wait to hear what the Elders had to say. He opened his door just as Raphael showed up on his doorstep.

"Well? I see you smiling, showing me your huge teeth!"

"That's right, my brother. I am happy today!" Raphael said as he walked in and went straight to the kitchen and looked for some elixir and a clean mug. "Gab, they bought it! They have granted Archie passage!"

"That's wonderful, Raphael! Does Michael know yet?"

"Nope. I am going to let it be a surprise."

"You are out of elixir! Let's go to my home and celebrate." Gabriel nodded in agreement as they walked out, shutting the door.

Raphael and Gabriel were enjoying some elixir when a dove flew at them, coming in from the balcony. It landed on the table in front of Raphael, dropping a scroll for him. He sat down with his mug in hand and looked at Gabriel.

"Wonder what this is?"

Gabriel just kept on drinking, waiting for Raphael to tell him what it said. He watched Raphael, who read and smiled, then looked up and said, "Let's go! It's time!"

They both stood, leaving their mugs on the table. Raphael went into his bedroom and came out with a decorative bottle full of elixir. He called out to Gabriel to grab the basket on the counter, and they walked out. Soon they were in flight, flying to the gates of Celestrian.

***

Sassy was in bliss lying in her tree holding the hand of her love. The tree was brilliant in vibrant colors. They were both so happy to be reunited and able to pick up right where they had left off. Their love was so easy and grew deeply when they were together.

Lounging and laughing so happy just being together, Michael noticed off in the distance Raphael and Gabriel walking over a hill in their direction. He knew his brothers wanted to see Sassy. So he thought he would make it a surprise by distracting her until they were there. He climbed over to the branch she was on and made sure her attention was elsewhere by grabbing her in his brawny arms.

He looked into her eyes and smiled as he said, "My twin flame. I like how that sounds." Sassy leaned into Michael as he kissed her.

She got lost in the passionate moment when suddenly a deep, roaring meeooow startled her! Looking around Michael, she saw Archie coming down the hill with Raphael. She couldn't believe what she saw! Instantly, she cried.

"Is this real?" she called out as she climbed down extremely fast. "Archie! Are you real?"

He responded with a roaring meeooww! Sassy hit the ground and ran in his direction as he began running to her. She fell to the ground as he rushed into her arms. They were so excited to be together again. Archie had his paws on her shoulders and purred and rubbed his massive head against hers. He had missed her so much! Sassy hugged him, feeling so blessed the Elders had changed their minds.

She looked up, thanking Raphael for everything and for bringing Archie here. Sassy was speechless, just lost in the love she shared with Archie. They played and rolled around on the emerald-green grass when everyone turned, looking toward Gabriel carrying Weegee in his arms while he had two goofy dogs playing chase around him as he led a younger Barney toward the group around the tree. Sassy called out to the dogs and Barney, who neighed, looking so healthy. It was a miracle. They had reunited her with her animals.

The brothers watched, intrigued by all the emotions shared between the animals and Sassy. Michael seemed to be the only one who understood the bond Sassy had with her furry friends. He could feel the love they all share.

All reunited together under the enormous tree of different colors, enjoying some delicious elixir. Raphael and Gabriel played with Scotty and Wookie. Having dogs was something different for them. Both brothers had so much while Barney grazed on the best sweet grass ever. Michael and Sassy, lost in each other's eyes, held each other as they swayed, dancing in the warm breezes of the early evening.

***

Archie was full grown and majestic. He made a new friend in Weegee. He allowed Weegee to climb up on his back as Archie jumped his way to a perfect lounging branch high in the tree. Archie stood there, looking out over the land with such pride, proud of his duties as a protector here in Celestrian.

Looking down at Sassy, he was proud of Michael and could feel his love for her. This pleased Archie, knowing now she finally found her love and will never be lonely again. Letting out an enormous yawn of pleasure, he lay down and crossed his paws. Life was finally perfect.

To be continued. . . .

Join us!

Sign up on our Mailing List that is available on website.

You will also get updates on new book release dates, discounts and freebies!